ASSESSING STUDENT LEARNING

ASSESSING STUDENT LEARNING
A Common Sense Guide

Linda Suskie
Towson University

ANKER PUBLISHING COMPANY, INC.

Dedication

To my husband Steve and my children Melissa and Michael, whose love and support made this book possible.

To the faculty and administration of Towson University, whose love of teaching and learning, passion for excellence, and collegiality continually inspire me.

To the thousands of faculty and administrators throughout higher education whose interest in and questions about assessment prompted me to write this book.

ABOUT THE AUTHOR

Linda Suskie is director of assessment at Towson University, near Baltimore, Maryland. Prior positions include serving as director of the assessment forum at the American Association for Higher Education (AAHE) and as a fellow at the Middle States Commission on Higher Education. Her 25 years of experience in college and university administration include work in assessment, institutional research, strategic planning, and continuous improvement.

For over 20 years, Ms. Suskie has been a frequent speaker, consultant, and workshop presenter on higher education assessment topics to audiences throughout the United States and across the globe. Her publications include *Assessment to Promote Deep Learning* (editor), *Questionnaire Survey Research: What Works,* and the frequently cited "Fair Assessment Practices: Giving Students Equitable Opportunities to Demonstrate Learning" in the *AAHE Bulletin.* Her professional service has included serving on a number of advisory groups for higher education organizations, as regional program chair for the Society for College & University Planning, and as treasurer of the North East Association for Institutional Research.

Ms. Suskie has taught graduate courses in assessment and educational research methods and undergraduate courses in statistics and developmental mathematics. She holds a bachelor's degree in quantitative studies from Johns Hopkins University and a master's degree in educational measurement and statistics from the University of Iowa.

TABLE OF CONTENTS

FOREWORD

Wedged between the table of contents and the preface, the foreword is a curious literary tradition. Neither introduction nor summary, review nor publicity blurb, perhaps the foreword is best seen as a sort of toast. Like a good toast, a good foreword should be personal, forward looking, and brief.

Assessing Student Learning: A Common Sense Guide deserves such a toast, for it contains much to celebrate. It is a notable contribution to the growing literature of academic assessment— one which will have a positive influence on assessment practices and publications for years to come.

In *Assessing Student Learning,* Linda Suskie sets a high standard for practicality, readability, breadth, and scholarship. It is, first and foremost, a practical, easy-to-read, what-to-do and how-to-do-it guide, providing readers with a wide range of good options and sage advice. In chapters that are both brief and rich with examples and illustrations, Ms. Suskie responds to the full range of issues faculty and administrators face when planning and implementing assessment. Drawing on extensive professional experience as an assessment specialist and as a teacher, she illuminates technical questions other assessment books rarely touch, such as writing items and calculating sample size. At the same time, she educates readers in the why-to-do-its of learning assessment, helping us weigh opportunity costs and make difficult choices. In short, this book aims to make us not simply more informed and skilled technicians, but also wiser, more independent practitioners.

Thanks to Glassick, Huber, and Maeroff (1997) and the Carnegie Foundation, we possess "a powerful conceptual framework to guide evaluation" (p. 25) of applied scholarship. This framework evaluates scholarly work on clarity of goals, adequacy of preparation, appropriateness of methods, significance of results, effectiveness of presentation, and reflective critique. Linda Suskie's goals for *Assessing Student Learning* are quite clear, her preparation for the task impeccable, her methods well chosen, results of her synthesis of research and practice significant, and presentation effective. She demonstrates reflective critique, having learned from her own mistakes and those of others. Consequently, I consider *Assessing Student Learning* a mature work by an accomplished scholar—an excellent example of the scholarship of assessment.

Lastly, as the subtitle announces, this is also a commonsensical book for busy, hard-working professionals. In this case, as Emerson noted, "Common sense is genius dressed in its working clothes."

May this worthy book find its way to all the right readers—those who will use and benefit from it—and may it and its author prosper through many future editions.

Reference

Glassick, C. E., Huber, M. T., & Maeroff, G. I. (1997). *Scholarship assessed: Evaluation of the professoriate*. San Francisco, CA: Jossey-Bass.

Thomas A. Angelo
Associate Provost for Teaching, Learning, and Faculty Development
University of Akron
November 2003

PREFACE

Interest in assessing student learning at institutions of higher education—and the need to learn how to do it—skyrocketed in the last two decades of the 20th century and continues to grow in the 21st century. All regional accrediting organizations and a growing number of specialized accrediting organizations have increasingly rigorous requirements that institutions and programs assess how well they are achieving their goals for student learning. Concurrently, the higher education community is growing increasingly committed to creating learning-centered environments in which faculty and staff work actively to help students learn, and the assessment of student learning is essential to gauging the success of these efforts. Both these trends have created a need for straightforward, sensible guidance on how to assess student learning.

Audience and Purpose

A number of years ago, a comment on one of my workshops cited its value to the "But how do we *do* it?" crowd. The phrase has stayed with me, and it is the root of this book. Yes, we in higher education are theorists and scholars, with an inherent interest in whys and wherefores, but there are times when all we need and want is simple, practical advice on how to do our jobs. Providing that advice is the purpose of this book.

Assessing Student Learning: A Common Sense Guide is designed to summarize current thinking on the practice of assessment in a comprehensive, accessible, and useful fashion for those without formal experience in assessing student learning. Short on background and theory and long on practical advice, this is a plainspoken, informally written book designed to provide sensible guidance for assessment practitioners on virtually all aspects of assessment. Assessment newcomers will particularly appreciate the minimal use of educational and psychometric jargon; this book discusses reliability, validity, and research design but avoids using those terms!

While this book is designed primarily to meet the needs of those charged with planning and implementing a program-wide or institutional assessment effort, much of the book, especially Part III, will be of interest to anyone involved in student learning, including faculty who simply want to improve assessments within their classes.

A Common Sense Approach to Assessment

This book is called *A Common Sense Guide* because its premise is that effective assessment is based on simple, common sense principles. Because every institution and program is unique and therefore requires a somewhat unique approach to assessment, this book presents readers not with a prescriptive "cookbook" approach but with well-informed principles and options that they can select and adapt to their own circumstances.

This book is also based on common sense in that it recognizes that most faculty do not want to spend an excessive amount of time on assessment and are not interested in generating scholarly research from their assessment activities. The book therefore sets realistic rather than scholarly standards for good practice. It does not, for example, expect faculty to conduct extensive validation studies of the tests they write, but it does expect faculty to take reasonable steps to ensure that their tests are of sufficient quality to generate fair and useful results, and it provides very practical suggestions on how to do that.

Overview of the Book

For assessment newcomers who want to gain a general understanding of all aspects of assessment, the book's four sections take readers roughly sequentially through the assessment process. Part I (Laying a Foundation for Assessment) sets the stage for successful assessment efforts by discussing the nature of and rationale for assessment, principles of good practice, and campus culture. Part II (Planning for Assessment Success) provides an overview of the many decisions that must be made in order to launch successful assessment efforts, including planning assessment strategies, establishing learning goals, and choosing appropriate assessment tools and approaches. Part III (The Assessment Toolbox) provides information on a wide range of assessment tools, including hands-on assignments (papers, projects, etc.), reflective writing, portfolios, traditional tests, surveys and focus groups, and published instruments. Part IV (Putting Assessment Results to Good and Appropriate Use) concludes the book with information on summarizing, analyzing, and communicating assessment results and using them effectively and appropriately.

For more experienced assessment practitioners who want to use the book as a reference guide, plenty of headings, charts, and bulleted lists help readers find answers quickly to whatever questions they have about assessment.

Using This Book

This book is intended to introduce readers to key assessment topics rather than provide exhaustive treatments of them. Each chapter concludes with key readings on the chapter's topics. If you find that a particular chapter whets your appetite and you'd like to learn more, these readings will give you more complete information and steer you to additional resources.

This book is not (as my husband reminded me when I was in the depths of despair over ever finishing it) an encyclopedia. Because this book focuses on general assessment principles applicable to a wide range of programs and situations, it does not specifically address assessment in specific programs such as general education curricula or student affairs programs; nor assessment of specific skills such as writing and critical thinking; nor assessment in special instructional settings such as online learning.

As you read this book, keep in mind that assessment is a nascent discipline. The science of educational testing and measurement is scarcely a century old, and many of the ideas and concepts presented here have been developed only within the last few decades. Assessment scholars and practitioners have yet to agree on many definitions, models, and principles, and some may disagree with some of the ideas expressed here. As you hear conflicting ideas, use your own best judgment—your common sense, if you will—to decide what's most appropriate for your particular situation.

You'll notice that, to keep this book as readable as possible, I have minimized citations, although ideas directly attributable to specific individuals and sources are clearly acknowledged. The text draws on the thoughts of many; they are listed in the Recommended Reading sections that conclude each chapter. You'll find that some references are not from higher education but from basic education and the business world. Each sector has much to learn from the others, and I encourage you to consider resources from outside higher education as seriously as those from within.

This book is designed to be suitable for professional development workshops and graduate courses in assessment. Each chapter concludes with prompts for thought, discussion, and practice that can be used in these settings. No answer key is provided, because these are mostly complex questions with no simple answers! Often the conversation leading to the answers will reinforce learning more than the answers themselves.

Acknowledgments

Some of the material in this book, particularly sections of Chapters 12, 14, and 15, is adapted from my earlier book, *Questionnaire Survey Research: What Works*, published by the Association for Institutional Research. I am grateful to the Association for permission to adapt this material. I also thank my daughter Melissa for writing the deliberately less-than-sterling essay in Figure 7.9.

This book would not be in your hands without the guidance, advice and support of many wonderful colleagues across the country. Assessment practitioners and scholars are the nicest, friendliest, and most supportive people in the world! I particularly want to acknowledge, with deep gratitude, the wise counsel and suggestions of Virginia Anderson, Towson University; Thomas Angelo, University of Akron; MaryAnn Baenninger, Middle States Commission on Higher Education; Christina Barrick, Towson University; Douglas Eder, Southern Illinois University–Edwardsville; Peter Gray, United States Naval Academy; Teresa Hall, Towson University; Christina Harnett, College of Notre Dame of Maryland; Sridharan Iyengar, Anne Arundel Community College; Ronald Montesi, formerly of Siena College; Marcia Mentkowski, Alverno College; John Muffo, Virginia Polytechnic Institute & State University; Thomas Ott, Community College of Philadelphia; Neil Pagano, Columbia College Chicago; Joseph Revelt, Millersville University; Glen Rogers, Alverno College; Ephraim Schechter, North Carolina State University; Peter Seldin, Pace University; and Lee Upcraft, Pennsylvania State University, on various aspects of this book. Special bouquets of gratitude go to Virginia Anderson and Thomas Ott, who patiently slogged their way through the entire manuscript and gave me a wealth of constructive feedback on *every* chapter! This book would not be half what it is without the contributions of these distinguished assessment practitioners and scholars.

Linda Suskie

LIST OF FIGURES

LIST OF TABLES

PART I
Laying a Foundation for Assessment

1
What Is Assessment? Why Assess?

W hile oral and written examinations have been a part of education for hundreds of years, only in the last century have the theory and science of assessment been studied systematically. Because assessment is relatively new compared to many other fields of study, and because it has been undertaken by people from disciplines with widely differing orientations, the vocabulary of assessment is not yet standardized. (This chapter, for example, discusses several ways that the term *evaluation* is used.) This book therefore begins by defining assessment and distinguishing it from some related concepts. Because it's also helpful to understand the value of a subject under discussion, this chapter also reflects on why assessment is important in higher education.

WHAT IS ASSESSMENT?

Assessment is the ongoing process of:
- Establishing clear, measurable expected *outcomes* of student learning.
- Ensuring that students have sufficient *opportunities* to achieve those outcomes.
- Systematically gathering, analyzing, and interpreting *evidence* to determine how well student learning matches our expectations.
- Using the resulting information to understand and *improve* student learning.

Many assessment practitioners, notably Angelo (1995), have put forth definitions of assessment. The previous definition summarizes their work.

These four steps do not represent a once-and-done process but a continuous four-step cycle (Figure 1.1). In the fourth step, assessment results are used to review and possibly revise approaches to the other three steps, and the cycle begins anew.

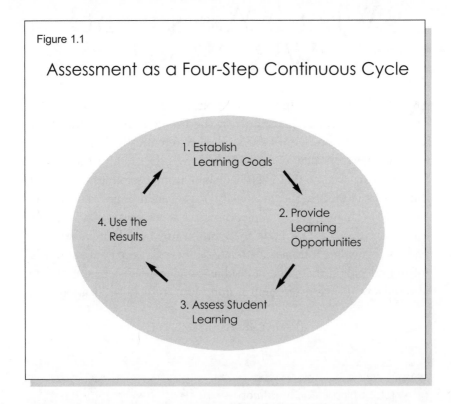

Figure 1.1

Assessment as a Four-Step Continuous Cycle

1. Establish Learning Goals

2. Provide Learning Opportunities

3. Assess Student Learning

4. Use the Results

While the term *assessment* can be used broadly—we can assess any goal or outcome in any discipline or any activity—in this book the term refers to the assessment of *student learning*.

WHAT IS THE DIFFERENCE BETWEEN ASSESSMENT AND TESTING?

Psychometricians define *testing* as the systematic measurement of a mental trait such as an aptitude, achievement, skill, or attitude. Testing thus describes much of the third step of the assessment process: systematically gathering and analyzing evidence of achievement of student learning outcomes.

To many educators and laypeople, however, *testing* brings to mind only traditional tests—multiple-choice, essay, and the like—and not the many other assessment strategies used today. Because of this widespread image of testing, assessment practitioners generally use the term only to refer to traditional tests (Chapter 11).

WHAT IS THE DIFFERENCE BETWEEN ASSESSMENT AND EVALUATION?

Evaluation is defined in many different ways. One definition equates evaluation with judgment: *evaluation is using assessment information to make an informed **judgment** on such things as:*

- Whether students have achieved the learning goals we've established for them;

- The relative strengths and weaknesses of our teaching/learning strategies; or

- What changes in our goals and teaching/learning strategies might be appropriate.

Evaluation defined this way is part of the assessment process: interpreting assessment evidence (part of Step 3) and using the results (Step 4). This definition points out that assessment results alone only guide us; they do not dictate decisions to us. We use our best professional judgment to make appropriate decisions. This definition of evaluation thus reinforces the ownership that faculty and staff have over the assessment process.

A second definition of evaluation is *determining the match between **intended outcomes** (Step 1 of the assessment process) and **actual outcomes** (Step 3 of the assessment process). Under this definition, the *assessment of student learning* and the *evaluation of student learning* could be considered virtually synonymous.

A third definition of evaluation is *investigating and judging the quality or worth of a program, project, or other entity* rather than student learning. We might evaluate an anthropology program, an employee safety program, an alumni program, or a civic project designed to reduce criminal recidivism.

Under this definition, evaluation is a broader concept than assessment. While assessment focuses on goals for student learning, evaluation addresses *all* the major goals of a program. An anthropology program, for example, might have goals not only for student learning but also to conduct anthropological research, provide anthropological services to local museums, and conduct its affairs in a cost-effective manner. An evaluation of the program would therefore consider not only student learning but also research activities, community service, and cost-effectiveness.

What Is the Difference Between Assessment and Grading?

Obviously there is a great deal of overlap between the concepts of grading and assessment. Both are attempts to identify what students have learned, and the grading process can therefore be an important component of an assessment program. But grades alone are usually insufficient evidence of student learning. Imagine applying for tenure or promotion and providing your students' grades as sole evidence of your teaching effectiveness and of what your students have learned. Would your tenure and promotion committee accept grades as sufficient evidence? Probably not, for the following reasons.

Grading and Assessment Criteria May (Appropriately) Differ

Some faculty base grades (appropriately) not just on evidence of what students have learned, such as tests, papers, presentations, and projects, but also on student behaviors that may or may not be related to course goals. Some faculty, for example, count class attendance toward a final course grade, even though students with poor attendance might nonetheless conceivably master course goals. Others count class participation toward the final grade, even though oral communication skills aren't a course goal. Some downgrade assignments that are turned in late.

These practices can all be very appropriate classroom management strategies and grading practices, but they illustrate how grades and assessment standards might not match. A student who has *not* achieved major learning goals might still earn a fairly high grade by playing by the rules and fulfilling other, less-important grading criteria. Conversely, a student who *has* achieved a course's major learning goals might nonetheless earn a poor grade if she fails to do the other things expected of her.

Grading Standards May Be Vague or Inconsistent

Sometimes grades are based on vague or inconsistent standards that do not correspond to major learning goals. While many faculty do base assignment and course grades on carefully conceived standards, grades can be inadequate, imprecise, and idiosyncratic, as Angelo points out in the preface to Walvoord and Anderson's (1998) *Effective Grading.* Faculty may say they want students to learn how to think critically but base grades on tests emphasizing factual recall. Faculty teaching sections of the same course may not agree on common standards and might therefore, theoretically, award different grades to the same student assignment. Sometimes individual grading standards are so vague that a faculty member might, conceivably, award an A to an essay one day and a B to the identical essay a week later.

Grades Alone May Give Insufficient Information on Student Strengths and Weaknesses

Grades alone don't always provide meaningful information on exactly what students have and haven't learned. We can conclude from a grade of B in an organic chemistry course, for example, that the student has probably learned a good deal about organic chemistry, but from that grade alone we can't tell exactly what aspects of organic chemistry she has and hasn't mastered. Similarly, we can conclude from a grade of B on a sociology research paper that the student has probably learned a good deal about sociology research methods, but from the grade alone we can't tell exactly what aspects of the research process he has and hasn't mastered.

Grades Do Not Reflect All Learning Experiences

As the Association of American Colleges & Universities' *Greater Expectations* (2002) report points out, grades give us information on student performance in individual courses or course assignments, not on how well students have learned key competencies, such as critical thinking or writing skills, holistically over an entire program. They also don't tell us what students have learned from ungraded cocurricular activities.

Do Grades Have a Place in an Assessment Program?

Of course they do! Grades can be useful evidence of student learning if the grades are based on direct evidence of student learning (tests, projects, papers, assignments, etc.) that is clearly linked to major learning goals and clearly delineated, consistent standards through test blueprints (see Chapter 11) or rubrics (Chapter 7). Walvoord and Anderson's (1998) *Effective Grading* gives a plethora of practical suggestions on how to tie grades more closely to explicit learning goals and standards.

What Is the Difference Between Assessment and Research?

Upcraft and Schuh (2002) note that assessment differs from traditional research in its purpose and therefore in its nature. Traditional research is conducted to test theories, while assessment is conducted to inform practice. Assessment is a form of *action research,* a distinct type of research whose purpose is to improve one's own work rather than make broad generalizations. Assessment's four-step cycle of establishing learning goals, providing learning opportunities, assessing student learning, and using the results to improve the other three steps mirrors the four steps of action research: plan, act, observe, and reflect.

While assessment, like any other form of action research, is disciplined and systematic and uses many of the methodologies of traditional research, most faculty and staff lack the time and resources to design and conduct rigorous, replicable empirical research studies with impartial distance. They instead aim to keep the benefits of assessment in proportion to the time and resources devoted to them. If you take the time and effort to design your assessments reasonably carefully and collect corroborating evidence, your assessment results may be imperfect but will nonetheless give you information that you'll be able to use with confidence to make decisions about teaching and learning. Chapter 2 discusses strategies for doing this.

WHAT IS THE DIFFERENCE BETWEEN ASSESSING STUDENT LEARNING AND ASSESSING INSTITUTIONAL EFFECTIVENESS?

Accreditation organizations, governing boards, legislators, and other stakeholders increasingly ask colleges and universities to assess *institutional effectiveness* as well as student learning. What's the difference? *Institutional effectiveness* is how well an institution is achieving its mission and major institutional goals. Since student learning is the heart of most institutional missions, the assessment of student learning is a major component of the assessment of institutional effectiveness (Figure 1.2).

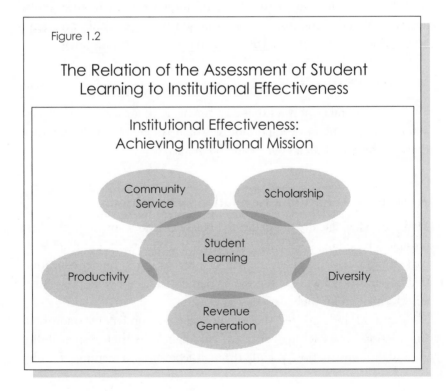

Figure 1.2

The Relation of the Assessment of Student Learning to Institutional Effectiveness

Institutional Effectiveness:
Achieving Institutional Mission

Community Service

Scholarship

Student Learning

Productivity

Diversity

Revenue Generation

But institutional effectiveness goes further; it includes other aspects of institutional mission, such as research and scholarship, community service, building a diverse community, or modeling certain values, and other major institutional goals, such as providing financial support to those without sufficient means to attend college, providing facilities and infrastructure that promote student learning, or developing collaborative partnerships with basic education.

Assessing institutional effectiveness thus involves assessing not only student learning but also each of these other aims through the same four-step cycle. Assessing an institutional mission of community service would begin, for example, by developing a clear statement of the major goals of the institution's community service programs (Step 1). Programs designed to achieve those goals are then implemented (Step 2). The programs are then assessed to see whether they are achieving their major goals (Step 3). (A goal to provide cultural programming to the local community might be assessed, for example, by counting attendance at cultural events and perhaps surveying local residents on how well the institution serves their cultural interests.) Finally, the results are used to modify the institution's community service goals, programs, and/or assessment strategies (Step 4), and the cycle begins anew.

WHY IS ASSESSMENT A GOOD IDEA?

There are a number of ways that assessment helps faculty, students, and administrators, the most important of which is helping faculty improve their teaching and their courses and programs.

Assessment Is Part of a Revolution in Education

Many of today's faculty are dedicated teachers who want to do the best possible job helping their students learn—and who want and need feedback in order to do so. They are part of a revolution in higher education that began in 1995 with a proposal by Barr and Tagg for what they called a new paradigm for higher education.

Barr and Tagg posited that faculty teaching under the traditional "instruction" or "teaching-centered" paradigm view their responsibility as providing instruction, usually through lectures and readings. Faculty teaching under this paradigm believe that if students don't learn the material and earn a poor grade, the fault lies with the students, not the faculty. Such faculty feel no sense of responsibility to reach out to students proactively and help them learn.

Today's faculty increasingly follow Barr and Tagg's "learning" or "learning-centered" paradigm. The paradigm draws on significant research (see Chapter 16) demonstrating that students learn more effectively when, among other things, they are actively involved in self-directed learning, they view their professor more as a guide than as a remote authority, and they receive frequent and prompt feedback on their work. Under this paradigm, faculty are more directly involved in helping students learn. While there will always be unmotivated students who deserve to fail, these faculty assume that, if a significant number of their students do not achieve their learning goals, the faculty's teaching/learning strategies are at least partly responsible.

Under the teaching-centered model, the major if not sole purpose of assessment is to assign student grades, but under the learning-centered model, assessment also provides the feedback essential to helping faculty understand what is and isn't working and how to improve their curricula and teaching/learning strategies to bring about even greater learning.

Assessment Has Many Other Benefits

Good assessment practices have many benefits beyond helping faculty improve their teaching. *Students* benefit because:

- The clear expectations that good assessment requires help them understand where they should focus their time and energies.

- Assessment, especially the grading process, motivates them to do their best.

- Assessment feedback helps them understand their strengths and weaknesses.

- Assessment information gives them documentation of what they've learned that they can use to apply for jobs, awards, and programs of advanced study.

Faculty benefit because:

- Assessment activities bring faculty together to discuss important issues such as what they teach, why, and their standards and expectations.

- Assessment activities help faculty see how their courses link together to form coherent programs and how the courses they teach contribute to student success in subsequent pursuits.

- Positive assessment results can be used as compelling evidence of the quality of their teaching when they apply for tenure, promotion, and salary increases.

Administrators benefit because:

- Assessment information documenting the success of a program or institution can be used to convince employers, donors, legislators, and other constituents of its quality and worth.

- Assessment can help ensure that institutional resources are being spent in the most effective ways possible—where they'll have the greatest impact on student learning.

- Assessment can help administrators make informed decisions about such matters as resource allocations and faculty hires.

WHAT OTHER FORCES ARE DRIVING ASSESSMENT?

Accrediting organizations, governing boards, and state governments are all increasingly calling upon, if not mandating, colleges and universities to assess student learning. Why?

Federal Requirements for Regional Accreditation

One force driving the assessment movement is the federal government, which sets conditions that regional accrediting organizations must meet in order to be recognized by the U.S. Department of Education. Regional accrediting organizations have always required institutions to provide evidence of their "quality" and that they are achieving their mission. Prior to the mid-1980s, the evidence provided by many institutions consisted of resources and other inputs into the teaching/learning process: number of books in the library, number of faculty holding doctorates, number of dollars spent on academic programs, and so forth. The assumption was that, if these resources were in place, learning and other good things were bound to happen.

The federal government changed this when it mandated that regional accrediting organizations must require institutions to provide *direct* evidence that they are achieving their missions. Since the primary mission of virtually all colleges and universities is the education of students, institutions must now provide direct evidence that students are achieving whatever learning goals the institutions have established.

Disciplinary Accreditation Requirements

Concurrently with regional accrediting organizations' increased emphasis on assessment, more and more disciplinary accrediting organizations are also increasing their focus on assessment. These organizations correctly recognize that the best evidence of the quality of an academic program is direct evidence that its students learn what the organization considers important.

Calls for Accountability

Another force driving the assessment movement is increasingly constrained resources. Governing boards, legislators, and others funding higher education are taking an increasingly businesslike approach and asking whether their investment is yielding adequate dividends. They are asking colleges and universities to justify their investment by being *accountable*: providing substantive evidence that their investment yields significant results.

Developing an assessment program is especially important for institutions not yet subject to an externally imposed system of assessments and standards. If these institutions assemble compelling evidence of student learning *now*, they have a much better chance of warding off such mandates.

Assessment is also important for those institutions that do not have a reputation for rigor, whose funding sources ask why faculty teach seemingly esoteric, impractical subjects, or whose tuition and fees are exceptionally high. If these institutions can demonstrate though assessment that their students develop important skills such as writing, critical thinking, and analysis, they are far more likely to receive support.

Other Forces

Other trends in education are also behind the increased focus on new approaches to assessment.

Critics of traditional paper-and-pencil tests increasingly advocate assessments that ask students to solve "messy" real-world problems rather than fabricated problems for which there is only one correct answer.

We are increasingly recognizing that that *student learning is greater than the sum of its parts.* Portfolios, capstone experiences, and other holistic assessments that draw a more complete portrait of student learning and help students see the big picture are increasingly encouraged.

The development of thinking and performance skills and attitudes is increasingly stressed more than the acquisition of knowledge (see Chapter 5). This dramatic change in learning goals requires rethinking approaches to assessment.

Our body of knowledge is changing so quickly that we now realize that students must not only learn while in college but develop a lifelong interest in learning and the ability to learn on their own, so they can continue to learn after they've left our institution. Again, this is a dramatic change in learning goals that requires rethinking assessment strategies.

We are increasingly recognizing that *students have different learning styles* and that any one assessment strategy may inadvertently favor some students over others (see Chapter 2). We thus aim to assess student learning using a variety of approaches and not solely through, say, essay tests.

WILL ASSESSMENT EVER GO AWAY?

Is assessment another higher education fad that we can simply ride out? It's not likely. One obvious reason is that federal regulations aren't likely to go away. A far more important reason, however, is that higher education's sharpened focus on helping students learn is likely to stay with us. Assessment is a critical tool to help ensure that teaching and learning in colleges and universities are the best that they can be.

Another emerging reason for the persistence of assessment is the growing trend to award certificates and licenses based on demonstrated learning rather than "seat time." It's possible that, within a few years, increased demand for this kind of certification will force college diplomas to bear seals certifying that graduates have, say, a certain level of writing skill or technology skill—and this can only happen with carefully designed assessment strategies.

TIME TO THINK, DISCUSS, AND PRACTICE

1) Brainstorm three possible goals for your college library. How might each goal be evaluated? Is each evaluation an example of assessing student learning or not?

2) Does each of these faculty have a learning-centered or a teaching-centered approach? Why?

- Dr. Alfred's term papers are due on the last day of class. He grades them during the following week, and students can pick them up when the next term begins.

- Dr. Berger wants students to discover principles on their own rather than absorb them through a lecture.

- Dr. Cowell views his job teaching calculus as identifying which students should continue as math majors and which should not.

- Dr. Dietz views her job as designing a learning environment for her students.

REFERENCES

Angelo, T. A. (1995). Reassessing (and redefining) assessment. *AAHE Bulletin, 48*(3), 7–9.

Association of American Colleges and Universities. (2002). *Greater expectations: A new vision for learning as a nation goes to college.* Washington, DC: Author. Retrieved June 2, 2003, from http://www.greaterexpectations.org

Barr, R. B., & Tagg, J. (1995). From teaching to learning: A new paradigm for undergraduate education. *Change, 27*(6), 12–25.

Upcraft, M. L., & Schuh, J. H. (2002). Assessment vs. research: Why we should care about the difference. *About Campus, 7*(1), 16–20.

Walvoord, B. E., & Anderson, V. J. (1998). *Effective grading: A tool for learning and assessment.* San Francisco, CA: Jossey-Bass.

RECOMMENDED READING

Angelo, T. A. (1993). A "teacher's dozen": Fourteen general, research-based principles for improving higher learning in our classrooms. *AAHE Bulletin, 45*(8), 3–7, 13.

Calhoun, E. (1993). Action research: Three approaches. *Educational Leadership, 51*(2), 62–65.

Callan, P. M., & Finney, J. E. (2002). Assessing educational capital: An imperative for policy. *Change, 34*(4), 25–31.

Chickering, A. W., & Gamson, Z. (1987). Seven principles for good practice in undergraduate education. *AAHE Bulletin, 39*(7), 5–10.

Crist, C., Guill, D., Harmes, P., & Lake, C. (1998, November). Purposes of assessment. In *CES fieldbook.* Oakland, CA: Coalition of Essential Schools. Retrieved June 2, 2003, from http://www.essentialschools.org/cs/resources/view/ces_res/126

Ewell, P. (2002). An emerging scholarship: A brief history of assessment. In T. Banta & Associates (Eds.), *Building a scholarship of assessment* (pp. 3–25). San Francisco, CA: Jossey-Bass.

Johnson, B. (1993). Teacher-as-researcher. *ERIC Digest*. Washington, DC: ERIC Clearinghouse on Teacher Education. (ERIC Document Reproduction Service No. ED355205)

Joint Committee on Standards for Educational Evaluation. (1994). *The program evaluation standards: How to assess evaluations of educational programs* (2nd ed.). Thousand Oaks, CA: Sage.

Knight Higher Education Collaborative. (1990). The lattice and the ratchet. *Policy Perspectives, 2*(4), 1–8.

Lake, C., Harmes, P., Guill, D., & Crist, C. (1998, November). Defining assessment. In *CES fieldbook*. Oakland, CA: Coalition of Essential Schools. Retrieved June 2, 2003, from http://www.essentialschools.org/cs/resources/view/ces_res/124

Leskes, A. (2002). Beyond confusion: An assessment glossary. *Peer Review, 4*(2/3), 42–43.

Mentkowski, M., & Associates. (2000). *Learning that lasts: Integrating learning, development, and performance in college and beyond.* San Francisco, CA: Jossey-Bass.

O'Banion, T. (1997). *A learning college for the 21st century.* Westport, CT: Oryx.

Pascarella, E. T., & Terenzini, P. T. (1991). *How college affects students: Findings and insights from twenty years of research.* San Francisco, CA: Jossey-Bass.

Romer, R., & Education Commission of the States. (1996, April). What research says about improving undergraduate education. *AAHE Bulletin, 48*(8), 5–8.

Seeley, M. M. (1994). The mismatch between assessment and grading. *Educational Leadership, 52*(2), 4–6.

2
What Are Good Assessment Practices?

Regardless of what or how we are assessing, our assessment activities should conform to six principles of good practice.

Good assessments:
- Give us *useful* information.
- Give us *reasonably accurate, truthful* information.
- Are *fair* to all students.
- Are *ethical* and protect the privacy and dignity of those involved.
- Are *systematized*.
- Are *cost effective*, yielding value that justifies the time and expense we put into them.

This chapter discusses each of these principles.

CREATE USEFUL ASSESSMENTS

Perhaps the most important assessment principle is that assessments be useful. If an assessment doesn't help improve teaching and learning activities, why bother with it? In order to be useful, *assessments must correspond to your key learning goals and your curriculum*. No one assessment is right for every course or program in every institution.

To ensure the usefulness of your assessments, periodically evaluate your assessment program and ask yourself whether your assessments are giving you useful information (see Chapter 16). If a particular assessment is not helping you or your students, stop doing it. Similarly, if a particular survey question isn't providing information that you can use to help make decisions about your program, stop asking it. And periodically compare your assessment tools against your learning goals to ensure that they continue to align.

CREATE ACCURATE, TRUTHFUL ASSESSMENTS

What is a "good" assessment? More than anything else, it is an assessment that gives us *truthful* information; it tells us what our students have *truly* learned. Students who have truly learned what we want them to will do well on a good assessment; students who truly have not learned what we want them to will not do well on it.

Unfortunately, it's not possible to determine with complete confidence exactly what our students have learned. We can't get inside their heads to find out what they truly know and what they don't. The best we can do is to look at samples of their behavior—what they write, produce, say, and perform—and from those samples try to estimate or infer what they truly know. Even under the best of circumstances, making an inference from these snapshots of behavior is bound to be at least somewhat inaccurate because of what psychometricians call "measurement error"—fluctuations in human performance that we can't completely control. We can't control, for example:

- Whether a student is ill on the day she completes an assignment or takes a test.

- Whether a student is preoccupied with an argument he's had and therefore isn't focusing sufficiently to do his best.

- Memory fluctuations (we all periodically "blank out" on key names and facts).

- Luck in whether a particular assignment or test question focuses on something a student knows well (we all learn some aspects of a subject better than others).

- Luck in guessing on multiple choice questions.

- Mental "set" (sometimes we have flashes of insight; sometimes we seem inexplicably in a mental rut).

While we thus can't create assessments that will give us absolutely accurate information about what students have learned, we must strive to make them sufficiently truthful that we will have confidence in our findings and can use them with assurance to make decisions about goals, curricula, and teaching strategies. The following approaches will help increase the accuracy and truthfulness of assessment strategies.

Start with clear statements of the most important things you want students to learn from the course or program. Learning goals are discussed in Chapter 5.

Teach what you are assessing. Purposefully help students learn the skills needed to do the assessment task. Matching goals, learning opportunities, and assessments is discussed in Chapter 4.

Because each assessment technique is imperfect and has inherent strengths and weaknesses, *collect more than one kind of evidence* of what students have learned. If you are assessing learning across an entire program, for example, rather than only give students a culminating examination, you might also look at samples of papers they've written and perhaps internship supervisors' ratings of their skills.

Before creating an assignment, *write a rubric:* a list of the key things you want students to learn by completing the assignment and to demonstrate on the completed assignment. Rubrics are discussed in Chapter 7.

Likewise, before writing test questions, *create a test "blueprint":* a list of the key learning goals to be assessed by the test and the number of points or questions to be devoted to each learning goal. Test blueprints are discussed in Chapter 11.

Make assignments and test questions crystal clear. Write them so that all students will interpret them in the same way and know exactly what you want them to do. Crafting effective assignments and creating test questions are discussed in Chapters 8 and 11, respectively.

Make sure that your assignments and test questions clearly relate to your key learning goals. Each test question, for example, should clearly correspond to the learning goal you've identified for it in your test blueprint. A writing assignment intended to assess how well students organize an essay shouldn't be graded primarily on grammar and spelling.

Ask colleagues and students to review drafts of your assignments, rubrics, and (using former students) test questions to make sure they're clear and appear to assess what you want them to.

Try out surveys and similar tools with a small group of students before using them on a larger scale. Check students' responses to make sure they are giving answers that make sense. Ask them if they found anything unclear or confusing. Ask some students to "think out loud" as they answer a test question; their thought processes should match those you intended.

Collect enough evidence to **get a representative sample** of what your students have learned and can do. Collect a sufficiently large sample that you will be able to use the results with confidence to make decisions about a course or program. See Chapter 6 for information on deciding on a sample size.

Score student work fairly and consistently. Before scoring begins, have a clear understanding of the characteristics of meritorious, satisfactory, and inadequate papers. Then use a rubric to help score assignments, papers, projects, etc., consistently. Other strategies for scoring fairly and consistently are discussed in Chapter 7.

Use assessment results appropriately. Never base any important decision on only one assessment. (Failure to adhere to this maxim is one of the major shortcomings of many high-stakes testing programs.) Assessments shouldn't make decisions for us or dictate what we should teach; they should only advise us as we use our professional judgment to make suitable decisions. Appropriate use of results is discussed further in Chapter 16.

Evaluate the outcomes of your assessment efforts and revise your assessment strategies to address any shortcomings. This is discussed in Chapter 16.

How Can Assessment Quality Be Documented?

Should you document evidence of the quality of your assessment methods? This depends on how the results may be used. An assessment used to make minor curricular modifications does not need as much evidence of its quality as one used to help determine who graduates, whether expensive modifications should be implemented, or whether a program should be terminated, or one whose findings are likely to be challenged.

Obviously, the more rigorous and extensive your evidence, the more compelling it is, but also the more time-consuming it is to collect and evaluate. Be forewarned that, no matter how extensive your efforts to document the quality of your assessment strategies, you can never *prove* that your assessments are accurate and truthful; you can only collect evidence that your assessments *appear* to be accurate and truthful. Someone who wants to dispute your findings will always be able to poke a hole in your assessment strategy.

Should you decide to document the quality of your assessment activities, here are some ways to do so.

Keep records of everything you've done to maximize assessment quality, including reviews of your assessment tools by others, tryouts of your assessment strategies, rubrics used to score student work, blind scorings by your colleagues, and other strategies discussed in the previous section.

Use other kinds of assessments to corroborate your findings. A student whose writing sample receives a high score, for example, should also receive a high score on a published writing test and a high rating from her professor on her writing skills.

See if results fall in appropriate patterns. Students at the end of a program should generally do better on an assessment than students at the beginning, while students with high grades should generally do better on an assessment than students with low grades. Some results should predict current or future performance; scores on a pre-calculus test, for example, should predict calculus grades at least somewhat accurately. And sometimes students should perform differently by major. Physics majors, for example, may score higher on a quantitative reasoning assessment, on average, than English majors.

These are only a few of the many approaches that can be taken to appraise and document the quality of assessment measures. To learn more, ask a psychology or education faculty member for information on reliability and validity.

CREATE FAIR ASSESSMENTS

A fair assessment is one in which students are given equitable opportunities to demonstrate what they know. This does not necessarily mean that all students should be treated exactly the same. Equitable assessment means that students are assessed using appropriate methods and procedures, which may vary from one student to the next depending on the student's prior knowledge, cultural experience, and learning style. For example:

- Marla is not a strong writer but great at visualizing concepts. She will better demonstrate her understanding of a complex concept if she can draw a diagram rather than write an explanation.

- Robert's culture values collaboration, and he learns more from working with others than by studying alone. He will better demonstrate his understanding if he can work with others on a group presentation rather than make a solo presentation.

- Janice is not a good test-taker but very creative. She will better demonstrate her understanding if she can create a video explaining a complex concept rather than take a test.

- Jason was home-schooled in a home without a computer, so he's still insecure on computers. He will better demonstrate his understanding on a paper-and-pencil test than on a computer-based test.

- Lisa attended a high school that stressed rote memorization and drill. She will better demonstrate her knowledge of American history on a fill-in-the-blank test than in a term paper that requires critical thinking skills.

- Dan has poor test-taking skills. If Question 2 stumps him, he'll likely spend the whole testing period on that question and never answer the remaining questions. He will better demonstrate his understanding by writing a term paper than by taking a multiple-choice test.

Creating custom-tailored assessments for each student is, of course, largely impractical, but we can work toward assessing students equitably by providing a variety of assessment venues. Instead of assessing students solely through multiple-choice tests or solely through writing assignments, assess them using a combination of tests, writing assignments, and other projects. Students might convey the essence of a novel's protagonist, for example, through a diagram, video, or oral presentation rather than through the traditional essay. Table 8.1 in Chapter 8 offers other suggestions for varying assignments.

CREATE ETHICAL ASSESSMENTS

A number of professional organizations engaged in the assessment of human performance have developed statements of ethical standards. Two pervasive themes in these statements are protecting the privacy and dignity of those being assessed and using results in a fair and appropriate manner. Virtually all these statements agree that ethical assessment programs:

Protect the privacy of those who are assessed. Take appropriate security precautions before, during, and after you conduct an assessment, and protect the confidentiality of individually identifiable information. Password-protect computer files with identifiable information and store paper records with identifiable information in locked file cabinets. If several people are reviewing samples of student work or accessing a computer file, removing information that identifies individuals may be a wise precaution.

While it's important to protect student privacy, faculty must have sufficient information to be able to do their jobs, and this can often involve sharing identifiable information. Some departments, for example, periodically hold faculty meetings to discuss the progress of each of the students in their program. Faculty also consult with their colleagues about their students less formally; a faculty member concerned about a student's slipping performance might consult with the student's advisor for ideas on how to help the student get back on track. Faculty are simply carrying out an important part of their responsibilities when they hold such conversations, and considering identifiable assessment results can make the conversations more fruitful.

Keep students informed about the nature and purpose of each assessment. Students should be informed as early in their programs as possible, in writing, of graduation or program completion requirements beyond successful completion of course work, such as compiling a portfolio, completing a survey, participating in a focus group, or taking a comprehensive examination. These statements should also make clear if, in order to progress or graduate, students are expected to earn a minimum score on a special assessment such as a portfolio or published test.

Minimize potential bias. Obviously we wouldn't want to use an instrument with stereotyping or offensive material. But an unbiased instrument goes farther than that; it describes activities that are equally familiar to all and uses words that have common meanings to all. An item on a quantitative skills test that asks students to analyze football statistics wouldn't be fair to women, for example.

A good way to detect potential bias is to ask yourself, "If someone wanted to see the exact opposite of the results that I'm hoping for, would he or she conduct the same assessment in the same way?" You're probably hoping, for example, that your assessments will demonstrate that your students are learning all kinds of important things. Imagine (however difficult this may be for you!) that someone is convinced that your course or program is of very poor quality and expensive to boot and wants it eliminated. What strategies to assess student learning might you both conceivably agree on?

To ensure further that your assessments are equitable and don't favor students of a particular gender or background, ask colleagues and students of varying backgrounds to review drafts of your assignments and test questions. And engage and encourage your students; the performance of some is greatly influenced by positive contact with faculty.

Give appropriate attribution to the work and ideas of others. Don't use items from someone else's test or survey in your own assessment instrument, for example, without obtaining permission from the author or copyright holder and acknowledging the contribution.

Make the following information available to anyone considering your assessment results:

- The exact wording of assignments and questions given to students.

- How the participating students were selected and any evidence that the students who participated are a representative, unbiased sample of the students you wanted to assess (see Chapter 4).

- The number of students or student works in the sample, the number actually participating, and the participation rate (for example, "A random sample of 50 seniors was invited to participate in exit interviews. Twenty students or 40% of those invited participated").

- Information on the precision of the results (see Chapter 14).

- A fair, objective presentation of the results, both intended and unintended, without censorship.

- Qualifiers and caveats regarding the conclusions drawn from the results. (You might, for example, want to caution your audience about a low survey participation rate, a test question that you've learned was misinterpreted by many students, or that male students are underrepresented in the group of papers you assessed.)

Discourage others from making inappropriate interpretations or otherwise false or misleading statements about assessment results.

Promote the use of multiple sources of information when making any major decisions.

What Is the Role of Institutional Review Boards in Assessment Programs?

Title 45, Part 46 of the Code of Federal Regulations (Office for Protection from Research Risks, 2001) describes federal policy for the protection of human research subjects. The regulations stipulate that institutional review boards (IRBs) must be established to ensure that research protects and poses no significant risk or threat to the rights and welfare of human subjects. There are three levels of review: full review (which requires appearing before the entire IRB), expedited review (in which at least one member of the IRB reviews the research plan), and exempted from review (under which the research plan must still be sent to the IRB).

The regulations state that "an IRB shall review and have authority to approve, require modifications (to secure approval), or disapprove all research activities covered by this policy." They define research as "a systematic investigation, including research development, testing and evaluation, designed to develop or contribute to generalizable knowledge." The regulations further state that:

Unless otherwise required by department or agency heads, research activities in which the only involvement of human subjects will be in one or more of the following categories are exempt from this policy:

(1) Research conducted in established or commonly accepted educational settings, involving normal educational practices, such as (i) research on regular or special education instructional strategies, or (ii) research on the effectiveness of or the comparison

Focus on those assessment strategies that give the greatest dividends for time and resources invested.

Limit the volume of assessment information you collect from students. Perhaps a one-page chart will give you just as much information on students' analysis skills as a three-page essay. Perhaps a two-page abstract will give you just as much information on students' writing skills as a 20-page term paper.

Use rubrics (Chapter 7)—they really speed up the process of evaluating student papers and projects.

Stop doing something else. Consider dropping your midterm examination to give you more time to assess student projects. Consider moving some of your more straightforward lectures to handouts that students read on their own, creating more class time for students to collaborate on assignments and for you to review assignments with individual students.

Look at samples rather than censuses of student work (see Chapter 6). If students maintain journals in your course, for example, spot check a random sample of them each week rather than read them all. If all students in a program complete a senior thesis, evaluate just a sample of them for writing and critical thinking skills.

Stagger your assessments. Stagger the due dates for assignments so each class's assignments are turned in a few weeks apart and you're not overwhelmed with papers at any one point in the term. Similarly, stagger program assessments across a multi-year period. A three-year assessment cycle might include an examination of student portfolios every first year, a survey of alumni every second year, and exit interviews of graduating students every third.

Adapt your assessment schedule to meet your evolving needs. Suppose that focus groups show high levels of student satisfaction but senior theses show poor organizational skills. You may want to put the focus groups on a back burner, conducting them only once every three years just to make sure student satisfaction isn't slipping, and begin reviewing theses every term to monitor the effectiveness of your efforts to strengthen organizational skills.

We're not talking dissertation-quality research here; establish realistic expectations for quality. As discussed in Chapter 1, assessment is a form of action research, a branch of research that, while disciplined and systematic, is inherently imperfect, so don't expect perfection. While it would be wonderful if every assessment project were designed to meet standards for publication in peer-reviewed research journals, realistically most faculty don't have the time—or interest—to do this. Aim not for replicable, generalizable research but for results that are simply good enough to use with confidence to make decisions about teaching and learning in your course, program, or institution.

Chapters 3 and 7 of this book and Chapter 8 of Walvoord and Anderson's (1998) *Effective Grading* have more suggestions on keeping the assessment burden manageable.

TIME TO THINK, DISCUSS, AND PRACTICE

1) Discuss what it means to have a "high-quality" assessment. Brainstorm three characteristics of a high-quality assessment.

2) The History faculty are assessing students' writing skills by evaluating senior theses for organization, focus, style, and mechanics.

- Brainstorm three ways that the faculty might help ensure that this assessment will give them accurate, truthful information.

- What should the faculty do to protect the privacy of the students and their professors as they conduct this assessment?

3) One of the goals of Mackenzie College's general education curriculum is for students to develop a tolerance for perspectives other than their own. Brainstorm three survey questions they might ask that you think would yield *unbiased* results.

References

Office for Protection from Research Risks. (2001, November 13). *Code of federal regulations: Title 45: Public welfare: Part 46: Protection of human subjects.* Washington, DC: National Institutes of Health. Retrieved June 2, 2003, from http://ohrp.osophs.dhhs.gov/human subjects/guidance/45cfr46.htm

Walvoord, B. E., & Anderson, V. J. (1998). *Effective grading: A tool for learning and assessment.* San Francisco, CA: Jossey-Bass.

Recommended Reading

American Association for Higher Education. (1996, July 25). *9 principles of good practice for assessing student learning.* Washington, DC: Author. Retrieved June 2, 2003, from http://www.aahe.org/assess ment/principl.htm

Anderson, J. A. (1988). Cognitive styles and multicultural populations. *Journal of Teacher Education, 24*(1), 2–9.

Badger, E. (1999). Finding one's voice: A model for more equitable assessment. In A. L. Nettles & M. T. Nettles (Eds.), *Measuring up: Challenges minorities face in educational assessment* (pp. 53–69). Boston, MA: Kluwer.

Campbell, D. T., & Fiske, D. W. (1959). Convergent and discriminant validation by the multitrait-multimethod matrix. *Psychological Bulletin, 56*(2), 81–105.

Conference on College Composition and Communication. (1995). *Writing assessment: A position statement.* Urbana, IL: National Council of Teachers of English. Retrieved June 2, 2003, from http://www.ncte.org/about/over/positions/category/assess/107610.htm

Conference on College Composition and Communication. (2001). *Guidelines for the ethical treatment of students and student writing in composition studies.* Urbana, IL: National Council of Teachers of English. Retrieved June 2, 2003, from http://www.ncte.org/about/over/positions/level/coll/107670.htm

Fleming, J. (1998). Correlates of the SAT in minority engineering students: An exploratory study. *Journal of Higher Education, 69,* 89–108.

Gonzalez, V. (1996). Do you believe in intelligence? Sociocultural dimensions of intelligence assessment in majority and minority students. *Educational Horizons, 75,* 45–52.

Greater Expectations Project on Accreditation and Assessment. (2002). *Criteria for recognizing "good practice" in assessing liberal education as collaborative & integrative.* Washington, DC: Association of American Colleges and Universities. Retrieved June 2, 2003, from http://www.aacu.org/gex/paa/assessment.cfm

Huba, M. E., & Freed, J. E. (2000). Applying principles of good practice in learner-centered assessment. In *Learner-centered assessment on college campuses: Shifting the focus from teaching to learning* (pp. 65–90). Needham Heights, MA: Allyn & Bacon.

Joint Committee on Standards for Educational Evaluation. (1994). *The program evaluation standards: How to assess evaluations of educational programs* (2nd ed.). Thousand Oaks, CA: Sage.

Joint Committee on Testing Practices. (1988). *Code of fair testing practices in education.* Washington, DC: National Council on Measurement in Education.

Lam, T. C. M. (1995). Fairness in performance assessment. *ERIC Digest.* Washington, DC: Office of Educational Research and Improvement. (ERIC Document Reproduction Service No. ED 391 982)

Linn, R. L. (1999). Validity standards and principles on equity in educational testing and assessment. In A. L. Nettles & M. T. Nettles, (Eds.), *Measuring up: Challenges minorities face in educational assessment* (pp. 13–31). Boston, MA: Kluwer.

McCabe, D. L., & Pavela, G. (1997). The principled pursuit of academic integrity. *AAHE Bulletin, 50*(4), 11–12.

National Council on Measurement in Education. (1995). *Code of professional responsibilities in educational measurement.* Washington, DC: Author. Retrieved June 2, 2003, from http://www.natd.org/Code_of_Professional_Responsibilities.html

National Research Council. (1993). *Leadership statement of nine principles on equity and educational testing and assessment.* Washington, DC: Author. Retrieved June 2, 2003, from http://www.ncrel.org/sdrs/areas/issues/content/cntareas/math/ma1newst.htm

Parkes, J. (2000, March 8). The relationship between the reliability and cost of performance assessments. *Education Policy Analysis Archives, 8*(16). Retrieved June 2, 2003, from http://epaa.asu.edu/epaa/v8n16/

Shavelson, R. J., & Huang, L. (2003). Responding responsibly to the frenzy to assess learning in higher education. *Change, 35*(1), 10–19.

Spangehl, S. D. (1994). Latent and leveraged benefits of assessment: Expanding the value of assessment information. In T. H. Bers & M. L. Mittler (Eds.), *New directions for community colleges: No. 88. Assessment and testing: Myths and realities* (pp. 13–21). San Francisco, CA: Jossey-Bass.

Suskie, L. (2000). Fair assessment practices: Giving students equitable opportunities to demonstrate learning. *AAHE Bulletin, 52*(9), 7–9. Retrieved June 2, 2003, from http://www.aahebulletin.com/public/archive/may2.asp

Thompson, B., & Daniel, L. G. (1996). Seminal readings on reliability and validity: A "hit parade" bibliography. *Educational and Psychological Measurement, 56*(5), 741–745.

3

Promoting an Assessment Culture

I t's the rare academic institution to which change comes easily. Why are so many people resistant to change?

- **Some people are satisfied with the status quo.** Some faculty, for example, are reasonably good teachers, with good evaluations from students and peers and a good life in general. They're not interested in stretching to achieve even greater excellence. Their attitude is, "If it ain't broke, don't fix it."

- **Others don't see the relevance of an initiative** to them and therefore try to ignore it. Some faculty, for example, are more engaged in their research than in the undergraduates they teach and are simply not very interested in improving their teaching or their department's curriculum.

- **Others feel that they're already too busy** with their current responsibilities. They see any innovation as just one more thing they have to do on top of everything else, with their time already stretched too thin.

- **Still others are old-timers who have seen many new initiatives come and go** over the years. They're convinced that, if they just wait, assessment too will fade away.

- **Some people think they will need to learn and use new skills** that will be difficult to master. Some people, for example, are uncomfortable with technology and worry that assessment means learning how to design and administer computer-based tests and surveys.

Others are "mathephobes" and worry that they'll have to figure out how to analyze mounds of data.

- *Others feel their status is threatened* by a new initiative. A faculty member who teaches with entertaining but lightweight lectures might feel threatened by the prospect of assessing students' critical thinking skills. Another faculty member who prizes her independence might feel threatened by the prospect of developing common learning outcomes collaboratively with her colleagues.

- *Some people have misconceptions about a new initiative.* Some faculty, for example, view assessment as a threat to academic freedom and their treasured autonomy. They fear that they'll be told exactly what and how to teach. Others worry that less-than-positive assessment results will hurt their promotion or tenure prospects.

On top of these sources of resistance to any kind of change, some people may be especially resistant to assessment because it carries the prospect of bad news: learning that something isn't working as well as it should. No one likes to hear bad news because it usually means that a problem needs to be fixed, which means more work, and few people want more work.

How can a culture of assessment be fostered if there is resistance to change and to assessment? The overriding key, as discussed in the next section, is that institutional leaders must be engaged in and committed to assessment. Beyond that, because institutional cultures vary, there's no one strategy that will work for everyone, and what works on one campus may not work on another. To identify effective strategies for your institution, think of another initiative that's been launched successfully, perhaps a reform of the general education curriculum, a first-year experience program, or a service learning initiative. How was faculty buy-in achieved with that initiative? You may be able to emulate those strategies.

CAMPUS LEADERS MUST BE ONBOARD

While there are many reasons why some institutions are engaged in assessment and others are not, assessment practitioners and scholars have found that one factor predominates. If campus leaders are committed to assessment, assessment gets done and it gets done well. If campus leaders—especially the chief academic officer (vice president for academic affairs, provost, or dean) and the chief executive officer (president or chancellor)—aren't onboard, there may be pockets of assessment efforts across campus but assessment doesn't permeate campus culture. Indeed, as you read the rest of this chapter, you'll see that very few of the suggestions offered can be implemented without the active support of institutional leaders.

How, specifically, do engaged campus leaders strengthen campus assessment efforts?

They are personally committed to assessment. They have taken the time to acquaint themselves with current thinking about the principles and practice of assessment. They are comfortable with the concept of assessment, they have worked through any reservations they may have about it, and they understand why assessment is important.

They inspire interest in assessment across campus. They have a clear vision of assessment that they share enthusiastically with others. They establish a sense of urgency, making clear why assessment is a priority and why it must be taken seriously. They talk up assessment in their formal remarks and informal conversations with faculty, students, and staff, explaining how assessment will benefit the institution, individual programs, and individual faculty and staff members. They sponsor consultants, speakers, and forums on assessment and support these programs with their active presence.

They promote communication. They help faculty and staff see how their work fits into the big picture of documenting overall institutional effectiveness (see Chapter 1). They have communication channels with campus assessment committees and actively use those channels to promote and facilitate assessment. A provost might, for example, ask a member of her staff to serve on an assessment committee and speak regularly with the staff member about the committee's activities and directions.

They encourage risk-taking. As discussed in Chapter 1, assessment is a form of action research: a process of trial-and-error experimentation, both in creating new assessment strategies and in using the results to modify curricula and teaching methods. Despite the faculty's best efforts, sometimes a new assessment strategy yields little useful information, and sometimes a change in curriculum or pedagogy is initially a failure. The wise campus leader exhibits patience in these circumstances and waits for the kinks to be worked out. Some campuses, for example, do not evaluate faculty teaching a redesigned course for the first semester or two, giving faculty time to refine the design.

They encourage a sense of community. They help faculty understand the importance of building a community with a common understanding of what is important and a curriculum with a purposeful structure, and they recognize and reward faculty who do this.

They keep their promises to, for example, keep assessment on a front burner and not to penalize faculty with less-than-positive assessment results.

Finally, as discussed later in this chapter and in Chapter 4, **they set clear expectations for assessment; they provide incentives, resources, support, and rewards for assessment efforts;** and **they use assessment results** to make decisions and set priorities.

Focus on Teaching and Learning Rather Than Assessment

Assessment is, sadly, viewed by some faculty and staff as a four-letter word; just bring up the term and you may hear mental doors closing. But assessment is really just a tool to bring about better teaching and learning. If you focus conversations not on assessment but on helping students learn, you will engage those faculty who are enthusiastic teachers, and their enthusiasm may bring others onboard. Focus, then, on cultivating a culture of learning rather than one of assessment per se.

So how can an institution and its leaders promote a culture of learning?

Frame assessment efforts as teaching/learning efforts. In the early stages of introducing assessment to faculty and staff, focus conversations not on the "A-word" but on "goal-setting," "curriculum design," "teaching methods," and the like. Then gradually introduce the concept of assessment as a tool for facilitating these conversations. If your campus has a teaching-learning center that helps faculty improve their teaching techniques, affiliate an institutional assessment program with that center, conveying visibly that assessment is simply a tool to improve teaching and learning.

Bring the right people onboard. Virtually every institution is experiencing considerable faculty turnover as those hired a generation ago to teach baby boomers now retire. Faculty vacancies are a great opportunity to move substantively on promoting a learning-centered environment. Give hiring preference to faculty candidates with documented success in creating a learning-centered environment for their students and in using assessment to strengthen teaching and learning. If you ask faculty candidates to give a teaching demonstration, give hiring preference to those whose demonstrations facilitate active learning rather than merely deliver a lecture.

Recognize and reward efforts to improve teaching. Many institutions base faculty tenure, promotion, and merit pay decisions on the triumvirate of teaching, scholarship, and service, with teaching and scholarship usually weighted the most heavily and defined narrowly. Teaching quality is often judged largely by student evaluations of teaching and perhaps peer observation of a lecture, while scholarship is often defined as what Boyer called scholarship of discovery: making an original, often research-based contribution to a discipline's body of knowledge. Efforts to assess student learning are usually considered only as service to the institution, often the least valued of the triumvirate.

There is probably no stronger incentive to faculty to engage in assessment than to have assessment considered as evidence of teaching and scholarship excellence as well as service. While student evaluations of teaching and peer observations can be helpful indices of teaching effectiveness, an even better indicator of good teaching is whether students have learned what they're supposed to—a strong argument to allow faculty to include assessment results as evidence of teaching effectiveness.

The idea of assessment as scholarship stems from Boyer's (1990) seminal book *Scholarship Reconsidered,* in which he proposed expanding our conceptualization of scholarship beyond the scholarship of discovery. One form that he advocated honoring is the scholarship of teaching: the systematic development of new and better ways to help students learn a discipline's concepts and skills. To be considered true scholarship, the scholarship of teaching requires faculty to document the effectiveness of their teaching through the assessment of student learning. Valuing the scholarship of teaching as a form of scholarship when making tenure, promotion, and merit pay decisions thus stimulates interest in assessment.

EMPOWER FACULTY AND STAFF WORKING ON ASSESSMENT

As discussed in Chapter 4, design an assessment structure that allows faculty to assume a leadership role in planning and implementing an assessment program. Faculty and staff should be able to make appropriate choices and decisions about what to do, how to do it, and how to use assessment results. Help them get right to work, with minimal review of assessment plans. If their assessments identify something that needs improvement, provide governance and administrative structures that help them implement relatively minor changes quickly, again with minimal reviews and approvals.

MAKE ASSESSMENT RELEVANT

Many people will approach a new project with more enthusiasm if they find it inherently interesting, useful, and intellectually stimulating, so help faculty and staff focus on assessment efforts that will meet their needs and give them useful information for important decisions. Angelo (1999) has a wonderful phrase for this: "A vision worth working toward." Encourage faculty and staff to articulate their visions and use assessment to answer the questions in which they're most interested. Perhaps they're tired of their program's image as mediocre and want to start aggressively countering this notion with solid evidence. Perhaps they're convinced that smaller classes would lead to more effective learning but need evidence to justify this to campus leaders. Perhaps they're frustrated with their students' inadequate writing skills and want to learn how best to improve those skills.

PROVIDE OPPORTUNITIES TO LEARN ABOUT ASSESSMENT

An interesting aspect of American education is that, while most basic education teachers must have formal training in instructional design, teaching techniques, human development, and assessment methods, many higher education faculty and staff don't even have the opportunity to learn about these things. The typical faculty member has few if any occasions to learn how to craft an assignment, write a multiple-choice test, or grade an essay. Helping faculty and staff develop their assessment skills makes the assessment process far less formidable.

An effective assessment program therefore includes a variety of opportunities for faculty and staff to learn how to do assessment. These opportunities can include:

- *Campus professional development programs,* such as workshops, speakers, and brown bag lunch discussions.
- A *"help desk":* an accessible office that can answer questions quickly and provide one-on-one consultation.
- *Sponsored attendance at assessment conferences, institutes, and workshops.*
- A *campus assessment web site* that includes brief readings, guides, examples, and links to off-campus resources.
- A *campus assessment newsletter* or a column in the employee newsletter.

SET CLEAR EXPECTATIONS

Any task we face is less daunting if we understand exactly what we are to do, and assessment is no exception. An effective assessment program gives faculty and staff clear expectations and guidance on precisely what they are expected to do, and Chapter 4 suggests strategies for doing this.

BE FLEXIBLE

While clear expectations are important, so is flexibility. Giving faculty and staff latitude gives them a sense of control that creates a better climate for assessment. Remember that the primary purpose of assessment is to help faculty and staff improve student learning, and if bending the rules encourages faculty to achieve that end, be willing to do so. While you may expect all programs to submit annual assessment reports, perhaps you can be flexible on the date they're due. While you may have an established format for annual assessment reports, perhaps faculty who must submit an assessment report to a state agency can simply submit a copy of that report rather than rewrite it into your format. If faculty in a particular department will spend the next year rewriting their curriculum, it makes little sense to require them to develop an assessment plan now for a soon-to-be-obsolete curriculum, and a one-year postponement may be advisable.

MINIMIZE THE BURDEN OF ASSESSMENT

One of the most common concerns expressed by faculty and staff about assessment is, "But when I am supposed to find the time to do this?" Chapter 2 offers many suggestions for ways to help faculty and staff find time to focus on assessment; here are some more.

Relieve faculty and staff of less-critical responsibilities as they embark on assessment. Faculty and staff launching assessment efforts might be exempted from committee service or writing the usual annual report of department activities, for example. Give released time to faculty leading particularly time-consuming projects, such as the assessment of a major institutional or general education goal.

Provide centralized leadership, coordination, and support for assessment, including help with the mundane but essential tasks of collecting, processing, and analyzing assessment results.

Keep paperwork minimal. For accountability purposes, most institutions need regular reports on how student learning is being assessed but, as discussed in Chapter 4, make every effort to keep these reports as short and simple as possible.

Provide resources and support to make the assessment process manageable, as discussed in Chapter 4.

START SMALL

Because the prospect of implementing a full assessment plan can seem overwhelming, and because quick results can help build enthusiasm for assessment, encourage faculty and staff to begin with small-scale assessment projects that can be expanded later. Don't ask them to wait until they have a full, approved plan in place to begin collecting assessment information; some simple assessments like Minute Papers (see Chapter 9) can be implemented almost immediately. If faculty want to try a portfolio (Chapter 10), encourage them to include initially just a couple of examples of student work that assess just one or two key learning goals. Once the faculty are more comfortable with new assessment tools and have worked out logistical kinks, they can gradually expand the scope of their assessment efforts.

Also focus initially on assessing those aspects of a program that can be most easily assessed and improved. It might be easier, for example, for faculty to agree on how to assess writing than on how to assess creative thinking.

START WITH SUCCESSES

Many faculty and staff have an instinctive sense of the relative strengths of their programs and have ready answers to, "What makes the graduates of your program so good? Why are they in demand by employers or more advanced academic programs?" Faculty in one program might agree that their students graduate with outstanding research skills, while faculty in another program might agree that their students are great at communicating with others. Assessment can't begin and end with only good news; however, because its fundamental purpose is to improve student learning, which means identifying weaknesses as well as strengths, encourage faculty to focus initially on assessing the strongest aspects of their programs. This creates a win-win situation:

- Faculty instincts about the program are validated with solid information.

- Students in the program see evidence that they're really learning what's important.

- Prospective students are attracted to the program because they see evidence that they will learn things that are valued and important.

- College administrators use the good news to convince alumni, foundations, and other donors to invest in the program.

- Faculty fears that assessment results will be used punitively are abated; even if disappointing results are found later, those results will be balanced by the good news of the initial assessment results.

INVOLVE STUDENTS

Students are, of course, a vital part of any assessment undertaking. Involving them in planning an assessment effort can help ensure that it:

- Is feasible.

- Appears relevant and worthwhile to students.

- Yields maximum student participation.

- Motivates students to make a serious effort.

- Is not unduly burdensome to students.

- Thanks students for participating.

While including student representatives on an assessment steering committee is one way to involve students, focus groups, tryouts of assessment strategies, student membership on work groups planning specific assessments, and informal conversations with appropriate students are other effective strategies. Engage students in ways that fit best with your campus culture, your students, and their interests and needs.

CELEBRATE AND REWARD ASSESSMENT EFFORTS

Faculty and staff reluctant to engage in assessment may rightly ask, "What's in it for me?" Why should a good and busy faculty or staff member add to an already full plate? The answer is to create convincing incentives and rewards that recognize and honor those faculty and staff who are making strong, systematized assessment efforts. Such strategies vary by campus culture but may include the following.

Give assessment efforts strong consideration in tenure, promotion, and merit pay decisions. As discussed earlier, this is one of the most compelling ways to recognize faculty and staff efforts.

Give faculty and staff written recognition that might be placed in their personnel files or submitted with applications for tenure, promotion, or merit pay. This might be a certificate or a personalized letter of commendation signed by the president, chief academic officer, department chair, assessment committee chair, assessment officer, or a combination of these people.

Hold an annual event celebrating assessment efforts. An awards program or an annual assessment fair with exhibits of assessment activities in a central location are two possibilities.

Encourage campus leaders to commend publicly, in spoken and written remarks, those engaged in assessment.

Allow faculty and staff who are fully engaged in assessment to submit less-frequent reports. If you ask most programs for annual reports on assessment, for example, allow those clearly engaged in ongoing, systematized assessment to submit biennial reports.

Provide special funding, such as budget supplements, stipends, or mini-grants to those making significant efforts to assess student learning. Or release annual operating budgets or a portion thereof only to those programs that have submitted acceptable assessment plans or reports.

Base budget decisions in part on the presence of an effective assessment program. Move programs engaging in serious assessment efforts to the top of the funding list and/or eliminate from consideration those without assessment plans.

Require new program proposals to include complete, feasible assessment plans.

Honor faculty and staff who obtain external grants that will strengthen assessment.

Another way to recognize assessment progress is to develop measurable outcomes of assessment endeavors so faculty and staff can see how far they've come. Such measures might include:

- The number of programs that have written assessment plans.

- The number of multi-section courses that have common learning outcomes for all sections.

- The number of programs or courses whose learning outcomes, curricula, pedagogies, or assessment strategies have been revised in response to assessment findings.

- Resources spent on assessment activities.

- Resources spent on professional development activities that strengthen assessment skills.

USE ASSESSMENT RESULTS APPROPRIATELY

We all like to know that our work is making a difference, so an important way to engage faculty and staff in assessment is to make sure the results are used—appropriately—to improve student learning. Here are some ways that institutional leaders can use assessment results to promote a culture of assessment. Chapter 16 discusses other ways to use results effectively and appropriately.

Require evidence of student learning for course and program continuation. If your institution requires periodic reapproval of courses or programs, include in the approval criteria evidence that students are achieving the course or program's key learning goals.

Make planning and resource decisions in support of needs identified by assessment results. Provide equipment funding, for example, to a department that learns through careful assessment that its students need more technological training.

Keep faculty, students, and staff informed on how assessment findings support major decisions.

Don't penalize faculty whose assessment results are less than positive, as discussed in Chapter 16.

Don't Expect Everyone to Get Onboard

As noted at the beginning of this chapter, cultural change is rarely rapid, and there are invariably pockets of stubborn resistance. It may be virtually impossible to engage some individuals in assessment. Accept them and don't be discouraged by them. Just as many new academic programs and other initiatives are launched without 100% faculty buy-in, you don't need to get every single faculty member onboard for assessment to happen. Focus your energies on those faculty who are skeptical but intrigued by assessment, as well as those who are enthused about assessment, and you'll see good progress.

TIME TO THINK, DISCUSS, AND PRACTICE

1) The president of a community college wants faculty to develop an assessment plan for the college's general education curriculum. Brainstorm three things that she might realistically do to help create a positive, supportive climate for this project.

2) The assistant provost of a research university knows that the university must do a lot more with assessment in order to meet accreditation requirements, but the president and provost are focused on the university's research mission, and they are not interested in assessing student learning. Brainstorm three things that the assistant provost might do, in the absence of institutional leaders' support, to help promote a culture of assessment.

3) Brainstorm three ways to celebrate and reward assessment efforts that would fit well with your campus's culture.

REFERENCES

Angelo, T. A. (1999, May). Doing assessment as if learning matters most. *AAHE Bulletin, 51*(9), 3–6

Boyer, E. L. (1990). *Scholarship reconsidered: Priorities of the professoriate.* Princeton, NJ: The Carnegie Foundation for the Advancement of Teaching.

RECOMMENDED READING

Brown, F. W., & Moshavi, D. (2002). Herding academic cats: Faculty reactions to transformational and contingent reward leadership by department chairs. *Journal of Leadership Studies, 8*(3), 79–93.

Brown, K. (2001). Community college strategies: Why aren't faculty jumping on the assessment bandwagon—and what can be done to encourage their involvement? *Assessment Update, 13*(2), 8–9, 16.

Burke, J. C. (1999). The assessment anomaly: If everyone's doing it, why isn't more getting done? *Assessment Update, 11*(4), 3, 14–15.

Cross, K. P., & Steadman, M. H. (1996). *Classroom research: Implementing the scholarship of teaching.* San Francisco, CA: Jossey-Bass.

Ferren, A. (1993). *Faculty resistance to assessment: A matter of priorities and perceptions.* Commissioned paper for the 8th Annual American Association for Higher Education Conference on Assessment in Higher Education, Chicago, IL.

Gray, P. J. (1997). Viewing assessment as an innovation: Leadership and the change process. In P. J. Gray & T. W. Banta (Eds.), New directions in higher education: No. 100. *The campus-level impact of assessment: Progress, problems, and possibilities* (pp. 5–16). San Francisco, CA: Jossey-Bass.

Grunwald, H., & Peterson, M. W. (2003). Factors that promote faculty involvement in and satisfaction with institutional and classroom student assessment. *Research in Higher Education, 44*(2), 173–204.

Hutchings, P., & Shulman, L. S. (1999). The scholarship of teaching: New elaborations, new developments. *Change, 31*(5), 11–15.

Kotter, J. P. (1995). Leading change: Why transformation efforts fail. *Harvard Business Review, 73*(2), 59–68.

Leviton, L. C. (2003). Commentary: Engaging the community in evaluation: Bumpy, time consuming, and important. *American Journal of Evaluation, 24*(1), 85–90.

Loacker, G., & Mentkowski, M. (1993). Creating a culture where assessment improves learning. In T. W. Banta & Associates (Eds.), *Making a difference: Outcomes of a decade of assessment in higher education* (pp. 5–24). San Francisco, CA: Jossey-Bass.

Maki, P. (2002). Moving from paperwork to pedagogy: Channeling intellectual curiosity into a commitment to assessment. *AAHE Bulletin.* Retrieved June 2, 2003, from http://www.aahebulletin.com/public/archive/paperwork.asp

Ott, T. (2003). Shaping classroom practices: The scholarship of teaching. *Viewpoints: A Journal for Developmental Education, 4*(3). Retrieved June 2, 2003, from http://faculty.ccp.edu/dept/viewpoints/s03v4n3/frshape.html

Palomba, C. A., & Banta, T. W. (1999). Encouraging involvement in assessment. In *Assessment essentials: Putting principles to work on college campuses* (pp. 53–84). San Francisco, CA: Jossey-Bass.

Rodrigues, R. J. (2002, September). Want campus buy-in for your assessment efforts? *AAHE Bulletin, 55*(1). Retrieved June 2, 2003, from http://www.aahebulletin.com/member/articles/2002-10-feature02_1.asp

Schneider, C. G., & Shoenberg, R. (1999). Habits hard to break: How persistent features of campus life frustrate curricular reform. *Change, 31*(2), 30–35.

Stufflebeam, D. L. (2002, July 15). *Institutionalizing evaluation checklist.* Retrieved June 2, 2003, from http://www.wmich.edu/evalctr/checklists/institutionalizingeval.htm

Suskie, L. (2003). Assessment at Towson University: Lessons learned on keeping assessment thriving. *Assessment Update, 15*(3), 8–9.

Young, C. C., & Knight, M. E. (1993). Providing leadership for organizational change. In T. W. Banta & Associates (Eds.), *Making a difference: Outcomes of a decade of assessment in higher education* (pp. 29–35). San Francisco, CA: Jossey-Bass.

PART II
Planning for Assessment Success

4

Creating an
Assessment Plan

A ny undertaking benefits from some kind of plan; even a shopping trip can be more successful if you start with some notes on what you want to buy and which stores you want to visit. Assessment is no different. Your assessment efforts will be more effective and successful if you first plan your work by considering a number of questions, including why you're assessing, what and how you'll assess, what support structures will be provided, and how you'll monitor and evaluate assessment activities. These questions are all addressed in this chapter.

WHY ARE YOU ASSESSING STUDENT LEARNING?

There are two major purposes to assessment: improving teaching and learning and demonstrating the effectiveness of current teaching/learning efforts.

Assessment Can Improve Teaching and Learning

The first and most important reason to assess student learning is to *improve teaching and learning* by answering questions such as the following:

- Are our students learning what we think is important?

- Are they learning what they need to succeed in their future endeavors?

- Should we modify our learning goals? Are we expecting too much or too little from our students?

- Are we getting better at helping our students learn?

- Should our curriculum and/or teaching strategies be modified?

- Do recent innovations, such as a move to online learning or learning communities, help students learn more effectively?

- Would new or increased resources help students learn more effectively?

To answer these questions, faculty and staff need detailed feedback on the strengths and weaknesses of their teaching/learning strategies so they can make specific improvements. They often need to assess student learning while it is taking place—perhaps midway through a course or program—so they can give students prompt feedback and make immediate modifications to classroom activities and assignments. This kind of assessment is called *formative* assessment.

Assessment Can Demonstrate the Effectiveness of Current Teaching/Learning Efforts

The second major reason to assess student learning is to *demonstrate the effectiveness of teaching/learning efforts* to governing boards and external audiences such as accreditation organizations and foundations. The questions for which they need answers might include the following:

- Is this course, program, or institution of appropriate quality and value?

- Is this course, program, or institution worthy of our investment or support?

- Should this program be expanded, maintained, cut back, or eliminated?

- Should we support proposed changes to this course, program, or institution?

To answer these questions, these audiences usually want an overall snapshot of what students have learned at the end of a course or program. Assessments designed to meet the needs of these audiences may not give students and faculty useful feedback on student strengths and weaknesses. A published writing test that yields a single score on writing performance, for example, may tell external audiences how well students are writing but give faculty and staff no guidance on how to strengthen a writing program. This kind of assessment is called *summative* assessment.

Can These Disparate Purposes Be Reconciled?

These two purposes of assessment—improvement and accountability—are very different and call for different approaches. Assessing for accountability often means looking for aggregated information on strengths, while assessing for improvement often means looking for detailed information on weaknesses. In reality most institutions assess student learning for both purposes and must design assessment programs that achieve both ends. As Chapter 3 suggests, it may be advantageous to focus initially on assessing successes, as this can build enthusiasm for assessment and reduce fears that assessment may be used punitively. But some faculty and staff may find assessing for improvement a more rewarding initial activity, as it's more likely to give them useful information.

WHO WILL USE YOUR FINDINGS?

Of all the characteristics of good assessment described in Chapter 2, perhaps the most important is that assessment efforts yield useful information that can help make worthwhile decisions. Assessment planning must thus begin with a clear understanding of your audiences and the decisions they need to make. Your audiences may be both internal and external and include:

- Faculty and staff involved with the program.
- Other faculty and staff.
- Assessment steering committee members.
- Institutional leaders.
- Governing board members.
- Current students and their parents.
- Prospective students and their parents.
- Alumni.
- Prospective employers.
- Accreditation organizations.

- State and Federal agencies.
- Legislators.

Talk to representatives of your audiences, or at least people who are familiar with them, so you can understand their needs and design assessments to meet those needs. Try to find out:

What are your audiences' perspectives? Do they understand your course, program, or institution, or do they see it only in terms of their own roles and responsibilities? Do they have any prejudices or biases regarding your course, program, or institution? Do they appreciate its history, values, culture, and environment? Are they aware of its strengths and weaknesses? Do they understand how your assessment might affect their responsibilities, actions, and decisions?

What are your audiences' needs and priorities? What matters to them? What do they value? Do they need assessment for improvement or for accountability? What kind of support and help do they need from this assessment effort? Is their most pressing need for more resources, more attention, or more respect? Do they want support for the status quo or for initiating change?

What decisions do your audiences need to make? What information do they need to make appropriate decisions?

WHAT UNDERLYING VALUES INFORM YOUR ASSESSMENT EFFORTS?

Every institution has unique values, some made explicit in a mission statement, others implicit. The missions of some institutions promote specific religious values, for example, while the missions of others promote civic responsibility. At some institutions, collaboration is a highly prized but unstated value, while at others individual autonomy is valued but again unstated.

Clarifying your institution's underlying values and understanding how they might affect your assessment efforts can help promote the success of your assessment program. At an institution that values community service, for example, an assessment of service learning activities might be a particularly effective way to engage faculty and staff in assessment. At an institution that values collaboration, involving a large group of faculty and staff in the development of assessment policies and procedures might be critical to an assessment program's success.

WHERE DOES STUDENT LEARNING TAKE PLACE?

Student learning takes place in many venues, not just in the classroom. If you are launching an institution-wide assessment effort, take an inventory of all possible student learning venues to identify where assessment should be undertaken. Student learning venues can include:

- Individual courses.

- Academic programs, including undergraduate and graduate degree programs, certificate and other nondegree programs, and noncredit programs.

- General education core curriculum.

- Cocurricular programs and student life programs designed to promote student learning and development, including many clubs and activities.

- Cohort-driven programs and other special programs designed to enhance student learning, such as first-year experiences, learning communities, developmental education programs, tutoring programs, honors programs, programs for at-risk student cohorts, and study abroad programs.

WILL YOUR CAMPUS CULTURE SUPPORT ASSESSMENT?

Faculty and staff resistance is perhaps the major obstacle to the successful implementation of assessment programs, so an important step in planning an assessment program is to evaluate the campus culture for assessment and take appropriate steps to ensure a climate that promotes assessment. This is discussed in Chapter 3.

WHAT POLICIES, PROCEDURES, AND GOVERNANCE STRUCTURE DO YOU NEED TO PROMOTE SUCCESSFUL ASSESSMENT?

We joke that students' most common questions about an assignment are, "How long should it be? When is it due?" but many of us find our work easier to accomplish if we have similar structure and guidelines. Faculty and staff need sufficient guidance to understand what they are to do without being overwhelmed with excessive rules, forms, and bureaucracy. Requests for elaborate, lengthy assessment plans and reports can alienate faculty and stifle creativity and flexibility, as the process of creating elaborate plans can be so onerous that faculty will be loath to face the seemingly monumental task of updating or amending them. Begin with structures that are too simple rather than too complex; simple structures can always be expanded and clarified as needed, but an overly complex, burdensome structure will overwhelm and discourage faculty and staff and threaten an assessment program's success. As noted in Chapter 3, be willing to bend the rules if doing so helps engage reluctant or overburdened faculty. If your campus has a program review process, embed assessment efforts within the program review process rather than keeping the two possibly duplicative.

Assessment structures should include the following elements.

A Campus Definition of Assessment

As faculty and staff are introduced to the concept of assessment, many won't be familiar with the term or will have conflicting ideas about what it means. Having one locally accepted definition helps prevent confusion or disagreement over exactly what is and is not expected. Chapter 1 provides more information on defining assessment.

A Local Statement of Principles of Good Assessment Practice

Just as students deserve to know the grading criteria for their assignments and what kinds of work will earn an A, faculty deserve to know what kinds of assessment practices are considered exceptional, adequate, and inadequate on your campus. They also need to be reassured that there will be campus support for their efforts and that assessments will be conducted and the results used ethically and appropriately. It's therefore a good idea to develop a local statement of principles of good assessment practice that describes 1) characteristics of good assessment and 2) institutional commitments to foster successful assessment practices (such as that appropriate resources will be provided and that assessment results will not be used in a punitive way).

While the principles of good practice discussed in Chapter 2 and listed in its Recommended Reading section are a good starting point for developing a local statement, it's usually not a good idea to adopt an existing statement wholesale. Your campus culture undoubtedly has unique perspectives, values, and concerns that should be addressed through a local statement. If faculty are unionized, for example, a local statement might relate assessment expectations to contractual rights and responsibilities.

Written Guidance on Who Does What When

Matters that often need to be decided and then shared in writing include the following. But keep in mind that flexibility and sensitivity to work-load are as important as clear guidelines.

Which programs and units are to assess student learning? Will only degree programs assess student learning? Or are certificate programs, support programs, and student life programs also expected to assess student learning?

Within each program or unit, who has lead responsibility for making sure that assessment gets done? Consider naming a faculty "assessment coordinator" within each program to handle this responsibility.

Who identifies and decides how to assess the key learning goals of each course and program? While faculty within each academic program obviously assume this responsibility for their courses and programs, in some instances the line of responsibility isn't clear. Exactly who will decide on the learning goals and assessment strategies for the social sciences requirement of a general education core curriculum, for example, when students can fulfill that requirement by taking any one of 20 courses offered by eight departments?

How and when is information on assessment activities and results collected? What kind of feedback is provided to assessment practitioners, and who provides it? These questions are discussed later in this chapter.

Faculty Leadership

Because assessment is part of the teaching/learning process, faculty should guide assessment activities just as they guide the curriculum. If you are launching an institution-wide assessment effort, consider charging an assessment steering committee, composed predominantly of faculty drawn from a representative cross-section of disciplines, with establishing assessment policies and guidelines and with reviewing and providing feedback on reports of assessment activities. If your institution has named someone to coordinate assessment activities, that person may draft assessment policies and guidelines, but to ensure faculty support the statements should be endorsed by the steering committee before being implemented and disseminated.

Also consider incorporating the steering committee into your existing governance structure, perhaps by making it a standing committee of a faculty senate. This legitimizes the committee and conveys to the campus community that assessment is a permanent part of institutional fabric, not a fad to be addressed by a short-lived ad hoc task force.

While faculty should predominate, students should also have a role in the assessment planning process, as discussed in Chapter 3.

WHAT ARE YOUR STUDENT LEARNING GOALS?

Once groundwork is in place, work can begin on the first step of the assessment process, as identified in Chapter 1: identifying what you want students to learn. Identifying and expressing student learning goals is discussed in Chapter 5.

Many institutions have overarching learning goals for all students, regardless of major, in addition to learning goals for individual courses and programs. Some institutions, for example, have goals that all students will develop certain values. Examine statements of institutional mission, vision, values, or strategic plans to identify institutional learning goals. If your institution has such goals, plan an institutional effort to examine how well they are being achieved. Ideally, every student's program of study should have at least some learning goals that help achieve institutional learning goals, just as most courses should have at least some learning goals that help achieve the learning goals of the programs within which they reside.

DO ALL STUDENTS HAVE SUFFICIENT OPPORTUNITY TO ACHIEVE EACH LEARNING GOAL?

Once key learning goals are identified, the next task is to match them to your curriculum and cocurricular opportunities to ensure that every student in your program or institution, regardless of curricular choices and level of cocurricular involvement, has sufficient opportunity to achieve every goal. If one of your institutional goals is to develop an appreciation of other cultures and perspectives, for example, the curriculum should ensure that every student, regardless of major or extracurricular involvement, will develop this appreciation before graduation. Simply offering multicultural programming that students may or may not attend at their option may not suffice. Similarly, if one of your program goals is that students write effectively, the program curriculum should ensure that all students in the program, regardless of curricular choices, take multiple courses that help them understand how your discipline defines good writing, teach them how to write in your discipline, and give them constructive feedback on drafts.

A good way to analyze curricular learning opportunities is by "mapping" learning goals against required courses. Create a grid listing your institution's or program's major learning goals down the left side and required courses and other curricular requirements across the top. Then ask faculty to check off which goals are addressed in each course or requirement that they teach. You may find that some important learning goals are not addressed anywhere or in only one or two elective courses that few students take. Other important goals that should be addressed continually throughout the curriculum may be addressed only minimally. And some goals may suffer from overkill, taking up time in too many classes that could be devoted to other important goals that need increased attention.

If you and your colleagues decide that the match between goals and curriculum is inadequate, these exercises and conversations may lead to changes in curriculum and teaching methods. The assessment process can thus lead to significant improvements in teaching and learning before any assessments are conducted!

WHAT DO YOU ALREADY KNOW ABOUT STUDENT LEARNING?

It never makes sense to reinvent the wheel. Once learning goals and learning opportunities are clarified, the next step in assessment planning is finding out what faculty and staff have already learned about teaching, learning, and assessing key learning goals. Begin by researching current thinking on how each learning goal should be taught and assessed.

Review published literature, search the web, contact appropriate professional associations, and talk to colleagues at your institution and elsewhere. Posting a query on an appropriate discussion list can generate a wealth of information.

Next, find out how each key learning goal is currently assessed at your institution. Ask your colleagues, "How do we know that our students are indeed learning this? How would we convince board members, employers, and other audiences that graduating students have in fact learned this? If we don't know for sure, do we at least have some clues?" Table 4.1 gives examples of information that may already be on hand. Even if the information is incomplete or isn't rigorous, it may still yield hints about what's working and what might be improved.

How Are You Using Assessment Information to Improve Student Learning?

Once you have a sense of assessment information already on hand, your next question is how, if at all, that information has been used to improve teaching and learning. Do scores on published tests, for example, give a sense of students' relative strengths and weaknesses? If so, have faculty discussed whether their curriculum or teaching methods should be modified to address student weaknesses? Chapter 16 discusses how to use assessment results effectively and appropriately.

Should You Change or Add to Current Assessment Practices? If so, How?

In all likelihood, your review of current assessment information will identify some gaps. While you may have good information on hand regarding some learning goals, you may have only inadequate evidence on other learning goals and no information on still others. You'll therefore probably need to design new or improved assessment strategies for at least some key learning goals. Chapter 6 provides an overview of many assessment strategies. As you identify potential approaches, keep the following in mind.

Set priorities. Because we want students to learn, grow, and develop in so many ways, at first glance the prospect of assessing all those aims can seem overwhelming. Calm your fears by recognizing at the outset that you won't be able to assess every single thing that you want

Table 4.1

Examples of Assessment Information That May Already Be on Hand

- Scores on published tests, such as tests for placement, certification, or licensure
- Ratings of students by field experience supervisors
- Assessment information assembled to meet specialized accreditation requirements
- Grading criteria and grades or scores on locally developed tests and assignments
- Retention and graduation rates
- Placement rates of graduates into appropriate careers and/or subsequent academic programs
- Surveys of students and alumni
- Course syllabi, which can be analyzed for learning outcomes, active learning opportunities, and assessment methods
- Student transcripts, which can be analyzed for course enrollment patterns
- End-of-course student evaluation forms, which can be reviewed for questions that ask about the course rather than the instructor
- Counts of students participating in cocurricular, extracurricular, and service-learning activities
- Library circulation statistics, including uses of electronic library resources

students to learn. As discussed in Chapter 5, assess only those learning goals that you and your colleagues feel are most important. Start with your three to six most important learning goals, no more.

Recognize that some important goals can't be assessed. Towson University's general education curriculum requires all undergraduates to take a course that fosters "creativity or creative thought." Some of the learning goals that faculty have identified for courses in this category are:

- Celebrate not knowing.
- Be spontaneous.
- Gain pleasure from life experiences.
- Be intuitive.

Can these learning goals be assessed? Probably not, at least not in a practical way. Theoretically we could survey alumni 20 or 30 years from now to see if they are, indeed, gaining pleasure from life experiences. But this would be impractical; while we could indeed survey today's graduates many years from now, we would be assessing the impact of an obsolete curriculum and retired faculty, a pointless task.

One way to decide if a learning goal is assessable is to ask if it's teachable. Ask faculty to share, in specific, concrete terms, how they help students achieve a particular learning goal. What tasks and assignments do they give to students to help them achieve it? Or do they simply hope that students will achieve the goal through osmosis? If the learning goal is teachable, it's probably assessable, and the faculty's teaching strategies will give you clues on how to assess it.

If some of your goals appear difficult or impossible to assess, that's not an excuse to abandon assessment altogether. You will doubtless have other important goals that you can assess. (The Towson faculty teaching creativity courses identified several assessable goals including, "Examine ideas from multiple perspectives" and "Generate multiple solutions to problems.")

And you can often create proxy measures for the hard-to-assess goals that at least give you clues about what students have learned. If your goal is to prepare civic leaders, for example, you can count the number of students who engage in community service or assume campus leadership positions while in college. As your students prepare to graduate, you can ask them to reflect (see Chapter 9) on their views about civic responsibility and community service. No, these efforts aren't ideal, but they will still give you some useful insight.

Work out the mechanics. Once you've identified those learning goals that will be the focus of your assessment efforts, you're ready to work out the details of exactly what will be done. If you are assessing student learning throughout a program by looking at samples of student work, Table 4.2 lists some of the questions you'll need to answer for each of the program's key learning goals. The table lists too many questions to be answered by any one person all at one time, so develop a schedule to get all these questions answered. Indicate who has lead responsibility for taking care of each step and deadlines for completing each step.

How Will You Monitor Assessment Activities?

To ensure that campus assessment activities follow principles of good practice, ask all departments and programs to submit assessment plans describing what they expect to do. As discussed earlier, give faculty and staff written guidelines on what the plans should include, when they are due, and to whom they should be submitted. At a minimum, an assessment plan should list the program's major learning goals and summarize how and when the faculty or staff plan to assess each of those goals.

Once assessment is underway, ask faculty in each program or department for periodic progress reports. Although an annual report may be viewed as burdensome, it's an impetus to keep working on assessment and thus helps make assessment efforts systematic (one of the characteristics of good assessment described in Chapter 2). Annual reports also make it easier to compile periodic institutional reports to governing boards, accreditors, state agencies, and other audiences. As with assessment plans, provide written guidelines on what annual reports should include, when they are due, and to whom they should be submitted. Assessment reports should include brief summaries of:

- The program's major learning goals.
- How, when, and how frequently each major learning goal is being assessed.
- What has been learned from each assessment.
- How assessment findings have been used to improve teaching and learning.
- Any additional information that helps the reader understand what's happening, such as plans to modify learning goals, curricula, or assessment strategies.

Table 4.2

Logistical Questions to Address When Planning a Systematic Assessment of Samples of Student Work

- What assessment strategy or strategies will you use to assess this learning goal? (Chapter 6 provides an overview of the many assessment strategies from which you can choose, with Part III providing more details.)
- In which course(s) will you use this assessment strategy? If this assessment strategy will not be embedded into coursework, how will you implement it?
- If those courses have multiple sections, from which section(s) will you collect samples of student work?
- How and when will you contact the faculty teaching those sections, explain what you're asking them to do, and seek their cooperation?
- What assignment(s) or test questions will you be reviewing? If they are not already in place, who will write them and distribute them to the faculty?
- How many samples of student work will you examine at one time (see Chapter 6)?
- How will you choose the samples (see Chapter 6)? Will faculty submit copies of all their students' work, with someone else choosing a sample, or will you ask faculty to submit only a sample? If so, how will they choose the sample?
- What steps will you take to ensure that identifiable information (e.g., student names) is kept absolutely confidential?
- By what date should faculty submit copies of student work? To whom should they send the copies?
- How will you evaluate the student work? If you need to use a rubric (Chapter 7), who will develop it?
- What are your standards for deciding whether student performance is acceptable (see Chapter 16)? What will you consider minimally acceptable work? What level of work will you consider unacceptable for a graduate of your program?
- How and with whom will you share the results of your assessment (Chapter 15)?
- How will you use the results (Chapter 16)? What questions will the results help you answer? What decisions will the results help you make?

Keep Reporting Requirements
Short, Simple, and Flexible

Assessment efforts can quickly drown under excessive reporting requirements. Aim for short, simple plans that are considered perpetual drafts and can be easily updated, and be willing to be flexible in your requirements and expectations. Ask initially for too little information rather than too much; you can always ask for additional information in subsequent plans and reports. To ease the reporting burden, consider preparing a report template that faculty and staff can complete and submit electronically on disk, as an email attachment, or as a web-based form. In subsequent years, you can simply return it to the report writer with a request for an update. Figures 4.1 and 4.2 give examples of simple templates for assessment plans and reports.

How Will You Evaluate Assessment Efforts?

Just as students benefit from constructive feedback on their work, faculty and staff benefit from feedback on their assessment reports that tells them what they're doing well and how, if at all, they might be even more effective. Plan a feedback mechanism that spells out:

Who provides the feedback? Given that faculty should have lead responsibility for undertaking assessment, it's appropriate that faculty peers should provide feedback. An assessment steering committee composed primarily of faculty may be a good way to accomplish this. If the committee members don't feel qualified to offer feedback, the faculty member or administrator who coordinates assessment can draft a response that the committee can review and finalize.

What kind of feedback will be provided? This is a good opportunity to model effective assessment practices by providing clear evaluation criteria. If you have developed a local statement of principles of good assessment practice, use it to create a rubric (Chapter 7) delineating the characteristics of exceptional, sufficient, and inadequate assessment practices. Share the rubric with faculty and staff to help them prepare their reports. Figure 4.3 is an example of a rubric used to evaluate and provide feedback on annual assessment reports.

When will feedback be provided? Prompt feedback fosters effective learning, so aim to provide feedback as soon as feasible.

Figure 4.1

A Simple Template for an Assessment Plan

Program/Department:

Assessment Coordinator:

Date This Plan Is Completed:

Key learning outcome: What should students be able to do AFTER completing the program?	Through what courses/assign-ments will you ensure that all students have the opportunity to learn this?	How will you assess how well your students are learning this?	When do you expect to begin collecting this assessment information?	How often will you collect this assessment information?	Comments (optional)
1					
2					
3					
4					
5					
6					

Figure 4.2 A Simple Template for an Annual Assessment Report

Program/Department:

Assessment Coordinator:

Date This Report Is Completed:

	Key learning outcome: What should students be able to do AFTER completing the program?	Through what courses/assign-ments do you ensure that all students have the opportunity to learn this?	How are you assessing how well your students are learning this?* How often do you conduct this assessment?	Summarize the results of your assessments: What have you learned about how well you are achieving this goal?	How have you used this information to help your students?	Optional comments (e.g., changes to goals, assessments, schedule)
1						
2						
3						
4						
5						
6						

* Please attach examples of your assessment tools (e.g., assignments, grading criteria, scoring guidelines, surveys).

Figure 4.3

A Rubric for Providing Feedback on Assessment Plans and Reports

Key Learning Goals

❑ *Best practice:* In addition to meeting the standard described below, key program learning goals are clearly and actively communicated to students and faculty in the program.

❑ *Meets standard:* Learning goals describe in explicit, observable terms, using action words, how students will be able to use their knowledge, what thinking skills and disciplinary dispositions they will have, and/or what else they will be able to do upon completion of the program.

❑ *Needs attention:* Learning goals do not meet the standard described above.

Teaching/Learning Strategies

❑ *Best practice:* In addition to meeting the standard described below, it is clear that every student in the major has ample opportunity to master the learning outcome, either through multiple courses or through intensive study in one course.

❑ *Meets standard:* Every student has sufficient opportunity to master each learning outcome; every student in the major takes at least one course in which the learning outcome is addressed.

❑ *Needs attention:* Does not meet the standard described above.

Assessment Methods

❑ *Best practice:* In addition to meeting the standard described below, evidence is provided that the assessment methods yield truthful, fair information that can be used with confidence.

❑ *Meets standard:* Each assessment method clearly matches the learning outcome being assessed, and multiple assessments are used systematically (repeatedly, on a schedule) over time.

❑ *Needs attention:* Does not meet the standard described above.

Use of Results

❑ *Best practice:* In addition to meeting the standard described below, standards have been established that clearly describe performance levels considered minimally adequate for students completing the program, and positive assessment results are shared with faculty, students, academic administrators, prospective students, and other audiences as appropriate.

❑ **Meets standard:** Assessment results are shared and discussed with faculty teaching in the program and are used to modify learning outcomes, teaching methods, curriculum, and/or assessment strategies, as appropriate.

❑ **Needs attention:** Does not meet the standard described above.

❑ **Not applicable:** This is a plan that is not yet implemented.

Who will receive the feedback? Obviously the program's assessment coordinator or assessment committee should receive it. Some institutions may wish to copy all faculty and staff in the program, and some may decide to copy the program's dean or vice president.

The overall institutional assessment plan also needs periodic review and evaluation; this is discussed in Chapter 16.

WHAT RESOURCES DO YOU NEED?

Although assessment efforts need not be costly, they do require a certain investment. Some of the resources you may need for assessment include:

- A faculty member or administrator with lead responsibility for planning and supporting assessment activities (not necessarily on a full-time basis).

- Access to faculty, staff, and/or consultants with expertise in assessment aspects such as testing, surveys, focus groups, and statistics.

- Professional development resources, including publications, videos, consultants, speakers, and travel to off-campus conferences and workshops.

- Incentives and rewards for faculty, staff, and students to participate in assessment activities.

- Compensation for faculty who help read and score large numbers of student papers or projects or are otherwise expected to spend unusual amounts of time on assessment.

- Technical and support staff to help process and analyze data (see Chapter 14).

- Published tests or surveys (Chapter 13).

- Hardware and software that support assessment activities, perhaps to:
  - Create paper and/or online tests.
  - Create "bubble sheet" and web-based surveys and telephone survey scripts.
  - Enter, process, and analyze assessment results.
  - Maintain portfolios online.
  - Maintain assessment plans and results.

Because hardware and software come and go and are continually evolving, none is specifically described here. Before you shop for software, know exactly what you want to do with it and what features are important to you. Also know your hardware requirements; some software requires printers, scanners, or computers with certain specifications. To identify potential hardware and software, use a good web search engine to search for "survey software," "test software," "assessment software," and the like, then use discussion lists, conference exhibits and presentations, published literature, and colleagues to get more information and recommendations.

As you identify resource needs, keep in mind one of the characteristics of good assessment discussed in Chapter 2: Assessments should be cost effective, yielding benefits that justify the time and expense put into them. If a particular resource is costly, ask yourself how likely it is to lead to significant changes in how, what, or why students learn. If dramatic benefits aren't likely, the expenditure is probably not worthwhile.

TIME TO THINK, DISCUSS, AND PRACTICE

1) Brainstorm a list of programs and activities at your institution, other than degree programs, where student learning takes place and that therefore might be included in an assessment program.

2) What might be a suitable membership composition of an assessment steering committee at your institution? Justify your choices, and reflect on what they tell you about your institution's values and culture.

3) Brainstorm a list of information on student learning that your institution might already have on hand.

RECOMMENDED READING

Association of American Colleges and Universities. (2002). *Greater expectations: A new vision for learning as a nation goes to college.* Washington, DC: Author. Retrieved June 2, 2003, from http://www.greaterexpectations.org

Council for the Advancement of Standards in Higher Education. (1998). *Outcomes assessment and program evaluation: Standards and guidelines.* Washington, DC: Author.

Gangopadhyay, P. (2002, September). *Making evaluation meaningful to all education stakeholders.* Kalamazoo, MI: Western Michigan University, The Evaluation Center. Retrieved June 2, 2003, from http://www.wmich.edu/evalctr/checklists/makingevalmeaningful.pdf

Maki, P. (2002). Developing an assessment plan to learn about student learning. *Journal of Academic Librarianship, 28*(1/2), 8–13.

Schuh, J. H., & Upcraft, M. L. (2000). Assessment politics. *About Campus, 5*(4), 14–21.

Stufflebeam, D. (2000). *Strategies for institutionalizing evaluation: Revisited* (Occasional Paper #18). Kalamazoo, MI: Western Michigan University, The Evaluation Center.

Suskie, L. (2003). Assessment at Towson University: Lessons learned on keeping assessment thriving. *Assessment Update, 15*(3), 8–9.

5
Developing Learning Goals

As discussed in Chapter 1, assessment begins not with creating or implementing tests, assignments, or other assessment tools but by first deciding on your goals: what you want your students to learn. This chapter discusses why goals are important, the meaning of the terms goals, objectives, and outcomes, how to express learning goals, the learning goals considered most important in today's world, and how to develop goals.

WHY ARE GOALS IMPORTANT?

Imagine that an English professor teaching 19th century poetry asks his students to keep journals in which they reflect on what they've learned as the course progresses. With no clear goals for the journal, his assignment may be something like, "After every class, jot down your thoughts about what we're learning." With such a vague assignment, his students won't know what to do and, lacking focus, many won't learn much from the experience. The journal won't be as effective as it would have been with explicit goals.

Furthermore, with such a vague assignment, it isn't clear how the professor should evaluate the journals. He could evaluate them for writing qualities such as organization, clarity, grammar, or accuracy in reflecting class lectures and discussions. Or he could look for signs that students are developing an increased appreciation of 19th century poetry. Or he could evaluate them in terms of how well students appraise scholarly interpretations of 19th century poetry. Or he could look at how students relate 19th century poetry to other literature, culture, and events of the times. Which of these is the "correct" way to evaluate the journals? There's no way to tell, because we don't know what the professor wants the students to learn from the journal-keeping experience.

As this example shows, without clear goals, both our students' learning experience and our assessment of it are ambiguous and unsatisfactory. Our students don't know what to learn, and we don't know what to assess.

WHAT IS THE DIFFERENCE AMONG GOALS, OBJECTIVES, AND OUTCOMES?

Goals. Objectives. Learning outcomes. Behavioral objectives. All these terms can describe what we want students to learn. While educators don't yet use them consistently, some of the more common uses of these terms are described here.

What Is a Goal or Outcome?

Goals state what you, your colleagues, or your institution aim to achieve. Goals can describe aims outside the teaching/learning process as well as within it. Within the teaching/learning process, an astronomy professor might have a goal that her students learn about our solar system, your colleagues may have a goal to offer a quality educational program, and your institution may have a goal to encourage students to engage in service to the community. Outside the teaching/learning process, you may have a goal to complete some research this year, your department may have a goal to sponsor a regional scholarly conference, and your institution may have a goal to raise $8 million in alumni gifts.

Effective goals refer to a destination rather than the path taken to get there—the end rather than the means, the outcome rather than the process. A goal that truly describes an outcome explains why we do what we do. A faculty member's real goal is not that students will write a term paper but that they will become effective writers. A student activities director's real goal is not to offer a student leadership development program but to prepare students to become leaders. An institutional goal is not to raise $8 million but to increase educational opportunities for deserving students through additional scholarships.

What Is a Learning Outcome or Learning Goal?

Learning outcomes, also referred to as learning goals, are the knowledge, skills, attitudes, and habits of mind that students take with them from a learning experience. Kirkpatrick's (1998) four levels of evaluation, shown in Table 5.1, show the relation of learning outcomes to other outcomes of learning experiences.

What Is an Objective?

Many people use the word objectives to describe detailed aspects of goals. Within the broad goal of learning about our solar system, for example, an astronomy professor might have an objective that her students will learn basic facts about each planet.

Other people use the word objectives to describe the tasks to be accomplished to achieve the goal—the means to the end, the process leading to the outcome. If a goal of the astronomy professor is for students to explain science concepts in writing, her objectives might be for them to write essays, critique drafts of their peers, and maintain a journal in which they reflect on their growth as science writers.

What Is a Behavioral Goal?

Learning goals are sometimes phrased using broad, nebulous terms such as "Students will learn . . . ," "Students will know . . . ," "Students will understand . . . ," Students will become aware of . . . ," or "Students will appreciate . . . ." Such vaguely stated learning goals can lead to confusion. Consider, for example, the goal that students will "understand basic concepts about our solar system." Astronomy professors may have differing opinions about what constitutes "basic concepts." Are we talking about basic facts about each planet or also theories about how the solar system was created? And what does it mean to "understand" those basic concepts? Does it mean memorizing basic facts? Or does it mean using information about our solar system to speculate about the characteristics of other solar systems? If a learning goal isn't clear to us and our colleagues, it certainly won't be clear to our students. They'll have difficulty figuring out what and how to learn, and we'll have difficulty coming up with an appropriate assessment.

Table 5.1

Kirkpatrick's Four Levels of Evaluation of Learning Experiences

Level 1. *Reaction to the learning experience:* Are students satisfied with their learning experience? Satisfaction is important, because dissatisfaction is a clue that students may not have learned some important things. But student satisfaction levels alone don't tell us directly whether students have learned what we value.

Level 2. *Learning:* Are students learning what we want them to learn? *Learning outcomes* or *learning goals* are the knowledge, skills, attitudes, and habits of mind that students develop and take with them from the learning experience. *The achievement of learning outcomes or learning goals is the focus of most assessment efforts.*

Level 3. *Transfer:* Are students using the knowledge, skills, attitudes, and habits of mind that they've learned in their later pursuits: in further study, on the job, in community service, etc.? While these are important outcomes, they're difficult to assess and therefore not usually the focus of assessment efforts.

Level 4. *Results:* Are the knowledge, skills, attitudes, and habits of mind that students have acquired helping them achieve their goals and our goals for them? Are students persisting through graduation? Are they successfully obtaining the positions for which they've prepared? Are they admitted to appropriate programs of advanced study? Are they achieving the other life goals they've identified for themselves? While retention, graduation, and placement rates are important outcomes of most teaching/learning activities, they're insufficient evidence of student learning because 1) they don't tell us exactly what students have and haven't learned and 2) it's hard to tie the effect of a particular course, program, or other learning activity to these kinds of outcomes—there are too many possible mitigating factors.

Behavioral goals—also called *behavioral objectives*—attempt to rectify this problem by stating the outcome of learning using *concrete action words;* they describe what students can *do* after they've learned the material. Upon completing the astronomy professor's solar system unit, for example, perhaps her students will be able to *describe* the key characteristics of each planet. Perhaps they will be able to *create a scale model* of the solar system. Perhaps they will be able to *explain* why each planet except Earth cannot support human life.

Many educators believe that behavioral goals are the best way to express goals about student learning, as students are more likely to understand what we want them to learn if our goals are expressed in concrete terms. Behavioral goals also make assessment easier; they can practically dictate what an assessment will be, as these examples show.

Behavioral goal: Describe the key characteristics of each planet.

Assessment: Write short descriptions of the key characteristics of each planet.

Behavioral goal: Create a scale model of the solar system.

Assessment: Create a scale model of the solar system.

Behavioral goal: Explain why each planet except Earth cannot support human life.

Assessment: Write a short explanation of why each planet except Earth cannot support human life.

Despite their obvious advantages, behavioral goals are not always the most effective way to express the major learning goals of a course or program. Suppose that a graduate program in educational assessment has a goal that students "understand the concepts of reliability and validity." This learning goal might be expressed as any of the following behavioral goals:

- Explain the difference between reliability and validity.

- Give examples of reliability and validity evidence.

- Evaluate the reliability and validity evidence for a given instrument.

- Design an experiment to provide evidence of the validity of a given instrument.

This example shows several potential limitations of behavioral goals:

- Sometimes there is no one behavioral goal that adequately describes a particular learning goal; the learning goal can only be described by a list of behavioral goals. With so much detail, the forest—the major learning goal—is lost among the trees of specific behavioral goals describing what students should be able to do.

- Behavioral goals can be too restrictive. Students in a program with the behavioral goals listed above will learn how to do these things but may not understand other important aspects of the concepts of reliability and validity.

- Behavioral goals can restrict possible assessments. The first behavioral goal listed above stipulates, for example, that students prepare an explanation; they cannot, say, answer multiple-choice questions.

WHAT ARE GOOD WAYS OF EXPRESSING LEARNING GOALS?

Writing effective goals is an art, not a science, that comes easily to some people and remains a struggle for others. Goals are more easily crafted for some courses and programs than for others. As with all other aspects of assessment, consider learning goals a work in progress; be prepared to refine them after you implement them and see how well they work. The following suggestions will help you get started.

Aim for goals that are neither too broad nor too specific. The best learning goals are at a midpoint between these two extremes.

Too vague:	Students will demonstrate information literacy skills.
Too specific:	Students will be able to use institutional online services to retrieve information.
Better:	Students will locate information and evaluate it critically for its validity and appropriateness.

When possible, **use concrete action words** that describe what students should be able to do in explicit, observable terms. Table 5.2 provides examples of effective learning goals that use action words and are neither too broad nor too specific. Recognize, however, that there may be occasions when terms like "know," "understand," "become aware of," or "appreciate" are more useful than action words.

Define fuzzy terms. If you feel you cannot state your key learning goals using action words, define "fuzzy" terms carefully. Examples of fuzzy goals include:

- Think critically.

- Write well or proficiently.

- Understand or be familiar with a particular concept.

- Demonstrate knowledge, skill, proficiency or understanding.

- Appreciate a viewpoint.

Each of these goals would be improved if its fuzzy terms were clarified. "Think critically," for example, could be defined more clearly as "Analyze and evaluate arguments."

Focus on the end, not the means: what students should be able to do *after* they've successfully completed your course or program, not the tasks they are to do while in your course or program. Ask yourself, "Why do we have students complete these tasks? What should students be able to do as a result of accomplishing them?"

Focus on your most important goals. Trying to assess every learning goal will soon have you smothering under a mountain of assessment information. Ask yourself, "What are the most important things we want students to learn?" As suggested in Chapter 4, limit the number of major program goals that you assess to three to six. Once you are comfortable assessing those goals, you can always add additional goals.

Work with colleagues. Some of us are more task- and detail-oriented while others have a more global, theoretical orientation. Writing effective goals requires both perspectives: the ability to see both the big final destination and the specific, detailed steps to get there. If you tend toward one orientation, developing goals with some-one of the opposite perspective may be helpful.

WHAT POTENTIAL LEARNING GOALS SHOULD YOU CONSIDER?

The task of identifying learning goals can seem overwhelming, particularly when establishing goals for a broad program, a general education

Table 5.2

Examples of Effectively Expressed Learning Goals

- *Biology:* Make appropriate inferences and deductions from biological information.
- *Business Administration:* Develop graphic, spreadsheet, and financial analysis support for positions taken.
- *Chemistry:* Design an experiment to test a chemical hypothesis or theory.
- *Communication Studies:* Systematically analyze and solve problems, advocate and defend one's views, and refute opposing views.
- *Earth Science:* Analyze the surface and subsurface (three-dimensional and four-dimensional) geologic characteristics of landforms.
- *English:* Present original interpretations of literary works in the context of existing research on these works.
- *Environmental Science:* Critically evaluate the effectiveness of agencies, organizations, and programs addressing environmental problems.
- *Health Care Management:* Apply basic problem-solving skills along with health care financial management knowledge to develop recommendations related to the financial issue(s) confronted by a health care organization.
- *Medieval & Renaissance Studies:* Write with clarity, unity, coherence, and correctness.
- *Metropolitan Studies:* Conduct and present sound research on metropolitan issues.
- *Speech-Language Pathology/Audiology:* Use appropriate interpersonal qualities and professional characteristics during interactions with peers, academic and clinical faculty, and clients.
- *Theater:* Use voice, movement, and understanding of dramatic character and situation to affect an audience.
- *Women's Studies:* Use gender as an analytical category to critique cultural and social institutions.

Adapted from goals created by the faculty of Towson University.

curriculum, or an institution. It can help to view learning goals as falling into just three basic categories: knowledge, skills, and attitudes, each of which is discussed in this section. Several educators have developed more detailed frameworks that can also be helpful in identifying and clarifying learning goals (see Anderson & Krathwohl, 2001; Angelo, 1991; Biggs, 2001; Herman, Aschbacher, & Winters, 1992; Marzano, Pickering, & McTighe, 1993).

Increase Knowledge and Basic Understanding

Knowledge and understanding goals include remembering, replicating a simple procedure, and defining, summarizing, or explaining concepts or phenomena.

Examples:
- Explain how to access the web from computers in campus labs.
- Summarize the distinctive characteristics of a particular novelist.
- Understand each element of the scientific method.

Several generations ago, American education focused heavily on memorization—of facts, vocabulary, formulas, poetry, and so on—with good reason: Many students didn't have access to books, maps, newspapers, and other media once they left school. Whatever they didn't commit to memory could well be lost to them forever.

Today, memorization and simple understanding are less important for several reasons. First, the amount of knowledge available to us has simply exploded. We know, for example, far more about the building blocks of matter than we did a generation ago. There is more history to understand than when our parents went to school, and our study of history has broadened from a Eurocentric model to a global one. The number of scholarly journals in almost every field has grown exponentially. Today there are so many important concepts that we can't expect students to remember them all.

Coupled with the explosion in knowledge is our increasingly easy access to it. Today, we have access to public libraries, bookstores, newsstands, and the web. Is it so important to remember a formula, date, or vital statistic when it can be looked up so effortlessly? With today's easily accessible information, many educators believe that we should change our focus from remembering facts and concepts to learning how to find them, use them appropriately, and appreciate their meaning and value.

Additionally, our knowledge base will continue to expand and evolve. Today's students will someday need information that hasn't yet been conceived and insight that hasn't yet been drawn, rendering obsolete some of the information we now teach. Should we focus on having students remember material that may soon be outdated or irrelevant, or should we focus on developing the thinking skills they'll need to master new concepts on their own, after they've left us?

Finally, as we understand better how people learn, we are learning that much of what students memorize is committed to short-term memory and quickly forgotten. Imagine how your students would do if you popped their final exam on them five years later, or even a few months later. How much would they remember from the first time they studied for it? Probably not much—and is it worth spending time teaching material that's quickly forgotten? Or should we focus instead on developing skills and attitudes that will last a lifetime, such as the ability to write well, analyze the difference between two theories, or appreciate American folk music?

Because of all these factors, today educators are increasingly emphasizing skills more than knowledge and simple understanding. Does this mean that students shouldn't memorize anything anymore? Absolutely not! We wouldn't want to fly in a jet whose pilot has to look up the meaning of that flashing light as the plane goes into a nosedive. We wouldn't want to be operated on by a surgeon who has to pause to read up on how to stop that excessive bleeding. Students will always need to remember and understand certain fundamental concepts. But today we expect college students not only to understand facts and concepts but to be able to use them.

Develop Thinking and Other Skills

Skills fall into at least three categories:

- **Thinking skills,** including skills in analysis, evaluation, and other thought processes needed to solve problems and make necessary decisions.

- *Performance skills:* physical skills such as the ability to manipulate a tool, wield a paint brush, hit a softball, or dance gracefully.

- *Interpersonal skills,* including the abilities to listen, work with people from diverse backgrounds, lead a group, and participate as an effective team member.

While all three kinds of skills are important, thinking skills are often the focus of higher education courses, programs, and institutions. Thinking skills include the following.

Application is the ability to use knowledge and understanding in a new context, such as applying scientific principles to research problems, provided that the problems are new to the student. Many mathematics word problems require application skill.

Examples:
- Locate online resources on a particular topic or issue.
- Apply scientific and economic principles to everyday life.

Analysis is the ability to break a complex concept apart to see the relationships of its components. Students who can analyze can identify the elements, relationships, and underlying principles of a complex process. Analysis is not merely understanding the components of a process or concept explained in class; that would be simple understanding. Students who can analyze can understand the structure of concepts *they haven't seen before*. They can think holistically, make a case, discover the underlying principles of a relationship, and understand organizational structure. They can integrate their learning, relating what they're learning to what they already know.

Examples:
- Explain chemical reactions not explicitly introduced in prior study.
- Explain the impact of the Korean War on U.S.–Far East relations today.
- Analyze errors.
- Analyze perspectives and values.
- Explain why a research paper is structured the way it is.

Synthesis is the ability to put what one has learned together in a new, original way. It includes the abilities to theorize, generalize, reflect, construct hypotheses, generate new ideas and new ways of viewing a situation, invent, and suggest alternatives.

Examples:
- Write a poem that uses imagery and structure typical of early 19th century American poets.
- Theorize what is likely to happen when two chemicals are combined, and justify the theory.
- Design and conduct a research study.
- Design a community service project.

Creative thinking skills include synthesis skills and also the abilities to be flexible and take intellectual risks.

Example:
- Conceive of original, unorthodox solutions to a problem.

Evaluation, problem solving, and decision-making skills constitute the ability to make an informed judgment about the merits of something the student hasn't seen before. They include the abilities to conduct research, make appropriate choices, solve problems with no single correct answer, and make and justify persuasive arguments. They do not consist of merely understanding and reflecting arguments that have been presented in coursework; that would be simple understanding.

Examples:
- Judge the effectiveness of the use of color in a work of art.
- Evaluate the validity of information on a particular web site.
- Research, identify, and justify potential careers.
- Choose the appropriate mathematical procedure for a given problem.
- Identify an audit problem in a financial statement and recommend ways to address it.

Metacognition is learning *how to learn* and how to manage one's own learning by *understanding how one learns*. Because, as noted earlier, knowledge is growing at an exponential pace, there is increasing recognition that we must prepare students for a lifetime of learning, often on their own, making metacognition an increasingly valued skill. Metacognition is discussed further in Chapter 9.

Examples:
- Develop a personal study strategy that makes the most of one's learning style.
- Identify the strengths and weaknesses of one's completed work.

Other **productive dispositions or habits of mind** include the abilities to work independently, set personal goals, persevere, organize, be clear and accurate, visualize, be curious, and be open-minded to new ideas.

Examples:
- Develop and use effective time management skills.
- Follow directions correctly.

These various kinds of thinking skills are not discrete! It would be hard, for example, to think of someone engaged in sound evaluation who does not bring analysis skills into play.

Critical thinking is a widely used term whose meaning lacks clear consensus. Critical thinking skills can include many of the thinking skills described here, including analysis, synthesis, evaluation, problem solving, and some of the productive habits of mind. Critical thinking can also include the abilities to seek truth, clarity and accuracy; distinguish facts from opinions; and have a healthy skepticism about arguments and claims. If critical thinking emerges as a potential learning goal, spell out the kinds of thinking skills it encompasses in your particular situation.

Develop Attitudes and Values

Attitudinal goals include appreciation; becoming more aware of one's own values, attitudes, and opinions and their evolution and maturation; integrity; character; and enjoying and valuing learning.

Examples:
- Be a passionate and curious lifelong learner.
- Appreciate the merits and value of a subject or discipline.
- Appreciate the perspective of people from backgrounds different from one's own.
- Choose ethical courses of action.

What Kinds of Learning Goals Are Most Important and Valued Today?

While every program can and should have unique goals, faculty, employers, and other higher education stakeholders often note that today's college graduates, regardless of major, should have the following capabilities:

- *Communication skills, especially in writing.* Virtually everyone needs to be able to express himself or herself clearly in writing and speech.

- *Information literacy and research skills.* Because virtually everyone needs to continue to learn independently after graduation, both to stay current in one's field and for personal enrichment, everyone needs to know how to find information and evaluate its merits and worth.

- *Thinking skills.* Most careers require the abilities to analyze, evaluate, organize, solve problems, make decisions, and so forth.

- *Interpersonal skills.* Many careers require the ability to work with and lead others.

While these skills are often addressed in general education curricula, students often need to develop these skills from a disciplinary perspective as well. A first-year composition course, for example, won't teach biology, psychology, or business students how to write in their discipline; faculty in the discipline need to do that.

HOW SHOULD KEY LEARNING GOALS BE IDENTIFIED?

Institutions, programs, and courses always fit into a larger context, so learning goals should never be developed in isolation. Look to internal and external resources, including colleagues, to ensure that learning goals are appropriate and meet student needs.

Identify Resources for Potential Goals

Begin the goal identification process by looking for goals that others have adopted and that your goals should relate to or build upon. Possible sources include:

- Your institution's mission and vision statements.

- Standards espoused by appropriate disciplinary associations and accreditation organizations.

- Course syllabi.

- Capstone experiences.

- Angelo and Cross's (1993) *Teaching Goals Inventory*.

- Surveys or interviews of prospective employers.

- Admissions criteria for academic programs your students pursue after program completion.

Make Goal Identification a Collaborative Process

Conversations on learning goals can be one of the most invigorating and rewarding aspects of an assessment program because they address the heart of the faculty's work: teaching and learning. Agreement on the fundamental learning goals of a course or program is important because all students, no matter which sections of a required course they happen to register for or which elective courses they choose, should have confidence that their classes will successfully prepare them for what lies next, be it the next course in a sequence, a subsequent program, or their life work. Ideally, course and program goals should be developed not only in collaboration with others teaching the same course or program but also with those teaching prerequisites, co-requisites, and subsequent courses, along with students and employers, to ensure that the course or program meets the needs of all concerned.

Prepare for these conversations by identifying common ground that already exists. Even if a course or program does not have formally articulated learning goals, its faculty doubtless have an implicit sense of what they want students to learn. Collect information on potential common goals by:

- Examining course syllabi.

- Asking faculty about what they aim to accomplish in each course that they teach.

- Asking faculty to list three things they think all students should know or be able to do five or ten years after graduation.

- Asking faculty to complete the *Teaching Goals Inventory* in Angelo and Cross's (1993) *Classroom Assessment Techniques*, in which they rate the importance of a variety of goals.

Whichever method(s) you use, compile and share the results in a handout or on a large chart for all to see. With this information in hand, faculty can discuss questions such as:

- What do we value about our discipline?

- What does our disciplinary association or major authorities in our discipline think is important for students to learn?

- Why do we have this program or requirement? Why should students study this? How do we want this experience to affect their lives?

- What do we want all students to get out of this program or requirement, regardless of the particular course or track they elect?

- What do our students do after they graduate? What are the most important things they need for success in those pursuits?

- What makes our graduates successful? What makes them attractive to potential employers, graduate programs, and the like?

- If our program prepares students for specific careers, what knowledge, skills, and attitudes will their employers and supervisors be looking for?

How Can Consensus on Common Goals Be Achieved?

What if faculty simply cannot agree on key learning goals for a course or program? There's no law that says 100% agreement is needed in order to move forward, and there are several techniques to help gauge consensus, make decisions, and proceed. One is to ask each faculty member to write three important goals, and then break the faculty into small groups and ask each group to identify three goals that everyone agrees are important. The groups then share their goals, and common goals across groups are identified.

Another method is the Delphi technique:

- Create a list of all possible learning goals for a course or program.

- Distribute the list to faculty members, and ask each to check off those goals that he or she thinks should be one of the key goals of the course or program.

- Collect the lists, tally the checkmarks, and share the results with the faculty.

- Strike those goals with no votes. (Your group may also agree to strike those goals with just one or two votes.)

- Sometimes a few goals will emerge as the top vote-getters, and the group will agree to focus on them, ending the process.

- If consensus cannot be reached after the first round, redistribute the (possibly abbreviated) list with the initial results noted, and ask the faculty to vote again. Sometimes it's agreed that everyone will vote for no more than, say, eight goals.

- Again collect, tally, and share the lists. Human nature is such that few people will persist in voting for a goal that's not supported by anyone else, so consensus on a few manageable goals is usually reached by this point. If not, the cycle is repeated until consensus is achieved.

Does Collaboration Impinge on Academic Freedom?

While some would argue that establishing common learning goals flies in the face of academic freedom, academic freedom doesn't justify preparing students inconsistently for whatever comes after a course or program is completed. If the majority of the faculty in a department agree on key learning goals for a course or program, or if colleagues in another department argue convincingly that certain key learning goals must be achieved in order to succeed in a co-requisite, or if employers say they need graduates with certain skills, the faculty have an obligation to ensure that all its students, regardless of the particular courses or sections in which they enroll, have sufficient opportunity to achieve those ends.

This does not mean, however, that faculty should teach identical curricula and use identical pedagogies. Once the faculty in a program agree on key common learning goals, individual faculty members should decide what other goals they have for their classes and how best to help students achieve all those goals, both common and unique.

SHARE GOALS WITH STUDENTS

As noted at the beginning of this chapter, students learn more effectively when a learning activity has clear goals. Knowing why they are studying something or completing an assignment helps them focus on what's most important and get the most out of their learning experiences. It's therefore a good idea to share institutional, program, and course goals with students so they understand:

- Why do we offer (or require) this course or program? Why is it important that you study this?

- What is this course or discipline all about? What are the most important things you will learn in this course or program? Why are those things important?

- What do we expect of you in this course or program?

- How will this course or program help you prepare for your career and life?

- How does this course relate to other courses in your program, or how does this program relate to other disciplines you may be studying?

TIME TO THINK, DISCUSS, AND PRACTICE

1) A local community college wants all its students, regardless of major, to graduate with "quantitative problem solving skills." Write a learning goal that describes this aim more clearly.

2) A professor has asked his students to write a paper in which they are to "discuss" an historical event. Under what circumstances would this assignment assess only simple understanding of the event? Under what circumstances would this assignment assess a thinking skill? What thinking skill(s) might it assess?

3) Write a learning goal for students in a program in which you teach or are enrolled as a student that would focus on developing analysis skills.

4) Write three other learning goals for the same program. Write them in terms of skills or attitudes that students will have after they complete the program.

REFERENCES

Anderson, L. W., & Krathwohl, D. R. (Eds.). (2001). *Taxonomy for learning, teaching, and assessing: A revision of Bloom's taxonomy of educational objectives*. Needham Heights, MA: Allyn & Bacon.

Angelo, T. A. (1991). Ten easy pieces: Assessing higher learning in four dimensions. *New directions in teaching and learning: No. 46. Classroom research: Early lessons from success* (pp. 17–31). San Francisco, CA: Jossey-Bass.

Angelo, T. A., & Cross, K. P. (1993). Teaching goals inventory. In *Classroom assessment techniques: A handbook for college teachers* (pp. 393–397). San Francisco, CA: Jossey-Bass.

Biggs, J. (2001). Assessing for quality in learning. In L. Suskie (Ed.), *Assessment to promote deep learning* (pp. 65–68). Washington, DC: American Association for Higher Education.

Herman, J. L., Aschbacher, P. R., & Winters, L. (1992). *A practical guide to alternative assessment.* Alexandria, VA: Association for Supervision and Curriculum Development.

Kirkpatrick, D. L. (1998). *Evaluating training programs: The four levels* (2nd ed.). San Francisco, CA: Berrett-Koehler.

Marzano, R., Pickering, D., & McTighe, J. (1993). *Assessing student outcomes: Performance assessment using the dimensions of learning model.* Alexandria, VA: Association for Supervision and Curriculum Development.

RECOMMENDED READING

Association of American Colleges and Universities. (2002). *Greater expectations: A new vision for learning as a nation goes to college.* Washington, DC: Author. Retrieved June 2, 2003, from http://www.greaterexpectations.org

Association of American Colleges and Universities. (2002). *Liberal education outcomes for the 21st century.* Washington, DC: Author. Retrieved June 2, 2003, from http://www.aacu-edu.org/gex/paa/outcomes.cfm

Crist, C., Guill, D., Harmes, P., & Lake, C. (1998, November). *Managing alternative assessment.* Oakland, CA: Coalition of Essential Schools. Retrieved June 2, 2003, from http://www.essential schools.org/cs/resources/view/ces_res/130

Erwin, T. D. (2000). *The NPEC sourcebook on assessment, volume 1: Definitions and assessment methods for critical thinking, problem solving, and writing* [Electronic version]. Washington, DC: National Center for Education Statistics. Retrieved June 2, 2003, from http://nces.ed.gov/pubs2000/2000195.pdf

Facione, P. A. (1998). *Critical thinking: What it is and why it counts.* Millbrae, CA: California Academic Press. Retrieved June 2, 2003, from http://www.insightassessment.com/pdf_files/what&why98.pdf

Facione, P. A. (1990). *Critical thinking: A statement of expert consensus for purposes of educational assessment and instruction.* Millbrae, CA: California Academic Press. (ERIC Document Reproduction Service No. ED315423). Retrieved June 2, 2003, from http://www.insightassessment.com/pdf_files/DEXadobe.PDF

Gronlund, N. E. (1999). *How to write and use instructional objectives* (6th ed.). Upper Saddle River, NJ: Prentice Hall.

Marzano, R. (2000). *Designing a new taxonomy of educational objectives.* Thousand Oaks, CA: Corwin Press.

National Postsecondary Education Cooperative. (1997). *Student outcomes information for policy-making: Final report of the National Postsecondary Education Cooperative working group on student outcomes from a policy perspective.* Washington, DC: Author. Retrieved June 2, 2003, from http://nces.ed.gov/pubs97/97991.pdf

Roth, R., Beyer, C., & Gillmore, G. (2002, February 27). *Student learning outcomes (SLOs): A faculty resource on development and assessment.* Seattle, WA: University of Washington Accountability Board. Retrieved June 2, 2003, from http://depts.washington.edu/grading/slo

6
Choosing an Assessment Strategy

T he many ways to assess student learning can be overwhelming. This chapter aims to help you sort through your options by introducing you to the abundance of approaches to assessing student learning and the variety of frameworks you can use to interpret assessment results. This chapter will also discuss how much assessment evidence you should examine.

WHAT ARE YOUR OPTIONS FOR ASSESSING STUDENT LEARNING?

As discussed in Chapter 2, the best assessment plans use multiple, diverse approaches. Depending on your interests and needs, these approaches may include:

- Formative and summative assessments.
- Assessments yielding direct and indirect evidence of student learning.
- Assessments yielding evidence of learning processes, inputs, and context as well as learning outcomes.
- Objective and subjective assessments.
- Performance assessments and traditional assessments.
- Embedded and add-on assessments.
- Local and published assessments.
- Quantitative and qualitative assessments.

Formative and Summative Assessments

Formative assessments are those undertaken while student learning is taking place—perhaps midway through a course or program. Their purpose is usually to improve teaching and learning; faculty can give students prompt feedback on their strengths and weaknesses and make immediate modifications to classroom activities and assignments.

Summative assessments are those obtained at the end of a course or program. Their purpose is usually to document student learning for transcripts and for employers, donors, legislators, and other external audiences. Students may not receive any feedback on their performance other than possibly an overall grade or score.

Formative and summative assessments are discussed further in Chapter 4.

Assessments Yielding Direct and Indirect Evidence

Direct evidence of student learning is tangible, visible, self-explanatory evidence of exactly what students have and haven't learned. Table 6.1 gives examples of direct evidence of student learning.

Indirect evidence, on the other hand, provides signs that students are probably learning, but the evidence of exactly what they are learning is less clear and less convincing. Placement rates and many of Kirkpatrick's Level 4 (Results) outcomes (see Chapter 5, Table 5.1) are indirect evidence. If we know, for example, that 95% of the graduates of a teacher education program find jobs as teachers, we can conclude that they've probably learned important things, because they're attractive to employers, but we can't tell from this statistic alone exactly what they have and haven't learned. Table 6.2 gives examples of indirect evidence.

Indirect evidence of student learning not only is less persuasive than direct evidence but may be misleading. A 95% teacher placement rate, for example, may be due as much to a regional shortage of teachers as to the quality of a teacher preparation program. Because of this, *no assessment effort should consist of indirect evidence alone.* Indirect evidence can nonetheless be an important part of an assessment program. Information on learning processes, discussed in the next section, can be especially useful indirect evidence.

Table 6.1

Examples of Direct Evidence of Student Learning

- Ratings of student skills by their field experience supervisors (see Chapter 7)
- Scores and pass rates on appropriate licensure/certification exams (e.g., Praxis, NCLEX) or other published tests (e.g., Major Field Tests) that assess key learning outcomes
- Capstone experiences such as research projects, presentations, theses, dissertations, oral defenses, exhibitions, or performances, scored using a rubric (Chapter 7)
- Other written work or performances, scored using a rubric (Chapter 7)
- Portfolios of student work (Chapter 10)
- Scores on locally-designed tests (Chapter 11) such as final examinations in key courses, qualifying examinations, and comprehensive examinations, accompanied by test blueprints describing what the tests assess
- Score gains between entry and exit on published or local tests or writing samples
- Employer ratings of the skills of recent graduates
- Summaries and analyses of electronic class discussion threads
- Student reflections on their values, attitudes, and beliefs (Chapter 9), if developing those are intended outcomes of the program

---

Assessments Yielding Evidence of Learning Processes, Inputs, and Context

Most direct evidence of student learning focuses on learning *outcomes:* the knowledge, skills, attitudes, and habits of mind that students develop and take with them. While information on learning outcomes can be the most compelling evidence of student learning, such evidence alone may not help us understand *why* students are or aren't learning. In order to understand what's happening and how student learning might be improved, look at learning processes, inputs, and context.

Table 6.2

Examples of Indirect Evidence of Student Learning

- Course grades (see Chapter 1)
- Assignment grades, if not accompanied by a rubric or scoring guide
- For four-year programs, admission rates into graduate programs and graduation rates from those programs
- For two-year programs, admission rates into four-year institutions and graduation rates from those programs
- Quality/reputation of graduate and four-year programs into which alumni are accepted
- Placement rates of graduates into appropriate career positions and starting salaries
- Alumni perceptions of their career responsibilities and satisfaction
- Student ratings of their knowledge and skills and reflections on what they have learned over the course of the program (Chapter 9)
- Those questions on end-of-course student evaluation forms that ask about the course rather than the instructor
- Student/alumni satisfaction with their learning, collected through surveys, exit interviews, or focus groups (Chapter 12)
- Voluntary gifts from alumni and employers
- Student participation rates in faculty research, publications, and conference presentations
- Honors, awards, and scholarships earned by students and alumni

Table 16.1 in Chapter 16 describes a number of *learning processes*, such as time on task and active learning opportunities, that research has shown helps students learn effectively. Evidence of these learning processes (Table 6.3) is thus important, albeit indirect, evidence that students are probably learning important things. Evidence of learning processes also helps us understand why students are or aren't learning. Angelo and Cross's (1993) *Classroom Assessment Techniques* suggests many specific strategies to assess learning processes.

Table 6.3

Examples of Evidence of Learning Processes That Promote Student Learning

- Transcripts, catalog descriptions, and course syllabi, which can be analyzed for evidence of such things as program coherence and opportunities for active and collaborative learning
- Logs maintained by students documenting time spent on course work, interactions with faculty and other students, nature and frequency of library use, and so forth
- Interviews and focus groups with students, asking them why they achieve some learning goals well and others less well
- Many of Angelo and Cross's (1993) classroom assessment techniques
- Counts of out-of-class interactions between faculty and students
- Counts of programs that disseminate lists of the program's major learning goals to all students in the program
- Counts of courses whose syllabi list the course's major learning goals
- Counts of courses whose stated learning goals include thinking skills (see Chapter 5) as well as just basic understanding
- Documentation of the match between course/program objectives and assessments
- Counts of courses whose final grades are based at least in part on assessments of thinking skills as well as basic understanding
- Ratio of performance assessments to paper-and-pencil tests
- Proportions of class time spent in active learning
- Counts of courses with collaborative learning opportunities
- Counts of courses taught using culturally responsive teaching techniques
- Counts of courses with service-learning opportunities, or the number of student hours spent in service-learning activities
- Library activity in the program's discipline(s) (e.g., number of books in the discipline that have been checked out; number of online database searches that have been conducted; number of online journal articles in the discipline that have been accessed)

- Counts of student majors participating in relevant co-curricular activities (e.g., the percent of biology majors participating in the biology club)
- Voluntary student attendance at disciplinary seminars and conferences and other intellectual/cultural events relevant to a program

Learning inputs—things in place before the learning process begins that might affect the learning process and/or its outcomes—can also yield insight into why students are or aren't learning. Students may not do well in a math class, for example, into which they've been incorrectly placed. They may not learn current laboratory techniques if they work in ill-equipped labs. Table 6.4 gives examples of learning input evidence.

Learning context refers to the environment in which the learning process takes place, particularly those aspects that might affect the learning process and/or its outcomes. Employer needs, for example, affect technical, vocational, or professional curricula: if a program doesn't graduate students with the skills that employers need, its graduates won't be able to find jobs. Table 6.5 gives examples of information on learning context or environment.

Objective and Subjective Assessments

An *objective* assessment is one that needs no professional judgment to score correctly (although *interpretation* of the scores requires professional judgment). Most objective test items have only one correct answer and could be scored accurately by a reasonably competent eight-year-old armed with an answer key. *Subjective* assessments, on the other hand, yield many possible answers of varying quality and require professional judgment to score. Multiple-choice, matching, and true-false test questions (Chapter 11) are generally designed to be objective; most other assessments are subjective.

Subjective assessments are increasingly popular for several reasons:

Subjective assessments assess many important skills that objective tests cannot, including organization, synthesis, and problem solving skills. Subjective assessments are the tool of choice when we want

Table 6.4

Examples of Evidence of Learning Inputs That Affect Student Learning

- Students' high school records, including curriculum, grades, and rank in class
- SAT or ACT scores
- Placement test scores
- Transfer articulation policies and agreements with other institutions
- Library holdings in the program's discipline(s)
- Faculty credentials, such as the percent holding terminal degrees in their discipline
- Opportunities and expenditures for faculty professional development in teaching and learning
- Institutional funding for academic programs
- Student-faculty ratio, average class size, and/or ratio of students to full-time faculty
- Instructional facilities, technologies, and materials
- Number and/or dollar value of grants awarded for improving student learning

to encourage creativity and originality, because traditional multiple-choice tests have, by definition, only one correct response and therefore encourage convergent thinking.

Subjective assessments can assess skills directly. Many faculty would agree, for example, that a writing sample is more convincing evidence of a student's writing skill than her answers to multiple-choice questions on how to write. Similarly, watching a student nurse draw a blood sample provides more compelling evidence of his skill than his answers to multiple-choice questions on how to draw blood.

Subjective assessments promote deep, lasting learning. You probably remember far more from the research papers you wrote in college than from the studying you did for multiple-choice final exams.

Scoring procedures for subjective assessments allow for nuances. On a subjective math test, for example, students can receive partial

---

Table 6.5

Examples of Evidence of Learning Context That Affect Student Learning

- Prospective students' interest in the institution or program
- Prospective employers' demand for graduates of the institution or program
- Needs and expectations of prospective employers and graduate programs
- Perceptions of the institution or program by employers and other external audiences
- Characteristics and comparative strengths and weaknesses of competing institutions and programs
- Regional and/or national trends in the discipline
- The regional climate for higher education, including public and private support for higher education

---

credit for doing part of a problem correctly, but on a multiple choice math test, they'll usually receive no credit for an incorrect answer, even if they do much of their work correctly.

Objective assessments, meanwhile, remain widely used for several reasons:

Students can provide a great deal of information on a broad range of learning goals in a relatively short time. Testing experts call this "efficiency." If you want to assess a wide array of concepts and skills, a 45-minute multiple-choice test will give you more comprehensive information than a 45-minute essay test.

Because of their efficiency, **objective assessments encourage broader—albeit shallower—learning than subjective assessments.** Asking students to write a paper on a particular poem by Wordsworth is a good choice if the learning goal is to develop a thorough understanding of that poem but a poor choice if the learning goal is to develop a general understanding of Romantic poetry. For this latter goal, an objective test asking students to react to a variety of Romantic poems might be a better choice.

While they are difficult and time-consuming to construct, ***objective assessments are fast and easy to score.*** If they are stored securely so they can be reused, the payback on the time spent writing them only increases.

Those who govern or fund institutions or programs often find objective tests appealing because ***the results can be summarized into a single number.*** Busy board members and legislators often want a single number describing student learning, even though it usually presents an incomplete, if not distorted, picture. They don't want to spend time examining samples of student work, even though this evidence can be more convincing. Until the education community develops an effective, compelling way to summarize and communicate the results of subjective assessments, objective tests will probably be part of many assessment programs.

Performance Assessments and Traditional Assessments

Traditional assessments are the kinds of tests that have been around for decades, if not centuries: objective tests, "blue book" essay questions, and oral examinations. Traditional assessments are often completed in a controlled, timed examination setting and are usually designed only to collect assessment information, not give students a learning opportunity.

Performance assessments ask students to *demonstrate* their skills rather than relate what they've learned through traditional tests. Performance assessments include field experiences, laboratory and studio assignments, projects, performances, and term papers and other writing assignments. Performance assessments are sometimes called *alternative* assessments because they're alternatives to traditional multiple-choice and blue book tests. Performance assessments that ask students to do real-life tasks, such as completing internships, analyzing case studies with bona fide data, or conducting realistic laboratory experiments, are called *authentic* assessments. Performance assessments have two components: the assignment or prompt that tells students what is expected of them (Chapter 8) and a scoring guide or rubric (Chapter 7) used to evaluate completed work.

Performance assessments are subjective and have all the advantages of subjective assessments described earlier. A further advantage of alternative assessments over essay tests and other traditional assessments is that they merge learning and assessment; students learn while they are working on performance assessments, unlike traditional testing periods during which they often learn nothing. Authentic assessments have the additional advantage of giving students realistic learning situations.

While essay questions, oral examinations, and the like have been characterized here as traditional assessments, in reality they straddle the line between traditional and performance assessments. They are traditional in the sense that they are usually not designed to give students a learning opportunity and because their timed setting with limited access to resources often doesn't mimic the real world. They are performance assessments, however, because they ask students to perform skills such as writing and critical thinking.

Embedded and Add-On Assessments

Course assignments can often serve a dual purpose, providing useful information not only on what students have learned in a course but also on how well they have achieved some important program goals. A paper that a student writes in an advanced course, for example, can give us information not only on what the student has learned in that particular course but also on the writing skill that she has developed over the entire program. These kinds of **embedded** assessments—program assessments that are embedded into coursework—often require far less work than add-on assessments. Convincing students to participate in program assessment activities is a non-issue, as students don't even realize that they're providing program assessment information.

Sometimes, however, embedded assessments don't answer all key questions about student learning across a program, so we must ask students to participate in **add-on** assessments beyond course requirements. Students might be asked to assemble a portfolio throughout their program (Chapter 10) or, as they prepare to graduate, take a published comprehensive test (Chapter 13) or participate in a survey or focus group (Chapter 12).

The major challenge with add-on assessments is convincing students to participate in them and to give the assessment tasks serious thought and effort. Here are some suggestions for doing this:

Make participation in the assessment a program requirement. This is obviously the most effective participation incentive.

Show the importance of the assessment activity. Cultivate a strong campus culture of assessment (Chapter 3) in which students continually hear from their professors and from campus leaders that assessment activities are inherent, valued parts of the academic program, not superfluous extras. Offer to send students a summary of the overall results and, if possible, give students feedback on their own strengths and weaknesses, how they compare to their peers, and how their contributions are leading to tangible improvements.

Provide a material incentive to encourage students to participate, such as:

- A token incentive enclosed with every invitation or mailed survey (perhaps a pencil, window decal, or coupon for a free ice-cream cone), as these can create a sense of obligation.

- Something more significant to those students who participate (perhaps a long-distance phone card, a complimentary meal, tickets to a popular campus event or, if the time contributed is significant, a check compensating students for their time).

- Perks that are highly prized but have little or no direct cost, such as registration or housing preference, a parking space in a prime lot, or extra graduation tickets.

- Entering the names of those participating in a random drawing for significant prizes such as gift certificates.

The effectiveness of material incentives varies dramatically, depending on campus culture and student values. Free pizza might work beautifully with some students and be a dismal failure with others. Ask some students to suggest incentives that would convince them to participate, and consider trying out incentives with small groups of students before launching a full-scale assessment. You may want to use incentives only with those subgroups of students whose participation rates are historically low.

Minimize the inconvenience of the assessment activity. Keep the length of the assessment as short as possible, schedule it at a convenient time and place, and give students plenty of advance notice. If it's not possible to conduct the assessment during regularly scheduled class time in appropriate courses, consider conducting the assessment on several days, at several times, so students can find an assessment period that they can attend regardless of their other obligations. Some colleges schedule an "assessment day" once each term or year, during which no regular classes are held and students instead participate in assessment activities.

Allow students to include test scores in their credentials at their discretion. This is especially effective, of course, if the test is recognized and valued by prospective employers or graduate programs. Many students might be intrigued by the prospect of strengthening job prospects or graduate school applications by having their academic record note that they scored at, say, the 87th percentile on a nationally recognized exam. Include scores in student credentials *only if the student so chooses*, or students who think they will do poorly will be unlikely to participate.

Give top scorers or the first students to return a survey some kind of recognition, perhaps one of the no-cost perks mentioned earlier. Students earning exceptional scores on important assessments might receive an award, a seal on their diplomas, or a notation on their transcripts.

While it may be tempting to promote student participation in an add-on assessment by establishing a minimum score as a graduation or progression requirement, single scores should never be the sole basis of any major decision such as retention or graduation. *Using a single assessment score as a "gatekeeper" graduation or progression requirement is an unethical use of assessment results,* as discussed in Chapter 2. Minimum scores may be used as graduation or progression requirements *only if* students may take the test repeatedly *and if* they have an alternative means of demonstrating competence, such as submitting a portfolio of their work for evaluation by a faculty panel.

Local and Published Assessments

Local assessments are those created by faculty and/or staff at an institution, while **published** instruments are those published by an organization external to the institution and used by a number of institutions. Chapter 13 discusses the pros and cons of local and published instruments.

Quantitative and Qualitative Assessments

Quantitative assessments use structured, predetermined response options that can be summarized into meaningful numbers and analyzed statistically. Test scores (Chapter 11), rubric scores (Chapter 7), and survey ratings (Chapter 12) are all examples of quantitative evidence. Quantitative assessments are far more common than qualitative, probably because many assessment practitioners are more familiar with quantitative techniques and some audiences find quantitative results more convincing.

Some people confuse quantitative with objective assessments; they assume that quantitative assessments must be objective. To the contrary, much quantitative evidence is developed through subjective professional judgment. Rubric scores, for example, are subjective ratings of student work that can be quantified and analyzed statistically.

Qualitative assessments use flexible, naturalistic methods and are usually analyzed by looking for recurring patterns and themes. Reflective writing (Chapter 9), notes from interviews and focus groups (Chapter 12), online class discussion threads, and notes from observations are all examples of qualitative evidence.

Qualitative assessments are underused and underappreciated in many assessment circles. Unlike quantitative assessments, which collect only predetermined information, qualitative assessments allow us to explore possibilities that we haven't considered. They can give fresh insight and help discover problems—and solutions—that can't be found through quantitative assessments alone. Qualitative assessments can also add a human dimension to an assessment program, enhancing the dry tables and graphs that constitute many assessment reports with living voices. Qualitative assessments are discussed further in Chapter 9.

WHAT QUESTIONS WILL THE ASSESSMENT AIM TO ANSWER?

Successful planning for any undertaking begins with a clear vision of what you want to accomplish and why. The shopping trip described in Chapter 4 will be even more successful if, before you write your list, you have a clear idea of why you need your purchases and how you will use them. Knowing whether the slacks you're buying will be used in your office or garden or in cold or hot weather will make your shopping trip far more successful.

Similarly, the assessment strategy you choose is far more likely to be effective and appropriate if you keep in mind the questions that the assessment aims to answer. Imagine that Michael, one of your students, scored a 65 on a particular test. Did he do well or not? It depends on what you mean by "doing well." There are at least six perspectives, frames of reference, or bases of comparison for deciding what doing well means. Each involves comparing Michael's 65 against something else and answers a different kind of question:

- Standards-based: Are your students meeting your standards?

- Benchmarking: How do your students compare to peers?

- Best practice: How do your students compare to the best of their peers?

- Value-added: Are your students improving?

- Longitudinal: Is your program improving?

- Capability: Are your students doing as well as they can?

The questions you aim to answer and the perspectives you therefore choose determine your assessment design.

Standards-Based Perspective: Are Your Students Meeting Your Standards?

A *standards-based* (or *competency-based* or *criterion-referenced*) perspective compares Michael's 65 against an established standard. Suppose that your disciplinary association has decreed that students should earn a 55 on the test Michael took in order to be considered worthy of a college degree in your discipline. Or suppose that your department colleagues agree that students should earn at least a 60 in order to earn a passing grade on the test. Under either of these standards-based perspectives, Michael did rather well.

Employers, legislators, and other external audiences are increasingly calling for evidence that college graduates have achieved a certain level of competence in the knowledge and skills that these audiences consider important, making the standards-based perspective an increasingly popular way to interpret assessment results.

If a standards-based perspective is appropriate for your situation:

- *Design your assessment to collect information at a suitable point in the course or program,* usually at the end.

- *Determine the standard: what level of performance is "good enough."* This can be a challenge, of course; strategies to do this are discussed in Chapter 16. Some disciplinary associations, such as the American Council on the Teaching of Foreign Languages, have explicit performance standards.

- *Compare your findings against that standard.*

Benchmarking Perspective: How Do Your Students Compare to Peers?

A *benchmarking* (or *peer-referenced* or *norm-referenced*) perspective compares Michael's 65 against the scores of his peers. Suppose that the average score earned by all your students on Michael's test is 75. Or suppose that the national average for this test is 80. Under either of these benchmarking perspectives, Michael didn't do very well with his score of 65.

The benchmarking perspective is helpful because it adds an external viewpoint, getting us out of our ivory tower. We may think that our students are poor writers but learn that, compared to the national average, they're actually writing quite well. Or we may think that our students are very satisfied with library facilities only to learn that they're less satisfied on average than students at peer institutions.

Benchmarking can also help inform faculty discussions about setting appropriate standards. If the average score for students in your course or program is 75, knowing that the national average is 80 can help faculty decide whether an average of 75 is "good enough." Benchmarking can be misused, however, when a peer average is set as the standard against which performance is judged. Unless everyone in the peer group is performing identically, there will always be someone below average and someone above average, and expecting everyone to perform at or above the average is inappropriate.

If a benchmarking perspective is appropriate for your situation:

- *Design your assessment to collect information at an appropriate point in the course or program,* usually at the end.

- *Identify appropriate peers.* The key word is appropriate. It might not be useful, for example, for an open-admission institution to compare its students' quantitative skills against those of students at highly selective institutions. Peer groups can include:
  - The "national norms" developed for some published instruments (see Chapter 13).
  - For some public institutions, fellow members of a state or regional system.
  - For private institutions, an information-sharing network such as the Higher Education Data Sharing (HEDS) Consortium.
  - Peer institutions that the institution identifies.
  - Peers within one's own institution (the writing skills of chemistry students, for example, might be compared against the writing skills of biology, physics, and earth science students at the same institution).

- *Collect comparable information from those peers.* This can sometimes be a challenge. If your assessment tool does not have national norms and you are not part of a system or consortium, you must often contact each potential peer institution and solicit its cooperation in providing you with information. Some peer information, such as student enrollment, may be available from an institution's web site, catalog, or other public document.

- *Compare your findings against those of your peers.* This comparison is facilitated if you have already discussed what performance level compared to peers is "good enough."

Best-Practice Perspective:
How Do Your Students Compare to the Best of Their Peers?

A *best-practice* (or *best-in-class*) perspective compares your results against the best of your peers. Suppose that you are at a community college whose students average 125 on the XYZ Quantitative Reasoning Test. While the national average for all community college students is 112, students at Potomac Community College average 148, one of the best institutional averages in the country. Under a best-practice perspective, although your students scored above the national average, you would nonetheless conclude that there is room for improvement because your students' average fell short of Potomac's.

While the benchmarking perspective usually focuses on whether performance is above or below average, the best-practice perspective compares a course, program or institution's performance against the very best of its peers, in order to help it be one of the best possible. If the faculty and staff of a best-practice course, program, or institution are willing to share what they are doing, you can gain valuable ideas on how you might achieve similarly outstanding results.

Use a best-practice perspective only if you and your colleagues have a strong commitment to improving your course, program, or institution further, no matter how good it may already be. If a best-practice perspective is appropriate for your situation, design your assessment as you would for a benchmarking perspective. Your challenge will be to identify peers that have "best practices" and to obtain their cooperation in sharing information about exactly what they do that makes them among the best in their class.

Value-Added Perspective: Are Your Students Improving?

A *value-added* (or *growth*, *change*, *improvement*, or *pre–post*) perspective compares Michael's 65 against his performance when he entered. Suppose that, a year ago, Michael scored a 35 on the same test. Under this value-added perspective, Michael shows considerable improvement.

The value-added perspective can give exceptionally compelling information on what students have learned during a course or program. If we assess students only at the end of a course or program using a standards-based or benchmarking perspective, students we identify as, say, superior writers may have been superior writers in high school who learned little from us.

While the value-added perspective was eagerly embraced during the early years of the assessment movement, it has fallen out of favor in recent years for several reasons. One reason is that it can be difficult to motivate students to do their best on "pre-assessments"—the assessments given at the beginning of a course or program. Another is that pre-assessments may not be available for students who transfer into the program.

A third reason that the value-added perspective has fallen out of favor is because assessment tools remain highly imprecise. The "error margin" (discussed later in this chapter) of assessments given at the beginning and end of a course or program can therefore be large, and the error margin of the change from pre-assessment to post-assessment will be even larger, often so large that it masks change or growth. Suppose, for example, that student essays are scored using a five-point scale, and the average score for entering freshmen is 3.2 and the average for rising sophomores is 3.4—a discouragingly small gain. Part of the reason for this relatively small change may be that faculty are not scoring the essays completely consistently, as discussed in Chapter 7.

A final reason why the value-added perspective has fallen out of favor is that, even if significant improvement is found, we often can't be sure that the improvement is the result of our program alone or of other experiences or normal maturation. Growth in a student's oral communication skills, for example, may be due more to her part-time job than to her speech communication course, while the refinement of her life goals may be due as much to normal maturation as to a special career exploration program. While it is theoretically possible to study concurrently a group of comparable individuals outside a course or program, in practical terms it can be difficult to identify people who are truly comparable and convince them to participate in such an assessment.

The value-added perspective may be nonetheless a good choice if it is important to document that a course or program yields significant gains in student learning. You might be asked to justify, for example, that the $200,000 your institution spends each year on mathematics tutoring improves students' mathematics skills significantly, and a value-added approach may provide the most convincing evidence of this.

The value-added perspective can also be helpful if your students are so different from typical students that a standards-based or benchmarking perspective would be inappropriate. Suppose that you have many students who never studied algebra in high school, leaving them far behind typical college students in quantitative skills. Under a standards-based or benchmarking perspective, you might conclude that your mathematics program is deficient, but under a value-added perspective, you may learn your students' skills improve significantly and your programs are actually quite effective.

The value-added perspective can also be helpful if you have too few students to compare with confidence against standards, benchmarks, or norms. If, for example, your program typically graduates only a handful of students each year, their average score on a particular assessment could fluctuate considerably from one year to the next, making it difficult to decide how successful the program is. In this case, it may be more useful to examine each student's individual growth.

A value-added perspective isn't needed in those disciplines about which most students know little or nothing when they enter, such as occupational therapy or aeronautical engineering.

If a value-added perspective is appropriate for your situation, design your assessment to collect the same information at both the beginning and end of the course or program. Determine the growth in your students, and decide if it is "good enough." Again, this decision is facilitated if you have already discussed how much growth is "good enough." If your results are quantitative, statistical tests (Chapter 14) can help you make this decision.

Longitudinal Perspective: Is Your Program Improving?

A *longitudinal* perspective compares current students against peers in prior classes. Suppose that, on Michael's test, all students this year averaged 70, while students last year averaged 55 and students the year before averaged 40. Under this perspective, this year's class did quite well.

The longitudinal perspective differs from the value-added perspective because it looks at changes in *successive* groups of students rather than change within *one* group or *one* student. This perspective is particularly helpful in evaluating the effectiveness of changes in courses or programs. As with the value-added perspective, the longitudinal perspective can also be useful if your students, courses, or programs are very different from the norm. Under a standards-based or benchmarking perspective, relatively low scores might lead you to conclude that your courses or programs are inadequate, but under a longitudinal perspective, you may learn this year's course or program is significantly more effective than last year's and you are making good progress.

If a longitudinal perspective is appropriate for your situation:

- **Design your assessment so that the same assessment is given to successive groups of students.** It's important to balance your need for longitudinal information with your need for information that's relevant to your current course or program. Review your assessment tool on a regular basis and revise any items or sections that are now outdated or irrelevant, even if that means losing some longitudinal information.

- *Determine the change in successive groups of students.* Again, examining the degree of change is facilitated if you have discussed in advance how much change is "good enough." If your results are quantitative, statistical tests (Chapter 14) can help you decide if changes are significant. Keep in mind that changes from one class to the next may be due to extraneous factors. If you see an improvement in writing skills, for example, perhaps it's because this year's class was better prepared in high school than last year's class.

Capability Perspective: Are Your Students Doing as Well as They Can?

A *capability* (or *potential*) perspective compares assessment results against what your students are capable of doing. Caitlyn is tone-deaf but loves to sing, so she's taking a choral class to meet a general education performing arts requirement. By the end of the course, she still can't sing in tune, but the tone and rhythm of her singing have improved. Josh is physically uncoordinated and, despite a semester of hard work in a fitness class emphasizing soccer, his kicks still miss the goal most of the time. Are these students successes or failures? By the criteria of most perspectives, they are clearly deficient in some important skills. But perhaps they are doing as well as they possibly can, given their inherent capabilities.

Now consider Emily, who won first prize at her state's high school science fair for two straight years. As a college senior, she scored at the 70th percentile on a national science test, and her senior research project was judged good, not outstanding, by faculty in her program. Is she a success or a failure? By the criteria of standards-based and benchmarking perspectives, she is successful, but a nagging thought remains: She could be doing better.

The capability or potential perspective can be helpful for understanding these kinds of "outliers"—students whose capabilities are significantly above or below those of typical students. The challenge to using this perspective is determining students' capability accurately.

Some published test "batteries" for basic (K–12) education are normed so that achievement scores can be compared against aptitude scores, but these kinds of tests are rare at the higher education level. This perspective is therefore seldom used in higher education, except informally.

If a capability perspective is appropriate for your situation, design your assessment to collect information systematically on student capability as well as achievements. Then compare your students' achievements against their capability, and decide if their achievement levels are satisfactory. This perspective usually requires subjective, professional judgment rather than statistical analysis to decide whether student performance levels are acceptable.

Which Perspective Should You Use?

Each perspective—standards-based, benchmarking, best practice, value-added, longitudinal, and capability—has advantages and disadvantages and each gives a somewhat incomplete picture of student learning. *Using multiple perspectives—as many as appropriate and feasible—will give you the most complete portrait* of how effectively your students are achieving your goals. If you are examining the performance of your students on a certification examination, for example, you might look at how they compare against national norms, against students in the best programs in the country, and against your students who took the examination a few years ago. Considering all these perspectives will give you a more balanced picture of how your students are performing.

How Much Evidence Should You Examine?

Obviously the more assessment evidence you collect and consider, the greater confidence you will have in your conclusions about student learning. Faculty who look at 300 essays will have more confidence in their conclusions about student writing skills than faculty who look at ten essays. But more evidence means more precious time spent collecting and examining it, so an important question is, "How much evidence is enough?"

To get a perspective on how much evidence you should examine when assessing program or institutional goals, consider that professional pollsters, trying to determine the opinions of hundreds of millions of Americans, rarely survey more than 1,000 people. If you've seen the results of such surveys, you may have noticed that pollsters note an "error margin" of about 3%. This means that if a pollster finds, for example, that 76% of Americans think the President is doing a good job, the pollster is very sure (actually 95% sure) that, if all Americans could be surveyed, between 73% and 79% (76% plus and minus 3%) would say that the President is doing a good job. Table 6.6 lists the error margins of various sample sizes.

Table 6.6

Error Margins of Various Sample Sizes

Random Sample Size	Error Margin
9,604	1%
2,401	2%
1,067	3%
600	4%
384	5%
264	6%
196	7%

While professional pollsters often aim for samples of about 1,000 people, with an error margin of 3%, unless your assessments may lead to major (read expensive) changes at your institution, a sample of 300 or 400 is probably sufficient.

What if 300 or 400 is still too large to be practical? What if faculty only have the time to score, say, 100 essays? Yes, you can use smaller sample sizes—whatever number you think is feasible—if you recognize that your sampling error will be larger and if you take careful steps to ensure the accuracy and truthfulness of your assessment findings (see Chapter 2).

What if you have a small program or institution? Table 6.7 lists the sample sizes you'd need for 5% sampling errors from some relatively small groups of students.

Table 6.7

Sample Sizes Needed From Small Groups for 5% Error Margins

Number of Students You're Sampling From	Random Sample Size
1,000	278
500	217
350	184
200	132
100	80
50	44

How Might a Sample Be Chosen?

Simple random samples—in which every student has an equal chance of being selected—are a straightforward way to ensure that your sample is representative of all your students. A simple random sample might be drawn by writing every student's name on a separate slip of paper, putting all the slips in a bag, shaking the bag, and drawing out as many names as you need. This can be done virtually by using software to generate a random sample. If such software isn't available (check with your computer center), select students based on the last few digits of their student identification numbers, as these last few digits are usually randomly distributed. If you have 250 students and wish to examine writing samples from 50 (20%) of them, for example, you could choose all students whose student identification numbers end in, say, 4 or 5 (20% of all possible digits 0 through 9).

Simple random samples aren't always practical. If you want to administer an in-class survey, for example, it wouldn't be feasible to choose a random sample of the entire student body, go to every class, and ask just the sampled students in each class to complete the survey while the rest of the students sit idle. If a simple random sample isn't realistic, other kinds of samples are possible.

Cluster random samples involve taking a random sample of subgroups of students and then collecting information from everyone in those subgroups. You could take a random sample of first-year writing classes, for example, and then assess essays written by everyone in those classes. Or you could take a random sample of floors in the residence halls and interview everyone on those floors.

Purposeful or judgment samples are carefully *but not randomly* chosen so that, in your best judgment, they are representative of the students you are assessing. Suppose that you want to assess essays written by students in first-year writing classes and you would like to select a cluster random sample of classes. Unfortunately, you know that while some faculty will gladly cooperate, others will decline to provide you with copies of student essays. You can still obtain a good sample of essays by choosing, from those classes with cooperating faculty, a sample of classes that meet on various days and at various times and seem to represent a good cross-section of all first-year writing classes.

Or suppose that you want to assess student learning in general education science courses and, while students may meet this requirement by taking any of 17 courses, 80% take one of just two courses: introductory biology and introductory geology. Collecting assessment information from just these two courses will be far simpler and more cost effective than collecting information from all 17 courses and will give you useful information on 80% of your students.

If you must use a small or non-random sample or if you have a low participation rate, it's especially important to collect information showing that your sample is representative of students in general (see Chapter 14).

TIME TO THINK, DISCUSS, AND PRACTICE

1) A chemistry faculty member wants to assess the writing and research skills of her department's graduating seniors. Brainstorm possible examples of:

- *direct* evidence of student learning
- evidence of learning *processes*
- *qualitative* evidence that could be helpful in assessing students' writing and research skills

2) The international studies faculty wish to interview graduating seniors on their perceptions of the program. Unfortunately, seniors in the program typically take many different courses in a variety of departments, so these interviews can't be conducted as a class activity. Brainstorm three approaches that the faculty might use to convince seniors to participate in an out-of-class interview.

3) For each of the following scenarios, decide which frame(s) of reference would be most appropriate—and realistically feasible—for interpreting the results. (At this point, don't discuss whether the department is achieving its goal; that topic is addressed in Chapter 16.)

- One of the foreign language department's goals is for its French seniors to surpass seniors nationally on the Major Field Test in French. This year 55% of seniors scored above the national average on the test.
- One of the social work department's goals is for its graduates to succeed in graduate study. A survey of alumni who graduated five years ago shows that 40% have earned an M.S.W.

4) The business program at Calvert College requires every student to compile a portfolio of his or her work. The program's ten faculty would like to assess student learning by examining a sample of portfolios from its 200 graduating students. It takes about 25 minutes to review each portfolio. How many portfolios would you recommend that the faculty examine? Why?

REFERENCE

Angelo, T. A., & Cross, K. P. (1993). *Classroom assessment techniques: A handbook for college teachers.* San Francisco, CA: Jossey-Bass.

RECOMMENDED READING

Astin, A. W. (1991). *Assessment for excellence.* New York, NY: Macmillan.

Campbell, D. T., & Stanley, J. C. (1963). *Experimental and quasi-experimental designs for research.* Chicago, IL: Rand McNally.

Coalition of Essential Schools. (2002, May 14). *Overview of alternative assessment approaches.* Oakland, CA: Author. Retrieved June 2, 2003, from http://www.essentialschools.org/cs/resources/view/ces_res/127

Duvall, B. (1994). Obtaining student cooperation for assessment. In T. H. Bers & M. L. Mittler (Eds.), *New directions for community colleges: No. 88. Assessment testing: Myths and realities* (pp. 47–52). San Francisco, CA: Jossey-Bass.

Ehrmann, S. C. (2003, March 19). *Increasing student response rates by making the study more valuable: A dozen principles of good practice.* Takoma Park, MD: The TLT Group, The Flashlight Program. Retrieved June 2, 2003, from http://www.tltgroup.org/resources/Flashlight/Participation.html

Jones, D. P. (2002, April). *Different perspectives on information about educational quality: Implications for the role of accreditation* (CHEA Occasional Paper). Washington, DC: Council for Higher Education Accreditation.

Jones, E., & Voorhees, R., with Paulson, K. (2002). *Defining and assessing learning: Exploring competency-based initiatives.* Washington, DC: National Center for Education Statistics. Retrieved June 2, 2003, from http://nces.ed.gov/pubs2002/2002159.pdf

Krejcie, R., & Morgan, D. (1970). Determining sample size for research activities. *Educational and Psychological Measurement, 30,* 607–610.

Pascarella, E. T. (2001). Identifying excellence in undergraduate education: Are we even close? *Change, 33*(3), 19–23.

Prus, J., & Johnson, R. (1994). A critical review of student assessment options. In T. H. Bers & M. L. Mittler (Eds.), *New directions for community colleges: No. 88. Assessment and testing: Myths and realities* (pp. 69–83). San Francisco, CA: Jossey-Bass.

Scheaffer, R. L., Mendenhall, W., & Ott, L. (1990). *Elementary survey sampling* (4th ed.). Boston, MA: PWS-Kent.

Stufflebeam, D. L. (2000). The CIPP model for evaluation. In D. L. Stufflebeam, G. F. Madaus, & T. Kellaghan (Eds.), *Evaluation models: Viewpoints on educational and human services evaluation* (2nd ed., Chapter 16, Evaluation in Education and Human Services, Vol. 49). Boston, MA: Kluwer.

Taylor, B. E., & Massy, W. F. (1996). *Strategic indicators for higher education*. Princeton, NJ: Peterson's.

Volkwein, J. F. (1999). *Managing a program of outcomes assessment.* Preforum workshop at the Association for Institutional Research Annual Forum, Seattle, WA.

Wiggins, G. (1990). The case for authentic assessment. *Practical Assessment, Research & Evaluation, 2*(2). Retrieved February 15, 2004, from http://www.pareonline.net/getvn.asp?v=2&n=2

PART III
The Assessment Toolbox

7

Using a Scoring Guide to Plan and Evaluate an Assignment

E ducators are increasingly recognizing the value of performance assessments: papers, projects, field experiences, performances, and other assignments that ask students to perform or demonstrate their skills. This chapter and Chapter 8 explain how to plan, create, and evaluate these kinds of assignments.

It may strike you as curious that this chapter, on creating a rubric or scoring guide for an assignment, comes before the chapter on creating the assignment itself. Shouldn't we first create the assignment and then the scoring guide? But think of planning a road trip: When we use a map to plot a route, we first locate our destination and then chart the most appropriate route to get there. Similarly, assignments are more effective if we first clarify what we want students to learn from the assignment and then design an assignment that will help them achieve those ends. Creating assignments thus begins not by writing the assignment itself but by writing the criteria or standards that will be used to evaluate it.

If this process differs from your experience and therefore seems daunting ("How can I possible create grading criteria when I don't know what I'm asking students to do?"), use an iterative process to create assignments. First, list the most important things you want students to learn by completing the assignment. Then draft the assignment itself (Chapter 8). Next, use the drafted assignment to refine your learning goals into more complete scoring criteria. Once the scoring criteria are spelled out, revise your assignment so it will elicit the work described in the criteria.

What Is a Rubric?

A rubric is a scoring guide: a simple list, chart, or guide that describes the criteria that you and perhaps your colleagues will use to score or grade an assignment. At a minimum, a rubric lists the *things you're looking for* when you evaluate a student assignment. The list is often accompanied by *guidelines for evaluating each of those things*.

Some faculty are put off by the "jargony" nature of the word "rubric." If you find this to be the case, simply substitute in your discussions a term such as "scoring guide" or "grading criteria."

Why Use Rubrics?

If you have never used a rubric to grade student assignments, you will find that using them makes your life easier and improves your students' learning in several ways.

Rubrics help students understand your expectations. If you distribute your rubric with the initial assignment, students will understand exactly what you want them to do and where they should focus their energies. You'll have fewer questions from students about what they are to do, and your students may find the assignment a richer, more rewarding experience.

Rubrics can inspire better student performance. Rubrics show students exactly what you value and what you'll be looking for when you evaluate their assignments. Knowing what you expect will motivate some (not all!) to aim for the target you've identified.

Rubrics make scoring easier and faster. While it may seem that using a scoring guide adds an extra burden to the grading process, faculty overwhelmingly report that rubrics actually make the grading process faster because rubrics give them a clear reminder of what they're looking for and they don't need to write as many comments on papers.

Rubrics make scoring more accurate, unbiased, and consistent. Rubrics ensure that every paper is evaluated using the same criteria. The consistency of rubrics can help track changes in student performance as you refine your teaching. Rubrics can help you determine, for example, whether introducing collaborative learning activities into your classes has helped improve students' analysis skills.

Rubrics improve communication with your students and help them understand their strengths and weaknesses. Marked rubrics give students a clear picture of exactly what they did well and what deficiencies they should address in future assignments. Rubrics give students a more complete picture of their performance than a few comments scrawled on their papers. They also give you feedback: If a number of students are not demonstrating understanding of a particular concept or skill, rubrics bring this to your attention.

Rubrics reduce arguments with your students. By making your scoring criteria explicit, rubrics stop student arguments ("Why did he get a B- when I got a C+?") cold. You can focus your conversations with students on how they can improve their performance rather than defending your grading practices.

WHAT DO RUBRICS LOOK LIKE?

Rubrics can be classified into four formats: checklists, rating scales, descriptive rubrics, and holistic rating scales, each of which has advantages and disadvantages.

Checklists

A checklist rubric is a simple list indicating the presence of the "things you're looking for." Figure 7.1 is an example of a checklist rubric.

Figure 7.1

A Checklist Rubric for a Web Site

❑ The purpose of the site is obvious.
❑ The site's structure is clear and intuitive.
❑ Titles are meaningful.
❑ Each page loads quickly.
❑ The text is easy to read.
❑ Graphics and multimedia help convey the site's main points.
❑ The design is clean, uncluttered, and engaging.
❑ Spelling, punctuation, and grammar are correct.
❑ Contact information for the author or webmaster is given.
❑ The date each page was last updated is given.

Checklist rubrics are used most often in primary grades (Did you write your name on your paper? Did you print neatly?). In higher education our expectations are more sophisticated (Did you summarize very well or merely adequately?) so checklist rubrics are used less often. Faculty might use them when they observe student performance in laboratory or studio settings (Did the student wear goggles? follow safe practices? clean up at the end of the lab?). Students might use them to self-assess their work before they turn it in (Did I revise this paper at least once? Have I proofread it? Does my bibliography use proper formatting conventions? Did I include at least eight references?).

Rating Scales

A rating scale rubric is a checklist with a rating scale added to show the degree to which the "things you're looking for" are present. Figures 7.2 and 7.3 are examples of rating scale rubrics.

The major shortcoming of the rating scale rubric format is that performance levels are usually vaguely described. In the rubric in Figure 7.3, the difference between "outstanding" and "very good" articulation of information and ideas isn't clear. The vague nature of rating scale rubrics can lead to several problems:

Faculty may be inconsistent in how they rate performance. One faculty member might rate a paper's organization "good" while another faculty member might rate the same paper's organization "adequate." Minimizing such inconsistencies is discussed later in this chapter.

Students don't receive thorough feedback. Yes, students can learn from a completed rubric that their paper's organization was relatively weak and their grammar was relatively strong, but from the scored rubric alone they won't know exactly how their organization was weak or how it might be improved.

Rating scale rubrics can lack credibility with some audiences. An accrediting body might, for example, look skeptically on faculty rating 85% of their students' essays "excellent" and the rest "very good," although external raters, such as faculty from another institution or prospective employers, would make the ratings more credible.

Rating scale rubrics are quick and easy to create and use, however, so they do have a place in many assessment programs, especially for relatively minor assignments.

Figure 7.2

A Rating Scale Rubric for an Oral Presentation

The presenter. . .	Strongly Agree	Agree	Diagree	Strongly Disagree
Clearly stated the purpose of the presentation.	❑	❑	❑	❑
Was well organized.	❑	❑	❑	❑
Was knowledgeable about the subject.	❑	❑	❑	❑
Answered questions authoritatively.	❑	❑	❑	❑
Spoke clearly and loudly.	❑	❑	❑	❑
Maintained eye contact with the audience.	❑	❑	❑	❑
Appeared confident.	❑	❑	❑	❑
Adhered to time constraints.	❑	❑	❑	❑
Had main points that were appropriate to the central topic.	❑	❑	❑	❑
Accomplished the stated objectives.	❑	❑	❑	❑

Adapted with permission from Drs. Sharon B. Buchbinder and Donna M. Cox from a rubric used by faculty in the Health Care Management Program, Towson University.

Descriptive Rubrics

Descriptive rubrics replace the checkboxes of rating scale rubrics with brief descriptions of the performance that merits each possible rating. Figures 7.4 and 7.8 are examples of descriptive rubrics. Other examples are in Huba and Freed's (2000) *Learner-Centered Assessment on College Campuses* and in Appendix C of Walvoord and Anderson's (1998) *Effective Grading.*

Descriptive rubrics are increasingly popular because their descriptions of each performance level make faculty expectations explicit and student performance convincingly documented. Students, faculty, accreditors, and other audiences all clearly understand exactly what is meant by an "outstanding" or "inadequate" rating. Descriptive rubrics are therefore a good choice when:

Figure 7.3

A Rating Scale Rubric for an Information Literacy Assignment

Please indicate the student's skill in each of the following respects, as evidenced by this assignment, by checking the appropriate box. If this assignment is not intended to elicit a particular skill, please check the "N/A" box.

	Outstanding (A)	Very Good (B)	Adequate (C)	Marginally Adequate (D)	Inadequate (F)	N/A
1) Identify, locate, and access sources of information.	❏	❏	❏	❏	❏	❏
2) Critically evaluate information, including its legitimacy, validity, and appropriateness.	❏	❏	❏	❏	❏	❏
3) Organize information to present a sound central idea supported by relevant material in a logical order.	❏	❏	❏	❏	❏	❏
4) Use information to answer questions and/or solve problems.	❏	❏	❏	❏	❏	❏
5) Clearly articulate information and ideas.	❏	❏	❏	❏	❏	❏
6) Use information technologies to communicate, manage, and process information.	❏	❏	❏	❏	❏	❏
7) Use information technologies to solve problems.	❏	❏	❏	❏	❏	❏
8) Use the work of others accurately and ethically.	❏	❏	❏	❏	❏	❏
9) What grade are you awarding this assignment?	❏	❏	❏	❏	❏	
10) If you had to assign a final course grade for this student today, what would it be?	❏	❏	❏	❏	❏	

- *You are undertaking important assessments* whose results may contribute to major decisions, such as accreditation, funding, or program continuance.

- *Several faculty are collectively assessing student work,* because these rubrics' clear descriptions make scoring more consistent across faculty.

- *It's important to give students detailed feedback* on exactly why their work wasn't scored more highly.

- *Outside audiences will be examining the rubric scores* with a critical eye.

The main disadvantage of descriptive rubrics is that coming up with succinct but explicit descriptions of every performance level for every "thing you're looking for" can be time-consuming and require tryouts and revisions. Thus, while descriptive rubrics might be considered the gold standard of rubrics, don't feel that you need to develop them for every assignment.

Holistic Scoring Guides

Sometimes it's not possible to come up with a list of "things you're looking for" that can be applied against all the assignments that are being assessed. If students are writing poems, creating sculptures, or completing capstone independent study projects, the works they submit may vary so much that scoring criteria may vary substantially from one project to the next.

Then sometimes assessment projects are so massive that we don't have time to complete a rubric for every assignment. Perhaps 1,500 entering students' essays must be read and scored to decide who should enroll in a developmental writing course. Perhaps 150 senior portfolios must be reviewed to get an overall sense of the writing skills of our graduates. The major purpose of such assessments is not to give feedback to individual students but to make decisions within a fairly tight timeframe.

In these situations, a holistic scoring guide may be a good choice. Holistic scoring guides do not have a list of the "things you're looking for." Instead, they have short narrative descriptions of the characteristics of outstanding work, acceptable work, unacceptable work, and so

Figure 7.4

A Descriptive Rubric for a Slide Presentation on Findings From Research Sources

	Well Done (5)	Satisfactory (4–3)	Needs Improvement (2–1)	Incomplete (0)
Organization	Clearly, concisely written. Logical, intuitive progression of ideas and supporting information. Clear and direct cues to all information.	Logical progression of ideas and supporting information. Most cues to information are clear and direct.	Vague in conveying viewpoint and purpose. Some logical progression of ideas and supporting information, but cues are confusing or flawed.	Lacks a clear point of view and logical sequence of information. Cues to information are not evident.
Persuasiveness	Motivating questions and advance organizers convey main idea. Information is accurate.	Includes persuasive information.	Includes persuasive information with few facts.	Information is incomplete, out of date, and/or incorrect.
Introduction	Presents overall topic. Draws in audience with compelling questions or by relating to audience's interests or goals.	Clear, coherent, and related to topic.	Some structure but does not create a sense of what follows. May be overly detailed or incomplete. Somewhat appealing.	Does not orient audience to what will follow.

	Well Done (5)	Satisfactory (4–3)	Needs Improvement (2–1)	Incomplete (0)
Clarity	Readable, well-sized fonts. Italics, boldface, and indentations enhance readability. Text is appropriate length. Background and colors enhance readability.	Sometimes fonts are readable, but in a few places fonts, italics, boldface, long paragraphs, color, or background detract.	Overall readability is difficult with lengthy paragraphs, too many fonts, dark or busy background, overuse of boldface, or lack of appropriate indentations.	Text is very difficult to read. Long blocks of text, small fonts, inappropriate colors, or poor use of headings, indentations, or boldface.
Layout	Aesthetically pleasing. Contributes to message with appropriate use of headings and white space.	Uses white space appropriately.	Shows some structure but is cluttered, busy, or distracting.	Cluttered and confusing. Spacing and headings do not enhance readability.

Adapted with permission from a rubric developed by Patricia Ryan, lecturer in the Department of Reading, Special Education, and Instructional Technology at Towson University.

on. Figure 7.5 is an example of a holistic scoring guide; Figure 8.4 in Chapter 8 includes another example.

The major shortcomings of holistic scoring guides are the difficulty achieving consistent scores across raters (discussed later in this chapter) and feedback that is not quite as explicit as in descriptive rubrics.

Figure 7.5

A Holistic Scoring Guide for Students in a Ballet Program

A: Active learner – Enthusiastic – Very energetic – Fully engaged in every class – Able to accept corrections – Able to make and synthesize corrections – Able to maintain corrections – Able to self-assess – Shows continuous improvement in major problem areas – Connects movement sequences well – Demonstrates strong dynamic phrasing – Very musical – Continuously demonstrates correct épaulment – Demonstrates advanced understanding and applies correct alignment, fully extended classical line, full use of rotation, and use of classical terminology – Daily demonstrates commitment to the art form and addresses areas of weaknesses without instructor input

B: Active learner – Enthusiastic – Energetic – Engaged in every class – Able to accept most corrections – Able to make and synthesize most corrections – Able to maintain most corrections – Able to self-assess – Shows improvement in major problem areas – Connects movement sequences relatively well – Demonstrates adequate dynamic phrasing – Generally musical – Generally demonstrates correct épaulment – Demonstrates understanding and generally applies correct alignment, classical line, and use of classical terminology – Continues to address areas of weakness and shows general improvement

C: Active learner but not fully physically/mentally engaged in class – Able to accept most corrections – Not quite able to make and synthesize corrections – Not yet able to maintain corrections – Unable to fully self-assess – Shows some improvement in major problem areas – Connects some movement sequences – Demonstrates limited dynamic phrasing – Almost musical – Working toward correct épaulment – Working on understanding and applying correct alignment, continuing to find classical line, unable to fully execute artistry and use classical terminology – Continues to address areas of weakness but unable to demonstrate consistent visible improvement

D: Not an active learner/lacks sufficient energy – Not physically or mentally engaged in class – Unable to accept/understand most corrections – Unable to make and synthesize corrections – Unable to maintain corrections – Unable to self-assess – Shows very little improvement in major problem areas – Seldom connects movement sequences well – Demonstrates marginal dynamic phrasing – Seldom musical – Unable to demonstrate correct épaulment – Unable to apply correct alignment, demonstrate classical line, execute artistry or use classical terminology – Seldom addresses areas of weakness – Unable to demonstrate visible improvement in most areas of weakness – Lacks self-motivation

Adapted with permission from a holistic scoring guide used by the faculty of the Department of Dance at Towson University.

WHAT ARE THE STEPS TO CREATING EFFECTIVE RUBRICS?

Rubrics are not difficult to create, although descriptive rubrics can be time-consuming; just follow these steps.

Look for Models

Rubrics are increasingly widespread assessment tools, so it makes sense to begin creating a rubric by looking for models that you can adapt to your circumstances. (If you use or adapt someone else's rubric, ask for permission and acknowledge the work of the original author.)

Start with a simple web search; many institutions, programs, and faculty post their rubrics there. If you subscribe to a discussion list on teaching in your discipline, post a query asking for examples of rubrics. Rubrics are far more common in basic (K–12) education than in higher education, so if you search for rubrics for, say, science laboratory reports, you may find more examples from high school than college. Don't despair; high school rubrics can still give you good ideas.

A number of web sites offer free templates and other simple software for creating and storing rubrics; use keywords like "rubric generator," "rubric builder," or "create rubrics" to find them.

List the "Things You Are Looking For"

Creating a rubric starts by listing the "things you're looking for"—the things you want students to demonstrate in the final product. Ask:

- Why are we giving students this assignment? What are its key learning goals? What do we want students to learn by completing it?

- What defines the skills we want students to demonstrate? What are the characteristics of good writing, a good presentation, a good lab report, good student teaching, and so forth?

- What specific characteristics of the finished project do we want to see?

Consider also the key characteristics of student assignments identified by Relearning by Design (2000):

- **Impact:** Does the assignment accomplish its purpose? Is the problem solved? Is the argument persuasive?

- **Quality:** Is the assignment of high quality? Are its components sound, clear, and well organized?

- **Methods:** Does the student follow correct procedures and use appropriate tools? Does the assignment show expected behaviors, such as evidence of careful research or collaboration?

- **Content validity:** Is the assignment accurate? Are arguments defensible?

- **Mastery:** Does the assignment demonstrate complex, mature understanding of the subject? Is the work insightful? fluent?

You may initially have a long list of things you're looking for! If so, the list probably needs to be pruned. A long rubric makes assignments more time-consuming to score and makes it harder for your students to understand the key skills that they are to focus on as they complete the assignment. Effective rubrics can have as few as three characteristics and often have no more than eight. Lengthy rubrics are more appropriate when the assignment is a holistic, culminating experience such as a senior thesis or field experience in which students are expected to demonstrate a broad range of learning goals.

So review your list and reduce it to only the most significant tasks, skills, or abilities that you'd like your students to demonstrate. Discard anything that isn't a high-priority goal or that isn't observable in this particular assignment. (Enthusiasm for science might not be observable in a lab report, for example.) Perhaps you can combine a group of similar skills into one category.

Now edit your list so that each characteristic is written using explicit, concrete terms, preferably action verbs or clear adjectives. "Writing quality" tells students and colleagues little about what you're looking for; "organization and structure" tells them far more. Be on the lookout for terms like "adequate organization," "appropriate vocabulary," or "acceptable grammar" that don't tell your students or colleagues what kind of organization, vocabulary, or grammar you consider acceptable.

Leave Room for the "Ineffables" and the Unexpected

Some faculty have found that students who are given rubrics along with an assignment do exactly what the rubric tells them that they need to do but no more, yielding solid but somewhat flat and uninspired products. To encourage originality, creativity, effort, and that unexpected but delightful "something extra," simply build these qualities into your rubric. You might tell students, for example, that ten percent of their assignment score will be based on things like effort, originality, or insight.

Create the Rating Scale

If you are creating any rubric other than a checklist, once you have listed the "things you're looking for," your next step is defining the performance levels that make up the rating scale. While there is no hard and fast rule for an optimal number of performance levels, there should be at least three, for exemplary, adequate, and inadequate performance. (The exemplary category is needed to motivate students to do better than merely adequate work.) Usually no more than five levels are needed; if faced with too many levels, faculty may have a hard time distinguishing consistently between, say, six and seven on a ten-point scale.

There's also no hard and fast rule on how to label each performance level. Use descriptors that are clear and relevant to you, your colleagues, and your students. Labels that work well for one assignment or discipline may not work for another. Examples of possible performance levels are:

- Exceeds standard, meets standard, approaching standard, below standard
- Complete evidence, partial evidence, minimal evidence, no evidence
- Excellent, very good, adequate, needs attention
- Letter grades (A, B, C, D, F)

Whatever labels you choose, make sure that you, your colleagues, and your students all have a clear, common understanding of which category represents minimally acceptable performance. If you use letter grades, for example, does C or D represent minimally acceptable performance?

If you are creating a descriptive rubric, once the performance levels are defined, your next step is to create brief descriptors for each trait at each performance level. If you are creating a holistic scoring guide, once the performance levels are defined, your next step is to create a written description for each performance level. What exactly do you want to see, for example, in an exemplary assignment? in an adequate assignment? What kind of work merits a failing grade?

Test the Rubric

Your final step is to try out the rubric by using it to score some actual samples of student work. Score some of your students' best and worst work. Are your standards appropriate, unrealistically high, or insufficiently challenging? Revise your rubric if necessary to improve its clarity and value.

HOW CAN RUBRICS BE USED AS TEACHING TOOLS?

Consider having students help you develop a rubric by discussing the characteristics of an effective assignment, drafting a rubric, and/or commenting on your draft rubric. Involving students in rubric design can get them thinking more actively about what they should learn from an assignment, where they should focus their efforts as they work on the assignment, and the performance level to which they should strive.

As noted earlier in this chapter, students often perform better if they know what they're aiming for, so give students copies of your rubric when you first distribute the assignment.

Finally, encourage your students to use the rubric to self-evaluate their work before turning it in, to make sure the assignment is complete and up to acceptable standards.

How Can Rubrics Be Used to Assess Program Learning Goals?

While rubrics are used most often to evaluate coursework—papers, projects, performances, and the like—they can also be used to assess program learning goals by looking at evidence of student learning from a number of sources.

Embedded course assignments. As discussed in Chapter 6, program assessments that are embedded into course assignments can be scored using a rubric and provide useful information not only on what students have learned in a particular course but also on how well they have achieved key program goals.

Capstone experiences. Many faculty encourage or require students approaching the end of their program to complete some kind of holistic project that helps them tie together the program's various elements. Theses, dissertations, oral defenses, exhibitions, performances, presentations, and research projects are examples of these kinds of capstone experiences. They can all be scored using a rubric and provide important evidence of the overall effectiveness of a program in achieving its major learning goals.

Field experiences. Many programs require students to participate in an internship, practicum, student teaching assignment, or some other kind of field experience. If these experiences give students opportunities to practice applying their knowledge and skills to real-life situations, their supervisors' ratings of their performance can be powerful evidence of the overall success of a program in achieving its major learning goals. Rubrics make it easy for supervisors to provide this information. Figure 7.6 is an example of such a rubric.

Employer feedback. Feedback from the employers of a program's alumni can be another important source of information on how well the program is achieving its major learning goals. Don't ask about the performance of an individual employee, as liability issues will discourage employers from providing such information. Ask instead about employers' overall perceptions of the program and its graduates.

Figure 7.6

A Rating Scale Rubric for Health Education Field Experience Supervisors

Please evaluate the student under your supervision using the following scale.

5 = Superior for an entry level health educator
4 = Slightly better than an entry level health educator
3 = Acceptable for an entry level health educator
2 = Slightly less than an entry level health educator
1 = Seriously deficient
N/O = Not sufficient observation for evaluation

	5	4	3	2	1	N/O
1) Accesses, uses, evaluates current, reliable health knowledge	❑	❑	❑	❑	❑	❑
2) Demonstrates word processing skills	❑	❑	❑	❑	❑	❑
3) Reads, interprets, and uses research information	❑	❑	❑	❑	❑	❑
4) Demonstrates problem-solving skills	❑	❑	❑	❑	❑	❑
5) Develops appropriate educational materials	❑	❑	❑	❑	❑	❑
6) Uses audiovisual equipment skillfully and appropriately	❑	❑	❑	❑	❑	❑
7) Demonstrates teaching skills	❑	❑	❑	❑	❑	❑
8) Demonstrates promotional/publicity skills	❑	❑	❑	❑	❑	❑
9) Uses knowledge of learning styles in development of presentations	❑	❑	❑	❑	❑	❑
10) Is sensitive to individual differences	❑	❑	❑	❑	❑	❑
11) Knows how and where to refer clients/ students for further help and information within organizational guidelines	❑	❑	❑	❑	❑	❑
12) Develops a professional network	❑	❑	❑	❑	❑	❑
13) Shows positive work attitude and ethic	❑	❑	❑	❑	❑	❑
14) Demonstrates willingness to work beyond minimum expectations	❑	❑	❑	❑	❑	❑

	5	4	3	2	1	N/O
15) Displays professional appearance appropriate to the organization	❑	❑	❑	❑	❑	❑

Adapted with permission from a rubric used by faculty in the Department of Health Science at Towson University.

Student self-assessments. While student ratings of their knowledge, skills, and attitudes aren't direct evidence of student learning, they can still provide useful indirect evidence. Self-assessments also help students develop metacognitive skills (see Chapters 5 and 9) and achieve deeper learning. Chapter 9 discusses student self-assessment, and Figure 9.2 in that chapter is an example of a rubric for self-evaluation.

Peer evaluations. Some faculty ask students to review and evaluate other students' work such as a presentation or a draft of a paper. If your learning goals include the development of interpersonal skills such as leadership or collaboration, you may wish to ask students to use rubrics to rate their peers in terms of these traits. Peer evaluations of contributions to collaborative learning activities can motivate students to participate fully and effectively in them, especially if the evaluations count in some way toward final grades. Figure 7.7 is an example of a peer evaluation rubric.

A major shortcoming of peer evaluations is that they can be highly inaccurate because they're transparent (it's obvious which ratings are positive), making them subject to rating biases and errors (discussed later in this chapter). Students may, for example, downrate a fellow student with good skills simply because they don't like him. Because of the potential for inaccuracies, use peer evaluations cautiously:

- Ask students to rate specific behaviors rather than the overall performance of their peers. Asking students, "Did this student complete his or her share of the group's work on time?" will yield more accurate information than, "Was this student an effective group member?"

- Use peer ratings in conjunction with other more direct evidence of the skills being evaluated.

Figure 7.7

A Rubric for Evaluating Fellow Group Members

Your name:
Name of the group member you're evaluating:

This group member . . .	Almost Always	Often	Sometimes	Rarely
1) Did his or her fair share of the work.	❑	❑	❑	❑
2) Participated actively in the group's activities.	❑	❑	❑	❑
3) Contributed useful ideas, suggestions, and comments.	❑	❑	❑	❑
4) Listened carefully.	❑	❑	❑	❑
5) Was considerate of others and appreciated their ideas.	❑	❑	❑	❑
6) Asked others to clarify their ideas, if necessary.	❑	❑	❑	❑
7) Expressed disagreements respectfully.	❑	❑	❑	❑
8) Did not dominate the conversation or interrupt others.	❑	❑	❑	❑
9) Tried to help the group reach consensus.	❑	❑	❑	❑
10) Helped the group stay on the topic.	❑	❑	❑	❑
11) Helped the group not waste time.	❑	❑	❑	❑
12) Helped me learn more than if I had worked alone.	❑	❑	❑	❑

- If you are counting peer ratings toward course grades, weight them minimally (perhaps no more than 5%).

Portfolios. Rubrics can be very helpful in evaluating portfolios of student work. Chapter 10 discusses portfolios and includes examples of rubrics for evaluating them.

WHAT ARE SCORING ERRORS AND BIASES? HOW CAN THEY BE AVOIDED?

No matter how carefully a rubric is constructed, rubric scores remain essentially subjective (see Chapter 6) and thus prone to unintentional scoring errors and biases. Rating scale rubrics and holistic scoring guides are especially prone to scoring errors and biases, which can include the following.

- *Leniency errors* occur when faculty judge student work better than most of their colleagues would judge it.

- *Generosity errors* occur when faculty tend to use only the high end of the rating scale.

- *Severity errors* occur when faculty tend to use only the low end of the rating scale.

- *Central tendency errors* occur when faculty tend to avoid both extremes of the rating scale.

- *Halo effect bias* occurs when faculty let their general impression of a student influence their scores, perhaps giving higher scores to a pleasant student or lower scores to a student whose attire they find offensive.

- *Contamination effect bias* occurs when faculty let irrelevant student characteristics (such as handwriting or ethnic background) influence their scores.

- *Similar-to-me effect bias* occurs when faculty give higher scores to those students whom they see as similar to themselves, such as students who share their research interests.

- *First-impression effect bias* occurs when faculty's early opinions distort their overall judgment. A student who presents her outstanding research in a sloppy poster display might suffer from first-impression effect bias, as might a student whose generally excellent essay opens with a poorly constructed sentence.

- *Contrast effect bias* occurs when faculty compare a student against other students instead of established standards. Faculty might, for example, give an "unacceptable" rating to the worst paper they read, even though the paper meets the minimally acceptable standards stated on the rubric.

- **Rater drift** occurs when faculty unintentionally redefine scoring criteria over time. Some faculty, as they tire from scoring student work, get grumpy and more stringent, while others skim student work more quickly and score more leniently.

To minimize these errors and biases and achieve greater scoring consistency:

- Remove or obscure identifying information from student work before it is scored. (This is called blind scoring.)

- If faculty are scoring student work together, practice scoring consistently. First discuss and come to agreement on the meaning of each performance level. Then score a few samples of student work, share your scores, and discuss and resolve any differences in your ratings. Once you're reasonably sure that you're all interpreting the rubric consistently, you can begin the actual scoring.

- Have each sample of student work scored independently by at least two faculty members. If those two faculty members disagree on any sample of student work, have that work scored by a third faculty member to break the tie.

- If faculty are scoring many samples of student work, rescore the first few samples after they finish to guard against rater drift.

- If faculty are scoring large numbers of papers, periodically schedule a refresher scoring practice session, in which they again all compare their scores and discuss and resolve differences.

These strategies are easier said than done, of course! Following all these steps can be time-consuming and expensive. (Faculty may expect extra compensation for spending hours or days scoring student work beyond that in the courses they teach.) To decide if these steps are worthwhile, consider the following questions:

Do we indeed have a problem with scoring errors and bias? Look at the scores faculty are awarding. Are they reasonably consistent across faculty, or are some faculty clearly more lenient or more stringent than the majority? If there is reason for concern, do a spot check:

Ask a faculty member or two to rescore—blind—a few student work samples.

What are the consequences of scoring errors or bias? If the scores are simply part of a variety of information used to inform faculty about teaching/learning successes and concerns, it may not be worthwhile to invest time and resources in rigorously eliminating scoring errors and bias. If, on the other hand, the scores are used to help make major decisions, such as whether students graduate or whether a program continues to be funded, ensuring accurate, consistent scoring becomes extremely important.

Are these scores of sufficient quality that we can use them with confidence for their intended purpose? As discussed in Chapter 2, if you don't feel you can use the results with confidence, you need to increase your investment in scoring accuracy and consistency.

How Can the Scoring Burden Be Kept Manageable?

One of the reasons that traditional multiple-choice tests continue to be popular is that busy faculty members can score them very quickly. Finding time to evaluate performance assessments can be a challenge, especially for faculty teaching courses with high enrollments. Chapters 2 and 3 offer many suggestions for minimizing the burden of assessment. Here are some more.

Don't waste your time scoring assignments with obviously inadequate effort. Establish what Walvoord and Anderson (1998) call gateway criteria and give them to students, in writing, with the assignment. Then return or fail assignments that don't meet those minimum standards.

Try Haswell's (1983) minimal marking strategy: Instead of correcting student writing errors, simply put a check in the margin on the line of the error and have the student figure out what's wrong on that line and what the correction should be.

Investigate software designed to score essays. While much available scoring software focuses on mechanics and less on organization and content, the latest software is based on artificial intelligence and is a promising means of scoring writing samples. If you are interested in exploring this approach, do literature and web searches for "computerized scoring" and "automated scoring."

SHOULD COMPLETED RUBRICS BE SUMMARIZED INTO AN OVERALL SCORE OR GRADE?

Whether and how completed rubrics are aggregated into an overall score or grade depends on the rubrics' purpose. If a rubric is used to assess a course assignment, completed rubrics probably should be aggregated into a single score or grade, both to give students feedback on their overall performance on the assignment and to help faculty determine course grades.

Sometimes, however, a rubric is used to assess a program's major learning goals and not for grading purposes. A department assessment committee might, for example, review senior theses after they have been graded, solely to learn about seniors' writing skills. In this situation, there may be no need to summarize the rubric's ratings of various attributes into an overall score; it may be sufficient to determine that, say, 84% of graduating students organize a paper effectively, 92% make compelling arguments supported with suitable information, and 78% use appropriate grammar and mechanics. But some assessment audiences may legitimately want to know simply, "Can students write effectively by the time they graduate?" and aggregating rubric ratings into a single score may be an appropriate response.

The most common approach for aggregating rubric ratings is shown in Figure 7.8, a rubric completed (in bold text) for Melissa, a hypothetical student. Each skill or attribute is assigned a certain number of possible points. Students scoring at the highest possible level earn the maximum number of points; students scoring at lower performance levels earn fewer points. Melissa earned 7 points for her introduction, 18 points for content, 20 points for organization, 18 points for conclusion/original thought, 7 points for writing style, 3 points for writing use/mechanics (obviously not her strong suit!), and 7 points for APA rules, for a total score of 80 points out of 100.

The "things you're looking for" in any rubric are rarely equally important, so if you use this model to aggregate rubric ratings, weight each skill or trait according to its importance. In Figure 7.8, organization is worth a maximum of 20 points while writing use/mechanics is worth ten points.

If you are aggregating rubric ratings in order to assign grades, make sure that the points you assign sum to totals that are appropriate for the performance levels they represent. In Figure 7.8, someone scoring "barely adequate" on every criterion would earn a total score of 70, widely regarded as a C-, an appropriate grade for barely adequate work. Someone scoring "good" on every criterion would earn a total score of 83, widely regarded as a B, an appropriate grade for good work.

Another model for summarizing rubric scores is that *students must show minimally adequate performance on **every** attribute in order to "pass"* or be considered minimally adequate overall. In Figure 7.8, a paper would have to score "barely adequate" or better in *every* category in order to be considered at least "barely adequate" overall. Under this model, Melissa's overall performance on this paper is Inadequate (failing), because her Writing Use/Mechanics score is Inadequate.

In yet another model, *students must show minimally adequate performance on just **certain** attributes in order to "pass"* or be considered minimally adequate overall. If the student passes this initial hurdle, the model in Figure 7.8 can be used to determine her overall score. Suppose that, in Figure 7.8, the faculty agree that Content is the most important criterion of the assignment, and students must score at least "barely adequate" in this category in order to pass the assignment. Melissa scored "good" on Content, so she would earn her overall score of 80 as described above. Suppose that Kelly, however, scored "inadequate" on Content and "exemplary" in every other category. Even though her total score would be 92, her paper would be considered "inadequate" (failing) overall.

Whichever model you choose, make sure your students understand how you plan to score their work and, if their work is to be graded, how you plan to arrive at a grade.

Figure 7.8

A Scored Rubric for Research Reports in Speech-Language Pathology/Audiology

	Exemplary	Good	Barely Adequate	Inadequate
Introduction (10 points)	The introduction smoothly pulls the reader into the topic, is organized, presents the main argument clearly, and states the author's views. (10)	The introduction is organized but does not adequately present the main argument or does not state the author's views. (8)	**The introduction presents the main argument and the author's views but is disorganized and does not flow smoothly. (7)**	The introduction is disorganized and difficult to follow. The main argument and the author's views are not introduced. (5)
Content (20 points)	Information is presented clearly, completely, and accurately across all sections. At least three major sections; at least one major section has two to three subsections. (20)	**Information is unclear and difficult to understand in one section. (18)**	Information is unclear and difficult to understand in two to three sections. (16)	The paper is unclear and difficult to understand across four or more sections. (12)
Organization (20 points)	**Organization is clear; good framework. Headers, preview paragraphs, topic sentences, and transitions aid in understanding main points. Information is presented logically. (20)**	Organization is unclear in one section (unfocused paragraphs, poor topic sentences, poor transitions). All other sections are logically organized. (18)	Organization is unclear in two to three sections OR headers and preview paragraphs or sentences are missing. (16)	Organization is unclear in four or more sections. (12)

	Exemplary	Good	Barely Adequate	Inadequate
Conclusion/ Original Thought (20 points)	Specific ideas for improving research or other ideas are presented in an organized manner with logical rationales. (20)	**Specific ideas are presented but the rationale for one idea may be weak. (18)**	Ideas are presented but in a vague, generic format OR rationales for two or more ideas are weak. (16)	Fewer than three original ideas related to the topic are presented OR all ideas are not well explained. (12)
Writing Style (10 points)	Tone is professional, vocabulary and syntax are mature, and easy to understand terms are used throughout the paper. (10)	**Syntax or vocabulary is complex, awkward, or filled with jargon in one to two sections of the paper OR words are used incorrectly in one to two sections of the paper. (7)**	Syntax or vocabulary is complex, awkward, or filled with jargon in three to four sections of the paper OR words are used incorrectly in three to four sections of the paper. (5)	Writing style makes more than four sections of the paper difficult to read and understand. (3)
Writing Use/ Mechanics (10 points)	The paper is free of spelling, syntax, formatting, punctuation errors. (10)	The paper has fewer than five spelling, punctuation, formatting, syntax errors. (7)	The paper has six to 15 spelling, punctuation, formatting, syntax errors. (5)	**More than 16 errors across the paper make it difficult to follow. (3)**
APA Rules (10 points)	All APA rules are followed for citations, headers, numbers, series, quotes, references, etc. (10)	**Fewer than three violations of APA rules, or one to two missing or incorrect citations and references. (7)**	Four to ten violations of APA rules and/or three to five missing or incorrect citations and references. (5)	Eleven or more violations of APA rules and/or six or more missing or incorrect citations and references. (3)

Adapted with permission from a rubric adapted by Sharon Glennen and Celia Bassich-Zeren in the Department of Communication Sciences and Disorders at Towson University.

Time to Think, Discuss, and Practice

One of Belleville College's general education goals is, "Students will be able to write effectively." The faculty has decided to assess this by asking all graduating students to write a one-page (400–500 words) review and analysis of arguments for and against making community service a college graduation requirement.

1) List the significant writing skills that the Belleville faculty probably want to see demonstrated in the paper.

2) Use your list to draft a rating scale rubric that the faculty might use to assess these papers.

3) The faculty has decided to make this assignment a 100-point requirement in a senior capstone course. Assign 100 points throughout your rubric so that 90–100 points represents what you consider A work, 80–89 points represents what you consider B work, etc.

4) Figure 7.9 is a student submission for this assignment. Use your rubric to score this paper and sum the ratings into a total score. Compare the grade earned against the student's submission. Do you all agree that the grade is appropriate for the performance documented by the rubric?

Figure 7.9

A Student Essay on Making Community Service a Graduation Requirement

Of all the requirements for graduation, community service is not usually one of them. However, some colleges are considering adding this as a prerequisite to receiving a diploma. This idea has caused disputes between some students, who do not wish to volunteer, and faculty, who feel that volunteering should not be required in order to graduate from an institute of higher learning.

One opinion is that as a graduating college student, you should not only be well educated, but also well rounded in general, and community service is one aspect that will help you to become a more well rounded person in general. This is the opinion of the people who advocate for community service. By requiring students to perform so many mandated hours of community service, they feel that the students will become enriched in ways that a classroom cannot provide.

Another opinion of faculty is that students do not have to volunteer in order to get a good education, which is the primary function of a university, and therefore, required community service should not be necessary in order to receive a diploma. Some students share this opinion also. They feel that community service should be a personal opinion based on personal interests and reasons for wishing to volunteer. They believe that if students are forced to volunteer in order to receive the diploma they have worked so hard for, since the community service work is not coming from their hearts, they will not be giving their all, simply going through the motions to satisfy the requirement.

If students are required to provide a certain number of community service hours, this may also detract from their attention to their school work, causing grades to suffer. Some faculty have taken this into consideration. They are not sure if creating mandatory community service hours is worth the possible decline in students' GPA's because they are so concerned with finding places to conduct community service and finding the time to perform their mandated hours.

Another question that is concerning the faculty of universities is whether or not there are enough locations in which students could perform community service. For some colleges that are not located around a large city, the number of places that needs volunteer work may not be sufficient enough to accommodate all the students that are attending the school. If there is not enough open spaces in volunteer organizations outside of the school, should the university be obligated to create situations in which volunteers are needed in the school so that students can perform their needed hours of community service?

All of these questions and concerns need to be adequately addressed before a decision is made at any university or post-secondary school. They should be addressed not only with faculty and staff of the school, but also students, in order to hear their points of view.

REFERENCES

Haswell, R. (1983). Minimal marking. *College English, 45*(6), 600–604.

Huba, M. E., & Freed, J. E. (2000). Using rubrics to provide feedback to students. *Learner-centered assessment on college campuses: Shifting the focus from teaching to learning* (pp. 151–200). Needham Heights, MA: Allyn & Bacon.

Relearning by Design, Inc. (2000). *Rubric sampler.* Ewing, NJ: Author. Retrieved June 2, 2003, from http://www.relearning.org/resources/PDF/rubric_sampler.pdf

Walvoord, B. E., & Anderson, V. J. (1998). *Effective grading: A tool for learning and assessment.* San Francisco, CA: Jossey-Bass.

RECOMMENDED READING

Andrade, H. G. (2000). Using rubrics to promote thinking and learning. *Educational Leadership, 57*(5). Retrieved June 2, 2003, from http://ascd.org/publications/ed_lead/200002/andrade.html

Center for Technology in Learning. (1997–2002). *PALS guide: Rubrics & scoring.* Menlo Park, CA: SRI International. Retrieved June 2, 2003, from http://pals.sri.com/guide/scoringdetail.html

Chicago Board of Education. (2000). *How to create a rubric from scratch: A guide for rugged individualists.* Chicago, IL: Author. Retrieved June 2, 2003, from http://intranet.cps.k12.il.us/Assessments/Ideas_and_Rubrics/Create_Rubric/create_rubric.html

Family Education Network, Inc. (2000–2003). *Creating rubrics: Inspire your students and foster critical thinking.* Boston, MA: Author. Retrieved June 2, 2003, from http://www.teachervision.com/lesson-plans/lesson-4521.html

Haladyna, T. M. (1997). *Writing test items to evaluate higher order thinking.* Boston, MA: Allyn & Bacon.

Mertler, C. A. (2001). Designing scoring rubrics for your classroom. *Practical Assessment, Research & Evaluation, 7*(25). Retrieved February 15, 2004, from http://www.pareonline.net/getvn.asp?v=7&n=25

Moskal, B. M. (2000). Scoring rubrics: What, when and how? *Practical Assessment, Research & Evaluation, 7*(3). Retrieved February 15, 2004, from http://wwwpareonline.net/getvn.asp?v=7&n=3

Moskal, B. M., & Leydens, J. A. (2000). Scoring rubric development: Validity and reliability. *Practical Assessment, Research & Evaluation, 7*(10). Retrieved February 15, 2004, from http://www.pareonline. net/getvn.asp?v=7&n=10

Pickett, N. (1999, March 31). *Guidelines for rubric development.* San Diego, CA: San Diego State University, Department of Educational Technology. Retrieved June 2, 2003, from http://edweb. sdsu.edu/triton/july/rubrics/Rubric_Guidelines.html

Pickett, N., & Dodge, B. (2001, June 20). *Rubrics for web lessons.* San Diego, CA: San Diego State University, Department of Educational Technology. Retrieved June 2, 2003, from http://webquest. sdsu.edu/rubrics/weblessons.htm

Shermis, M. D., & Barrera, F. D. (2002). Automated essay scoring for electronic portfolios. *Assessment Update, 14*(4), 1–2, 10–11.

Taggart, G. L., Phifer, S. J., Nixon, J. A., & Wood, M. (Eds.). (1998). *Rubrics: A handbook for construction and use.* Nevada City, CA: Performance Learning Systems.

8

Creating an Effective Assignment

Effective assignments not only help assess what students have learned but also help students learn what we value. Whether we ask students to write an essay, complete a research project, create a work of art, demonstrate laboratory skills, or give a speech, giving them instructions and guidance that tell them clearly what to do and why will help them both learn and demonstrate what they've learned. This is where prompts—the subject of this chapter—come in.

WHAT IS A PROMPT?

A prompt is simply an assignment: the (usually written) statement or question that tells students exactly what they are to do. A good prompt inspires students to give the assignment their best effort and achieve the assignment's learning goals.

There are two basic kinds of prompts. *Restricted-response* prompts ask everyone to provide pretty much the same response, just in his or her own words. An example would be giving all students the same chart and asking them to write a paragraph summarizing its major points. Many mathematics problems and science laboratory assignments are restricted-response prompts.

Extended-response prompts give students latitude in deciding how to complete the assignment, so completed assignments may vary considerably in organization, style, and content. Suppose, for example, that students are asked to speculate, with appropriate justification, on how our daily lives might be different today if the United States had never engaged in space exploration. The visions and supporting evidence in equally outstanding papers might vary a great deal.

WHY ARE PROMPTS IMPORTANT?

Carefully crafted prompts are critical in the teaching/learning process because, regardless of what we state in syllabi or say in class, the assignments we give students are the most powerful way we communicate our expectations to them. Without a well-written prompt, students may complete an assignment without learning what we want them to learn. Suppose, for example, that history faculty want students to be able to analyze the impact of a noteworthy individual on the outcome of World War II, but they simply ask students to write a term paper on "a person involved with World War II" with no further guidance or direction. Some students might complete the assignment by only summarizing the life history of a particular individual, doing nothing to develop their analysis skills.

Carefully written prompts are also critical to the success of assessment efforts because poorly written or inappropriate prompts may mask evidence of student learning. If student portfolios show little evidence of evaluation skill, for example, this may be not because students are poor at evaluation but because the assignments included in the portfolios never explicitly asked the students to evaluate.

HOW ARE PROMPTS USED?

Prompts are used to communicate virtually everything we ask students to do except to complete objective tests and rating forms. They can be used to convey our expectations for a wide array of student learning experiences.

Course assignments: A world of possibilities. While course assignments often consist of essays, term papers, and research reports, a broader range of assignments can stimulate student creativity, make plagiarism more difficult, and help students with diverse learning styles (see Chapter 2) demonstrate what they've learned. Table 8.1 gives just a few examples of assignments beyond the usual term paper or essay. Most of these assignments are performance assessments (see Chapter 6) that ask students to demonstrate skills—often in realistic settings—rather than simply describe or explain those skills.

Table 8.1

Examples of Assignments Beyond Essays, Term Papers, and Research Reports

- Abstract or executive summary
- Advertisement or commercial
- Annotated bibliography
- Autobiography or realistic fictional diary from a historical period
- Briefing paper
- Brochure or pamphlet
- Campaign speech
- Case study/analysis
- Client report
- Collaborative group activity
- Database
- Debate or discussion (plan, participation, and/or leadership)
- Debriefing interview preparation
- Dramatization of an event or scenario, in writing or as a presentation
- Editing and revision of a poorly written paper
- Evaluation of opposing points of view or the pros and cons of alternative solutions to a problem
- Experiment or other laboratory experience
- Field notes
- Game invention
- Graph, chart, diagram, flowchart, or other visual aid
- Graphic organizer, taxonomy, or classification scheme
- Handbook or instructional manual
- Journal or log (see Chapter 9)
- Letter to an editor or business
- Model, simulation, or illustration
- Narrative
- Newspaper story or news report on a concept or from a historical period
- Oral history recording of an event
- Plan to conduct a project or provide a service

- Plan to research and solve a problem
- Portfolio (see Chapter 10)
- Poster, display, or exhibit
- Presentation, demonstration, or slide show
- Process description
- Proposal for and justification of a solution to a problem
- Reflection on what and how one has learned (see Chapter 12)
- Review and critique of one's own work, that of a peer, a performance, an exhibit, a work of art, a writer's arguments, or how something could have been done better
- Selected portions of an essay or term paper (e.g., only the problem statement and the review of literature)
- Survey, including an analysis of the results
- Teaching a concept to a peer or a child
- Video or audio recording
- Web site

Embedded assessments of program learning goals: The same world. As discussed in Chapter 6, course assignments—in all their variety—can often give us useful information not only on what students have learned in a particular course but also on how well students have achieved important program goals.

Capstone experiences such as senior theses, performances, and research projects help students tie together the various elements of their programs. Such experiences provide richer learning opportunities if students receive carefully written prompts that inspire them to synthesize their learning and experiences meaningfully.

Self-reflections, discussed in Chapter 9, help students develop their metacognitive skills and achieve deeper learning. Table 9.1 in Chapter 9 gives many examples of prompts to stimulate student reflection on what and how they have learned.

Portfolios are an increasingly popular means of assessing student work. Chapter 10 offers suggestions on creating an effective portfolio prompt, and Figure 10.3 in that chapter is an example of a prompt for a portfolio.

Classroom assessment techniques are a special type of prompt designed to give faculty quick feedback on how effectively the teaching/learning process is working in their classes. One example is the Minute Paper, discussed in Chapter 9. Angelo and Cross's (1993) *Classroom Assessment Techniques* provides more information on these very useful assessment tools.

WHAT ARE THE STEPS TO CREATING A GOOD PROMPT?

To create prompts that create deep learning experiences and inspire your students' best work, follow these suggestions.

Identify specific, important learning goals for the assignment. Begin creating a good prompt by deciding what you want your students to learn from the assignment. The assignment should focus students on those skills and conceptual understandings that you consider most important. If you are giving a writing assignment, for example, make sure that it will elicit the kinds of writing skills that you most want students to strengthen. If you want students to learn to present a persuasive argument, make sure the assignment clearly requires convincing justifications. The best way to identify the learning goals you want students to achieve by completing an assignment is to develop a rubric (Chapter 7).

A good assignment asks students to demonstrate not just simple understanding but also thinking skills such as analysis, evaluation, and creativity. Focusing on these kinds of skills makes the assignment more challenging, worthwhile, and interesting and promotes deeper learning.

Create a meaningful task or problem that corresponds to those goals. Once you have clarified the key learning goals of the assignment, identify a task that corresponds to those goals and will help your students achieve them. (A writing assignment would obviously be a poor way to learn presentation skills!) While textbooks and other curricular materials may give you some ideas for tasks, a better approach is to think of a task that might be done by someone "in real life," as such assignments engage students and help them see that they are learning something worthwhile. Try "You are there" scenarios: "You are an expert chemist (statistician, teacher, anthropologist, or whatever) asked to help with the following situation . . ." Such role-playing need not be completely realistic: "You are one of President Andrew Jackson's closest advisors . . ."; "You are a member of the first space team traveling to Mars. . . . "

Make the assignment a worthwhile use of learning time. Consider carefully whether the time students put into your assignment will yield an appropriate payoff in terms of their learning. Will students learn twice as much from an assignment that takes 20 hours of out-of-class time as from one that takes 10 hours? Will students learn significantly more from a 30-page assignment than from a 5-page assignment (which may take you one sixth the time to evaluate)? Sometimes your learning goals may not demand a traditional term paper or research project; your students may achieve your learning goals just as effectively by completing an annotated bibliography or a research proposal.

Aim students at the desired outcome. Give your students clear, written directions and scaffolding upon which they can successfully create their best work. Begin with an introductory sentence that's an overview of what you want them to do and then answer the questions in Table 8.2.

If you like, you can provide additional scaffolding by:

- Underlining key words in the prompt.

- Reminding students of relevant readings or discussions and/or asking them to focus on these things.

- Providing a checklist that students can use to review their work, as suggested in Chapter 7.

- Making available model work from past classes. (If you do this, obtain the permission of the students whose work is being shared and ask if they want their names and any other identifying information removed.)

Good prompts for major assignments such as portfolios or term projects can run a page or more. Brevity is important, however, when you are asking for very short responses, such as the Minute Papers described in Chapter 9, or when you are giving timed in-class assignments such as an essay exam. In these situations, every minute counts, and time spent reading your prompt is time that can't be spent thinking or responding.

Give the assignment a meaningful name. Walvoord and Anderson (1998) point out that the title of an assignment is a powerful way to

Table 8.2

Questions to Address in a Prompt for an Assignment

- Why are you giving students this assignment? What do you expect them to learn by completing it?
- What should the completed assignment look like?
    - What skills and knowledge do you want students to demonstrate? (Explain terms that may be fuzzy to your students even if they're clear to you, such as *compare, evaluate,* and *discuss.*)
    - What should be included in the completed assignment?
    - How should the completed assignment be formatted?
- How are students to complete the assignment? How do you expect them to devote their time and energy?
    - How much time do you expect them to spend on this assignment? If this is a class assignment, how much will it count toward their final course grade?
    - If the assignment is to write something, what's an optimal length for the paper?
    - What reference materials and technologies are they expected to use?
    - Can they collaborate with others? If so, to what extent?
    - What assistance can you provide while they're working on the assignment? (Are you willing to critique drafts, for example?)
- How will the assignment will be scored or graded? (The best way to address this is to give students a copy of the rubric to be used to evaluate completed assignments.)

convey to students what you want them to do. They suggest terms like "argumentative essay," "original research project," or "sociological analysis," which make the assignment clearer than the usual "term paper."

Set challenging (but realistic) expectations. Often when students know exactly what they need to do to achieve a high score, they will rise to meet that standard, even if it means accomplishing things to which they never thought they could aspire. If you give students a copy of the rubric you will use to evaluate their completed assignments (Chapter 7), make sure it states clearly what you consider outstanding work.

Break apart large assignments. Rather than distribute an assignment for a term paper on the first day of class and collect the papers on the last day, break the paper into pieces that are handed in or checked at various points during the course. You might, for example, ask students to first submit an outline of a research paper and next an annotated bibliography for it. This helps students manage their time and, more importantly, gets those heading in a wrong direction back on track before it's too late for them to salvage their project. Breaking an assignment into pieces also makes your job of evaluating the completed assignments more manageable and can discourage plagiarism.

Depending on your students' needs, your goals, and your time constraints, at these checkpoints you might:

- Simply check off that this portion of the project is complete or in progress.

- Review and comment on this portion of the project.

- Give this portion of the project a tentative grade (pending subsequent revisions) or a final grade.

- Have student peers evaluate this portion of the project using a rubric that you provide.

Provide equitable opportunities for students with diverse learning styles and backgrounds to demonstrate their learning. Using assignments with scenarios involving football may be biased against women, and using scenarios involving personal computers may be biased against students with lower-income backgrounds, unless you are specifically assessing understanding of these topics. If all your course assignments are oral presentations, unless one of your major learning goals is to strengthen oral communication skills you may unfairly penalize those who have truly mastered the material but are poor speakers. As suggested in Chapter 2, give students a variety of ways to present what they've learned. You might make one assignment a panel presentation, another a chart or diagram, and a third a written critique. Table 8.1 offers many other possibilities.

Encourage students to reflect on their work, as reflection can promote deeper, longer-lasting learning. As suggested in Chapter 9, you can ask students to attach written reflections to their assignments.

Share your prompt with colleagues, especially those teaching the same, similar, or related courses such as the next course in a sequence. You'll help promote communication on what you're all collectively trying to accomplish, and your colleagues may be able to give you suggestions that strengthen the assignment.

WHAT DOES AN EFFECTIVE PROMPT LOOK LIKE?

Figures 8.1 through 8.4 are examples of effective prompts. More examples are in Huba and Freed's (2000) *Learner-Centered Assessment on College Campuses* and Walvoord and Anderson's (1998) *Effective Grading.*

Figure 8.1

A Prompt for a First-Year Composition Essay Assignment

In *The Color Purple,* by Alice Walker, Celie and her husband Albert, known simply as Mr. ___, have a heated exchange in which Celie reveals to him that she is leaving him to move to Memphis to start her own business. Afterwards, he retorts with the following remarks: "Look at you, you black, you pore, you ugly, you a woman. . . . You nothing at all."

Some men who have engaged in physical and mental abuse of women have been asked to attend a program on abuse. As part of the program, they will be asked to read an essay in which you persuade them not to engage in the kind of behavior that Mr. ___ displays.

Write this essay. Keep in mind that most of the men will be unfriendly or hostile to your ideas, so you must really convince them with your arguments.

Your essay will be graded in terms of content, organization, style/expression, and grammar/mechanics.

Adapted with permission from a prompt by Dr. Lena Ampadu, associate professor of English at Towson University.

Figure 8.2

A Prompt for a Wellness Research Paper

Research a topic of interest related to the components of wellness, and submit a formal paper written according to APA format. The paper will become part of your group project and presentation and be incorporated into the final class project, the development of a Wellness web page. Your paper must be typed and five to seven pages in length, including a selected bibliography.

Your paper should be divided into five sections:

1) Introduction to your wellness issue
2) Relevance of your issue to the college population
3) Steps needed to develop high functioning in this wellness area
4) Cautions: things to avoid related to this wellness issue
5) Resources available related to this wellness issue

Be sure to include an introduction and conclusion. Using articles, books, web sites and textbooks as your references, write a well-organized paper addressing your wellness issue. This is not an article review. Ideas from a variety of sources must be merged in each section to achieve a well-organized, well-written, interesting paper that thoroughly examines the issue. Each section should have three or more references. This is a formal research paper, not an opinion paper.

Note: In order to write a good paper, you need to find good, informative articles. Quote information from text sparingly.

The paper will be graded based on the following criteria:

5 pts.   Paper follows guidelines; information divided into appropriate sections

10 pts. Introduction

10 pts. Conclusion

30 pts. Coverage of topic and thoroughness

10 pts. Creativity

25 pts. Depth of understanding

20 pts. Accuracy

10 pts. Currency of information

 5 pts. Length (five to seven pages)

-10 pts. Poorly written

-10 pts. Poor grammar and spelling

-10 pts. Improper referencing

-10 pts. No in-text referencing

-10 pts. No bibliography

 -5 pts./day Late paper

Adapted with permission from a prompt by Dr. Kandice Johnson, assistant professor of health science at Towson University.

Figure 8.3

A Prompt for a Multimedia Presentation on the History of a Fairy Tale

Your group will present to the class a 30-minute, multimedia talk on the fairy tale that you researched this semester. You will present a "history" of your tale, detailing the ways that it has changed from its origins to the present. You comment not only upon character- and plot-based changes but upon changes that have resulted from changes in the media that deliver the story. In short, I would like you to explain to your colleagues the process by which the printed story that I distributed at the beginning of the semester was transformed into the most recent movie or web site.

Each member of the group must present for at least six minutes. You must incorporate into your presentation at least four of the six media considered in English studies: oral, manuscript, print, performance, film/video, and electronic.

Your presentations should be learned and professional, but that does not mean that they should be dry or wholly scripted. Rather, aim to emulate the performance of the most effective speaker that you know. Use notes or an outline if necessary, but do not stand there and read from a script. Vary your pitch and tone, move around, make eye contact with the people in the audience, and use your space. You have become an expert on your particular fairy tale. Now is your chance to share that expertise with a group of other fairy-tale experts who are eager to acquire your specialized knowledge.

Remember that you are presenting as part of a group. This means that you should rehearse not only your part of the presentation but the entire presentation as a whole. Pay particular attention to transitions between speakers and to the ways that people who are not speaking can help the person who is (passing out handouts, operating the TV/VCR, etc.). Time your group's presentation. Does each speaker speak for at least six minutes? Is the whole presentation precisely 30 minutes in length? Does your group employ at least four media during its presentation? How well does it incorporate those media? Practice!

Sixty percent of your grade will consist of a letter grade for your group's performance, and 40% of your grade will consist of a letter grade for your individual performance. Thus, you would be wise to devote the bulk of your efforts to ensuring the excellence of the group's overall performance, and then worry about your individual performance as time permits.

Adapted with permission from a prompt by Dr. Don-John Dugas, assistant professor of English at Towson University.

Figure 8.4

A Prompt for an Educational Research Problem Statement

To help you be an intelligent consumer of educational research, your major task in this course will be to write a proposal to conduct an educational research project. You won't actually conduct the research, but by writing a proposal you will demonstrate that you understand what "good quality" research is. You will also be able to learn more about a topic in education that interests you.

The first part of the research proposal is a statement of the problem to be investigated that will constitute 15% of your final grade. If you submit the statement before the due date, I will critique your work and give you a tentative grade. If you're satisfied with that grade, you may stop work, and if you'd like to improve your grade, you may submit a revision by the due date.

The statement of the problem should:

- Be no longer than two pages.
- Include a statement of the research problem to be investigated, the reason(s) you chose this topic, and what you hypothesize would be the results of your research.
- Include definitions of any key terms relevant to your topic, woven into the discussion rather than listed separately.
- Be accompanied by a completed reflection page that shows evidence of serious thought.

An outstanding (A) paper has the following characteristics:

1) It meets all the *content requirements* of the assignment, as described above.

2) It is *error-free*. For example, it has no erroneous conclusions or misunderstandings of research concepts.

3) It uses *appropriate language*. Sentence and paragraph structure and vocabulary are all simple ("because" instead of "due to the fact that"). Unemotional, professional terms and phrasings are used (*not* "I was amazed to find..."). There are no contractions.

4) It is *well written*. It is clear, understandable, and well organized, with an appropriate flow and headings. There are sound rationales for conclusions and decisions, evidence of serious thought, and no inconsistencies in what is said.

A good (B) paper is well done, but with some significant flaws not in an A paper (e.g., some errors or unclear statements).

Continued on page 164

An adequate (C) paper meets the content requirements and its major points can be understood, but it has several significant flaws not in an A paper (e.g., the content is not uniformly clear or consistent, or the paper has minimal discussion).

An inadequate (F) paper seriously fails to meet most of the characteristics of an A paper. Most critically, it does not meet the content requirements and/or is so poorly written that its major points cannot be understood.

SHOULD YOU LET STUDENTS CHOOSE FROM SEVERAL PROMPTS?

Thinking on this is mixed. On one hand, giving students choices lets them choose a prompt in which they will be interested and in which their learning may be demonstrated most effectively. A selection of prompts geared to an assortment of learning styles may help students of various backgrounds demonstrate their learning optimally.

On the other hand, because it's impossible for faculty to create assignments that are precisely equally difficult, scores on the completed assignments aren't strictly comparable; some students may inadvertently penalize themselves by choosing a prompt that's harder or more time-consuming than the others. Offering a choice of essay questions in a timed examination setting is particularly discouraged because students must spend some time reading and mentally framing answers to all the questions in order to choose the one to answer, losing time spent actually preparing a response.

HOW CAN YOU COUNTER PLAGIARISM?

The work of others is so readily available via the web that student plagiarism is a growing concern. While there's no way to eliminate plagiarism, these strategies may help.

- Provide plenty of instruction and assignments that help students understand exactly what plagiarism is. Test their understanding through realistic test questions and assignments on plagiarism.

- Set an example by citing the sources to which you refer.

- Give creative assignments that don't lend themselves to plagiarism. Oral or visual presentations, for example, don't lend themselves to plagiarism as readily as traditional written papers. Assignments that cross two courses might also be less susceptible to plagiarism.

- As suggested earlier in this chapter, break assignments into smaller pieces.

- After assignments are turned in, ask students to summarize them.

- Use web sites and software designed to detect plagiarized work. Contact your instructional technology center for information on available tools.

- Inspire and motivate students so they will want to complete the assignment properly (admittedly easier said than done)!

TIME TO THINK, DISCUSS, AND PRACTICE

Choose one of the following (poorly written!) prompts:

- What is your attitude toward health maintenance organizations?
- Compare the writing styles of F. Scott Fitzgerald and Ernest Hemingway.
- Compare the Republican and Democratic parties.
- Describe the operation of a microscope.
- Research the demographics of various ethnic groups in the United States.

1) Choose one person in your group to play the role of the faculty member who wrote the prompt. That person will answer your group's questions about the course or program for which the prompt was written and the learning goal(s) that the prompt is intended to assess.

2) Decide what makes the prompt ineffective.

3) With input from the role-playing group member, rewrite the prompt so it meets the criteria of good prompts.

REFERENCES

Angelo, T. A., & Cross, K. P. (1993). *Classroom assessment techniques: A handbook for college teachers.* San Francisco, CA: Jossey-Bass.

Huba, M. E., & Freed, J. E. (2000). Assessing students' ability to think critically and solve problems. In *Learner-centered assessment on college campuses: Shifting the focus from teaching to learning* (pp. 201–232). Needham Heights, MA: Allyn & Bacon.

Walvoord, B. E., & Anderson, V. J. (1998). *Effective grading: A tool for learning and assessment.* San Francisco, CA: Jossey-Bass.

RECOMMENDED READING

Carey, L. M. (1994). *Measuring and evaluating school learning* (2nd ed.). Boston, MA: Allyn & Bacon.

Cashin, W. E. (1987). *Improving essay tests* (IDEA Paper No. 17). Manhattan, KS: Kansas State University, Center for Faculty Evaluation and Development.

Chicago Board of Education. (2000). *Performance assessment tasks*. Chicago, IL: Author. Retrieved June 2, 2003, from http://intranet. cps.k12.il.us/Assessments/Ideas_and_Rubrics/Assessment_Tasks/as sessment_tasks.html

Coalition of Essential Schools. (2002). *How to analyze a curriculum unit or project and provide the scaffolding students need to succeed*. Oakland, CA: Author. Retrieved June 2, 2003, from http://www.essen tialschools.org/cs/resources/view/ces_res/85

Haladyna, T. M. (1997). *Writing test items to evaluate higher order thinking*. Boston, MA: Allyn & Bacon.

Herman, J. L., Aschbacher, P. R., & Winters, L. (1992). *A practical guide to alternative assessment*. Alexandria, VA: Association for Supervision and Curriculum Development.

Keenan, J. (1983, September 28). A professor's guide to perpetuating poor writing among students. *The Chronicle of Higher Education*, p. 64.

McColskey, W., & O'Sullivan, R. (1993). *How to assess student performance in science: Going beyond multiple-choice tests: A resource manual for teachers*. Tallahassee, FL: Southeastern Regional Vision for Education.

Moskal, B. M. (2003). Recommendations for developing classroom performance assessments and scoring rubrics. *Practical Assessment, Research & Evaluation*, 8(14). Retrieved February 15, 2004, from http://www.pareonline.net/getvn.asp?v=8&n=14

Rudner, L. M., & Boston, C. (1994). Performance assessment. *ERIC Review*, 3(1), 1–12.

Testa, A., Schechter, E., & Eder, D. (2002). Web corner: Authenticating student work in the digital age. *Assessment Update*, 14(2), 11.

9

Encouraging Student Reflection

O ne of the most intriguing developments in education has been the increasing value placed on reflection: encouraging students to reflect on what, how, and why they have learned. This chapter discusses why reflection is important, how to elicit student reflections, and how to summarize and analyze reflections and other qualitative assessment information.

WHY SHOULD WE ENCOURAGE REFLECTION?

While there are many reasons to include reflection in an assessment program, the most important benefit is that it helps students learn by encouraging metacognition and synthesis.

Reflection Helps Students Learn

The best assessments are learning experiences for students as well as opportunities for us to see what they've learned, and this is where reflection shines as an assessment strategy. As noted in Chapter 5, an increasingly important skill is *metacognition:* learning how to learn and how to manage one's learning by reflecting on how one learns best, thereby preparing for a lifetime of learning. Metacognition includes:

- Using efficient learning techniques.

- Discussing and evaluating one's problem solving strategies.

- Critically examining and evaluating the bases for one's arguments.

- Correcting or revising one's reasoning or arguments when self-examination so warrants.

- Forming efficient plans for completing work.
- Evaluating the effectiveness of one's actions.

Another important skill discussed in Chapter 5 is *synthesis:* the ability to put together what one has learned and see the big picture. Asking students to reflect at the end of a course or program on the major lessons that they've learned throughout the curriculum, the learning strategies they used, and how the pieces fit together can help them develop metacognition and synthesis skills.

Reflection Assesses Attitudes, Values, and Other "Ineffables"

Many faculty want students to develop an appreciation for a subject or discipline. Faculty teaching science courses, for example, often want students to develop a lifelong interest in science, continuing to read about and reflect on scientific developments throughout their lives. Faculty teaching art courses often want students to develop an openness to new ideas and a willingness to take risks as they create or view works of art.

These kinds of attitudes often can't be assessed accurately through graded tests or survey rating scales. In such structured assessment formats, students are more likely to give us the answers they think we're looking for than their true views. Carefully worded assignments for reflective writing, however, can encourage open, honest reflection that is far more useful both to us and to our students.

Some faculty believe that attitudes and values simply can't be assessed meaningfully. They argue that these traits take years to develop and that the only accurate way to assess their development would therefore be to observe students many years from now and see if a course or program has indeed affected their attitudes, values, and lifestyle. This would be a pointless exercise, of course, because by that time we would be assessing an obsolete curriculum. While it's true that there is no perfect way to assess attitudes or values (there's no perfect way to assess anything that students have learned), we can assess attitudes and values to a certain extent by using student reflection as a proxy measure that gives some worthwhile clues on how students may think and feel later in their lives.

Reflection Balances Quantitative Assessments With Qualitative Information

Most student reflection is a form of qualitative research: collecting information using flexible, naturalistic methods. As discussed in Chapter 6, qualitative assessments give us fresh insight, allow us to explore possibilities that we haven't considered, and help us discover problems—and solutions—that we wouldn't find through quantitative assessments alone.

Reflection Yields Useful Information Quickly and Easily

What makes student reflection a particularly appealing assessment strategy is that it can be implemented extraordinarily quickly. You can use the short questions discussed below, literally, in your next class. If you ask students for very brief reflections, analyzing the results can also be easy: Simply read through the responses (or, if you have hundreds, a sample of them) for a quick sense of the most common themes.

How Might Students Reflect?

Students can be asked to convey their reflections through Minute Papers, other questions and prompts, journals, and self-ratings. Interviews and focus groups, two other opportunities for student reflection, are discussed in Chapter 12.

Minute Papers

The easiest, fastest way to encourage reflection is to give students just a couple of thought-provoking questions and ask them to write no more than a sentence in response to each. The Minute Paper, developed by Weaver and Cotrell (1985) and described in Angelo and Cross's (1993) *Classroom Assessment Techniques*, is one of the best ways to do this. It's called a Minute Paper because students take no more than a minute or two to complete it, usually answering just two questions:

- What was the most important thing you learned during this class?
- What important question remains unanswered?

These questions can be modified; the first question could be stated as "What was the most useful or meaningful thing you learned in this class?" while the second could be stated as "What question remains uppermost in your mind as we end this class?"

As you review completed Minute Papers, compare students' answers to the first question against what you think is the most important idea of the class. If your students' answers match yours, you've delivered the curriculum with appropriate balance. But if a number of students mention ideas that you consider relatively trivial, you have a clue that you may not be getting your main points across effectively.

Next, look at students' responses to the second question. If students' responses are all over the map, you may be able to conclude that your class had no major sticking point. But if a number of students raise questions about a particular point, you have a clue that you may need to modify your curriculum or pedagogy to make that idea more understandable.

To encourage honest feedback, faculty often ask students to complete Minute Papers anonymously. But consider giving students the option of adding their name if they would like a response from you. This lets you provide individual assistance to students and makes Minute Papers a stronger learning opportunity.

Other Short Questions and Prompts

The Minute Paper concept—asking students for very brief reflections on what they have learned—can be modified to ask students about other aspects of their learning process or their developing attitudes and values. Table 9.1 presents a host of questions upon which you might ask students to reflect. To preserve one of the Minute Paper's strengths—its brevity—ask no more than three questions at one time.

The questions in Table 9.1 are not an exhaustive list; use them as inspiration for developing your own. To ensure honest feedback, take care to phrase your questions so that there are no obviously right or wrong answers. If you teach a course in 20th century art appreciation, for example, and ask your students, "What is your attitude toward modern art?" you're likely to elicit fairly generic, unenlightening responses such as "I like it" or "I've learned a lot about it." If, on the

Table 9.1

Examples of Prompts for Self-Reflection on an Assignment, Course, or Program

1) What was the one most useful or meaningful thing you learned in this assignment (course, program)?

2) What suggestions would you give other students on ways to get the most out this assignment (course, program)?

3) In what area did you improve the most? What improvement(s) did you make?

4) What one assignment for this course (program) was your best work? What makes it your best work? What did you learn by creating it? What does it say about you as a writer (teacher, biologist, sociologist, etc.)?

5) Describe something major that you've learned about yourself from this assignment (course, program).

6) What did you learn about writing (research, other skill) from this assignment (course, program)?

7) List three ways you think you have grown or developed as a result of this assignment (course, program).

8) What goals did you set for yourself in this assignment (course, program)? How well did you accomplish them?

9) If you were to start this assignment (course, program) over, what would you do differently next time?

10) What strategies did you use to learn the material in this assignment (course, program)? Which were most effective? Why?

11) What risks did you take in this assignment (course, program)?

12) What did you learn from this assignment (course, program) that is *not* reflected in your work?

13) If you could change any one of the assignments you did for this course (program), which one would it be? What would you change about it?

14) What problems did you encounter in this assignment (course, program)? How did you solve them?

15) What makes a person a good writer (teacher, biologist, sociologist, etc.)?

16) What are your strengths as a writer (teacher, biologist, sociologist, etc.)? Your weaknesses?

17) In what ways have you improved as a writer (teacher, biologist, sociologist, etc.)?

18) What have you learned in this course (program) that will help you continue to grow as a writer (teacher, biologist, sociologist, etc.)?
19) What would you like to learn further about this subject (discipline)? Why?
20) In what area would you like to continue to strengthen your knowledge or skills?
21) Write one goal for next semester (year) and tell how you plan to reach it.

other hand, you ask students, "Which work of art studied in this course would you most like to display in your home, if you could? Why?" you're far likelier to elicit thoughtful responses and learn more about your students' true attitudes toward 20th century art.

Before-and-After Reflection

Sometimes it can be helpful to ask students to reflect at both the beginning and end of a course or program and compare their responses to give you a sense of their growth and development. You might ask students to rate their skills and attitudes; to define a key, overriding concept ("What is chemistry?" "What is poetry?"); or to explain why a subject or discipline is important. Table 9.2 gives examples of student definitions of leadership before and after participating in a leadership development program. You can see how the pairs of responses powerfully convey what students learned in the program.

Longer Self-Reflection Assignments

While short questions and prompts for reflective writing are excellent ways to gain insight into student learning quickly and easily, longer assignments such as essays reflecting on learning experiences throughout a program can help students synthesize what they've learned and clarify their attitudes, values, and learning strategies.

These kinds of assignments require clear, specific instructions (prompts) to students. Figure 9.1 is an example of such a prompt. See Chapter 8 for more information on creating effective prompts.

Table 9.2

Student Definitions of Leadership Before and After Participating in a Leadership Development Program

Initial Definition of Leadership	Later Definition of Leadership
The ability to give and take orders and being able to take charge of a large group of people.	I have learned that leadership is not a one-man/woman show. To be a good leader, you must have the respect of your committee and you must be able to communicate.
The presence of a strong, task-oriented and social-oriented yet compromising force or person.	Leadership isn't as easy as it looks! Leadership takes a lot of hard work and there are ups and downs to the position of a leader. My definition has changed to include the importance of diverse people.
Leadership is a responsibility or a skill/trait one possesses that makes a person stand out above everyone else.	Leadership is a collective process. You need leaders and followers to make an event/organization successful.
Leadership involves taking control in an organizational way. A leader must know how to dictate responsibility as well as work with others to achieve a goal.	Leadership has a lot to do with confidence. Most of the confidence lies within yourself but you also have to have confidence in the people you're working with. My definition of leadership has changed in the sense that I feel like it is more delegating and following up with your delegations than actually taking a lot of work upon yourself.
Leadership is an important element of life that can only be fulfilled by individuals possessing the motivation, insight, and communication skills to fulfill the mission, goals, and objectives of an organization.	Leadership is ever changing. Now I think leadership is defined by the people being led.

Adapted with permission from responses to prompts by Tess Shier, coordinator for campus programs in the Office of Student Activities at Towson University.

Figure 9.1

A Prompt for a Reflective Paper on an Internship

Write a reflective paper on your internship experience. The purpose of this assignment is for you to develop and demonstrate the ability to:

- Set explicit goals for your own work.
- Monitor your progress toward meeting goals.
- Seek out and use feedback from others.
- Evaluate your learning and performance.
- Assess personal strengths and weaknesses.
- Communicate clearly and professionally through writing.

Your reflective paper should be five pages long, double-spaced, 10- or 12-point font with one-inch margins. Use the objectives listed above as a basis for your reflection and answer the following questions:

- How valuable was the internship experience to you?
- What specific experiences do you think made you stretch and grow as a professional?
- What could you have done differently during your internship to improve the learning experience?
- Would you recommend this placement to others? Why or why not?

Adapted with permission from a prompt created by Drs. Sharon B. Buchbinder and Donna M. Cox in the health care management program at Towson University.

Journals

Journals are documents in which students make repeated entries during a course or program. Journals may be designed to help students develop any of the following:

A skill through repeated practice. One of the most effective ways to learn is through time on task, and journals can help ensure that students routinely practice an important skill such as writing, critical thinking, or problem solving. Students in a first-year composition course might be asked to write a paragraph each day in a journal, while students in a literature course might be asked to write in a journal short critical analyses of each reading assignment.

Study skills, by ensuring timely progress on major projects. Students might be asked to make weekly journal entries on their work on a term paper or project to ensure that they're staying on track toward its timely completion.

Conceptual understanding, by writing brief summaries of lessons or readings. Faculty can review these summaries periodically to ensure that students are grasping key points correctly.

Metacognitive and synthesis skills, by reflecting on individual readings or assignments or on the entire journal. Students might be asked to record in a journal what they learned from each assignment, how they solved each problem, their reactions to each reading, or how each assignment or reading has affected their attitude toward the subject. After making routine entries on a regular basis, students might be asked to look back through their journals and reflect on how their skill or attitude has developed.

As with any other assignment or assessment, journals are worthwhile only if they are carefully planned. Effective journals require, first and foremost, *a clear learning goal.* Students should understand the journal's purpose and what they will learn by creating it.

Effective journals also require *clear instructions or prompts* (Chapter 8). Students should understand exactly what they should write in the journal and how often.

Finally, effective journals require *useful feedback* from faculty on how well students are achieving the journal's goals. If your journal's purpose is to strengthen writing, critical thinking, and/or other skills, students should receive feedback on the quality of those skills, and a simple rubric (Chapter 7) can be used to provide this.

If your journal's purpose is to encourage metacognition or the development of attitudes or values, providing constructive feedback is more of a challenge, as you want to encourage honest reflection that won't be marked right or wrong. But you can offer feedback on whether the journal includes the underlying elements necessary for valid statements on attitudes, values, and insight. You can note, for example, whether the student has:

- Made an adequate effort to complete the journal assignment.

- Demonstrated sufficient understanding of the lesson, reading passage, and so forth to be able to reflect on it meaningfully.

- Included meaningful personal responses and opinions in the journal entry.

- Connected his or her opinions to what has been learned in class.

Journals can be very time-consuming to read and evaluate. If you don't have time to read and comment on every journal entry, try asking students to read and comment on each other's journals, following your guidelines, or read and comment on random excerpts.

Self-Ratings

Students can reflect on what they've learned by rating themselves on their knowledge, skills, and attitudes using a rating scale (see Chapter 12). Figure 9.2 is an example of such a rating scale.

While self-ratings, unlike reflective writing, can be easily tallied and summarized, they are transparent: "Right" and "wrong" answers are self-evident, and students may be tempted to give you the answers they think you want to hear rather than their honest self-appraisals. Because of this, self-ratings should be viewed with caution and used only in conjunction with more direct evidence of student learning.

If you want to include self-ratings in your assessment program, see Chapter 12 for information on creating rating scales.

HOW ARE REFLECTIVE WRITING AND OTHER QUALITATIVE ASSESSMENTS SUMMARIZED AND ANALYZED?

Qualitative results can be analyzed through quick read-throughs, tallies, and thematic analysis. These processes are far more subjective than those used to summarize and analyze the results of quantitative assessments such as rubrics, ratings scales, and multiple-choice tests (Chapter 14), and careful, consistent judgment in interpreting results is essential.

Quick read-throughs. The fastest way to get a sense of qualitative results is to read through them quickly for general impressions. Simply reading through Minute Paper responses, for example, will give you a good sense of what your students are finding most difficult. If you have too many responses to read them all, read through a random sample of them.

Tallies. If your qualitative assessment information is composed of brief statements that fall into reasonably discrete categories, you may

Figure 9.2

A Self-Assessment of Library Skills

For each of the following skills, please make TWO ratings:
1) How strong are your skills in each of the following areas?
2) How much have the library session(s) in this course helped you to develop each of the following skills?

| | Your skill level | | | | | How much library session(s) have helped | | | | |
| | Low | | | | High | Low | | | | High |
	1	2	3	4	5	1	2	3	4	5
1) Identify potential sources of information related to this course.	☐	☐	☐	☐	☐	☐	☐	☐	☐	☐
2) Find information that's appropriate for and relevant to this field of study.	☐	☐	☐	☐	☐	☐	☐	☐	☐	☐
3) Critically evaluate information that you find, including its accuracy, authority, coverage, objectivity, and currency.	☐	☐	☐	☐	☐	☐	☐	☐	☐	☐
4) Cite the work of others accurately and ethically.	☐	☐	☐	☐	☐	☐	☐	☐	☐	☐

Adapted with permission from a rubric developed by the library faculty of Towson University.

Quick read-throughs. The fastest way to get a sense of qualitative results is to read through them quickly for general impressions. Simply reading through Minute Paper responses, for example, will give you a good sense of what your students are finding most difficult. If you have too many responses to read them all, read through a random sample of them.

Tallies. If your qualitative assessment information is composed of brief statements that fall into reasonably discrete categories, you may wish to tally the results. Figure 9.3 gives a tally of qualitative feedback on an assessment workshop. This simple summary makes clear that rubrics were most often mentioned as the most useful thing participants learned about at this particular workshop, with multiple-choice tests coming in second.

Thematic analysis. More extensive qualitative assessment results, such as reflective essays and transcriptions of focus group interviews, don't lend themselves to simple tallies. Such results are best analyzed using thematic analysis: synthesizing the results into a holistic description by organizing them into categories or groups and looking for common themes, patterns, links, and relationships among results. For more information on thematic analysis, see the Recommended Reading section at the end of this chapter.

Ensuring consistent, fair analysis. As noted earlier, the analysis of qualitative results is a highly subjective process that requires careful, consistent professional judgment. Suppose that one of the comments in Figure 9.3 was "Using rubrics for student self-ratings." Would this be categorized under rubrics, self-reflection, both, or in a separate category? These kinds of decisions must be made deliberately and consistently. Taking steps to ensure consistent, appropriate categorizations of qualitative results is particularly important if the results are part of a major, important assessment effort. Create some written rules or examples for categorizing ambiguous results such as this example. After all results have been categorized, review your decisions to make sure they have been consistent. Better yet, consider having two people independently read and categorize results and compare. It's also a good idea to corroborate your conclusions by comparing them against the results of other assessments, as discussed in Chapter 2.

Figure 9.3

A Simple Summary of Qualitative Participant Feedback on an Assessment Workshop

What was the one thing you learned in this workshop that you'll find most useful?

Rubrics (13 comments):

- Characteristics and advantages of different types of rubrics.
- Descriptive rubrics seemed useful.
- Examples of rubrics.
- Reinforcing understanding and validity of rubrics.
- Using rubrics.
- Rubrics are a very good thing when instructors buy into using them.
- Developing rubrics.
- Holistic scoring.
- The three different kinds of rubrics and how to begin writing them. (I'm going to begin soon!)
- How to construct a rubric—from basic to complex.
- Creating rubrics may be an excellent collaborative exercise by which department colleagues establish common goals and compare their grading definitions (scales).
- The potential range and flexibility of rubrics.
- Examples of different types of rubrics and examining purpose of rubric to select one.

Multiple-choice (9 comments):

- Tips for writing multiple-choice.
- Creating multiple-choice questions.
- Multiple-choice tests—I haven't used in a long while and will rethink.
- The criteria for writing good MC tests.
- How to avoid pitfalls in the writing of multiple-choice exams.
- Options for multiple-choice questions.
- Interpretive exercises—I think these will be most useful.
- I learned how to use scenarios effectively!
- Interpretive exercises may work well in my comparative literature course—where I usually emphasize essay-writing.

Self-reflection (5 comments):
- The self-reflection info will really work for my students.
- Reflective writing—I think these will be most useful.
- The role of self-reflection and metacognition.
- Role of self-reflection in assessment as a strategy.
- Examples of self-reflection questions.

General/misc. (3 comments):
- How to process and assess the assessment tools we use on a daily basis.
- Great tips and tools for assessing student learning.
- That assessment encompasses test design and grading.

Technological Support for Qualitative Assessments

If your qualitative results are voluminous, consider using qualitative research software to summarize and analyze them more efficiently. After responses are keyed in, qualitative research software typically highlights words and phrases and counts their frequency. Some software also organizes responses (e.g., groups all comments on one theme together) to facilitate review and analysis. For further information on such software, consult the Recommended Reading section at the end of this chapter, speak to a social science faculty member interested in qualitative research, or do a web search for "qualitative research" or "qualitative analysis."

If qualitative research software isn't available to help analyze voluminous results, examine a sample (see Chapter 6). Use an assortment of highlighting markers to code each theme, or develop a simple coding scheme. You might, for example, code reflections mentioning writing as the most important thing learned as 1, code those mentioning oral presentation skills as 2, and so on.

CAN AND SHOULD STUDENT REFLECTIONS BE SCORED OR GRADED?

Opinions on whether student reflections can or should be scored or graded are decidedly mixed. On one hand, one of the purposes of reflection is to elicit honest, truthful information on a student's attitudes, values, and learning strategies. Scoring student reflections may stifle that honesty, encouraging students to write only what they think we want to hear instead of what they truly think and feel. Indeed, it's possible that even asking students to put their names on their reflections may dissuade them from providing trustworthy information.

On the other hand, reflection is an opportunity to develop skill in analysis and synthesis, and we can certainly score how well students are demonstrating these kinds of skills in their reflective writing. Evaluations and grades can also be important incentives for students to give careful thought to their reflections. Example 11 in Walvoord and Anderson's (1998) *Effective Grading* is a rubric for evaluating journal entries.

Both positions have merit, and it's likely that the best approach will depend on your students and what you are asking them to do. Some students, for example, may be more comfortable reflecting anonymously until they develop increased confidence in their ability to reflect. Other students, however, may need the incentive of credit toward a final grade to complete a journal.

TIME TO THINK, DISCUSS, AND PRACTICE

1) Draft three prompts for self-reflection that might be given to students graduating from your institution to help assess your institution's major learning goals.

2) Choose one person in your group who teaches a course and develop guidelines for a journal for students to create during that course. Draft:

- The learning goal(s) for the journal.

- A prompt (assignment) explaining what students should record in the journal.

- Guidelines on how the journal will be evaluated.

REFERENCES

Angelo, T. A., & Cross, K. P. (1993). *Classroom assessment techniques: A handbook for college teachers.* San Francisco, CA: Jossey-Bass.

Walvoord, B. E., & Anderson, V. J. (1998). *Effective grading: A tool for learning and assessment.* San Francisco, CA: Jossey-Bass.

Weaver, R. L., & Cotrell, H. W. (1985, Fall/Winter). Mental aerobics: The half-sheet response. *Innovative Higher Education, 10,* 23–31.

RECOMMENDED READING

Anderson, J. (1992–1993). Journal writing: The promise and the reality. *Journal of Reading, 36*(4), 304–309.

Aronson, J. (1994). A pragmatic view of thematic analysis. *The Qualitative Report, 2*(1). Retrieved June 2, 2003, from http://www.nova.edu/ssss/QR/BackIssues/QR2-1/aronson.html

Association of American Colleges and Universities. (2002). *Greater expectations: A new vision for learning as a nation goes to college.* Washington, DC: Author. Retrieved June 2, 2003, from http://www.greaterexpectations.org

Boud, D. (1995). *Enhancing learning through self assessment.* London, United Kingdom: Kogan Page.

Catholic Community Forum. (2000, November 18). *Assessing metacognition.* Ballwin, MO: Author. Retrieved June 2, 2003, from http://www.catholicforum.com/catholicteacher/english_METACOGNITION.htm

Chandler, A. (1997). Is this for a grade? A personal look at journals. *English Journal, 86*(1), 45–49.

Costa, A. L., & Kallick, B. (2000). Getting into the habit of reflection. *Educational Leadership, 57*(7), 60–62.

Denzin, N. K., & Lincoln, Y. S. (2000). *Handbook of qualitative research* (2nd ed.). Thousand Oaks, CA: Sage.

Hoepfl, M. C. (1997). Choosing qualitative research: A primer for technology education researchers. *Journal of Technology Education, 9*(1). Retrieved June 2, 2003, from http://scholar.lib.vt.edu/ejournals/JTE/v9n1/hoepfl.html

Huba, M. E., & Freed, J. E. (2000). Using feedback from students to improve learning. In *Learner-centered assessment on college campuses: Shifting the focus from teaching to learning* (pp. 121–150). Needham Heights, MA: Allyn & Bacon.

Krueger, R. A. (1998). *Analyzing and reporting focus group results* (The Focus Group Kit, Vol. 6). Thousand Oaks, CA: Sage.

Mittler, M. L., & Bers, T. H. (1994). Qualitative assessment: An institutional reality check. In T. H. Bers & M. L. Mittler (Eds.), *New directions for community colleges: No. 88. Assessment and testing: Myths and realities* (pp. 61–67). San Francisco, CA: Jossey-Bass.

Patton, M. Q. (2002). *Qualitative research & evaluation methods* (3rd ed.). Thousand Oaks, CA: Sage.

Silverman, D. J. (2001). *Interpreting qualitative data: Methods for analyzing talk, text and interaction.* Thousand Oaks, CA: Sage.

10

Assembling Assessment Information Into Portfolios

Portfolios may be the most exciting, the most misunderstood, and the most challenging assessment tool that we have. They can be extremely valuable learning opportunities and assessment tools, but they can also take a tremendous amount of time to manage and evaluate. This chapter explains what a portfolio is and discusses when and how to use portfolios effectively.

WHAT IS A PORTFOLIO?

You may remember keeping a folder of your work in one or more of your elementary school classes. What are the differences between that folder and portfolios of student work as they're used today?

First, while many folders simply serve as repositories for student work, portfolios usually have three *clear educational purposes*:

- Helping students learn.

- Assessing what students have learned.

- Providing feedback to the portfolio's audience on what students have learned and how their learning might be improved.

Second, while the contents of folders are specified by the teacher and often include everything students do in a particular class, *students participate in choosing* what goes in their portfolios, using *selection criteria* provided by faculty. Students might be asked, for example, to include four assignments: one assignment that best shows their research skills, one assignment that best shows their writing skills, one assignment that best shows their ability to use a particular concept to solve a problem, and one assignment from which they feel they learned the most.

Third, while folders are often not evaluated systematically, portfolios are assessed using *evaluation criteria* developed by faculty, often in the form of a scoring guide or rubric (Chapter 7).

Fourth, while folders are often composed only of final products, portfolios often *illustrate growth,* either by including student work from the beginning as well as the end of a course or program or by including documentation of the process students went through in producing their work, such as notes, drafts, or work logs.

Fifth, while folders are added to but not refined, portfolios are *continually updated* with one assignment substituted for another. As students' writing skills evolve, for example, students may substitute a different assignment for the one they think best shows their writing skills.

Finally, while folders often do not represent a substantive learning opportunity, portfolios include written *student reflections* on the significance and contribution of each item in the portfolio. In this way, portfolios help students develop the ability to synthesize what they've learned and develop metacognition: the ability to "learn how to learn" by reflecting on what and how they have learned (see Chapter 9).

WHY USE PORTFOLIOS?

A portfolio is compelling evidence of what a student has learned.

- It assembles in one place evidence of many different kinds of learning and skills.

- It forces us to examine student learning holistically—seeing how learning comes together—rather than through compartmentalized skills and knowledge.

- It shows not only the final outcome of a course or program but also how the student has grown as a learner. It is thus a richer record than test scores, rubrics, and grades alone.

- By giving information on not only what students have learned but also how they have learned, it helps us refine what and how we teach.

- It integrates instruction and assessment, as students engage simultaneously in learning and assessment.

- It encourages diversity rather than conformity in student learning activities.

- As noted above, it encourages student reflection, which develops skill in synthesis and metacognition.

WHEN ARE PORTFOLIOS MOST EFFECTIVE AND USEFUL?

Portfolios can be used by faculty to document and evaluate student learning within a course, within another learning opportunity such as a service learning experience, and across an entire academic program. In this chapter, portfolios assessing student learning within a course are referred to as *course-based portfolios*, and portfolios assessing student learning across an entire program are referred to as *program-based portfolios*.

While portfolios can be used in virtually any learning experience, they are particularly appropriate in courses and programs that:

Focus on developing thinking skills rather than conceptual understanding. The papers and projects typically included in portfolios provide strong evidence of thinking skills such as writing, analysis, and evaluation but do not paint a comprehensive picture of students' knowledge. If your goals are largely to develop broad, comprehensive understanding (e.g., to understand the principal figures and events affecting East Asian history), traditional tests (Chapter 11) will help you assess these goals more effectively than portfolios.

Focus especially on developing synthesis and metacognition skills. As noted earlier, the self-reflection element of portfolios makes them ideal for developing these skills.

Have small numbers of students. When a program graduates only a handful of students a year, assessment measures such as tests, surveys, or capstone projects may not be very useful, because changes and differences in results may be due more to fluctuations in student characteristics than to changes in teaching/learning processes. Portfolios are a better choice in this situation because they give a more complete picture of student growth and development.

IS A PORTFOLIO APPROPRIATE AND FEASIBLE FOR YOUR COURSE OR PROGRAM?

A great deal of thought, time, and effort precedes successful portfolio implementation. The biggest problems are time and logistics. Portfolios can take a tremendous amount of time, both for students to compile and for faculty to monitor and assess, making them a particular challenge in large classes and programs. Storing portfolios securely yet accessibly can be another challenge. Electronic portfolios, discussed later in this chapter, solve the storage problem but not the time problem.

The questions below can help you decide whether a portfolio is an appropriate element of your assessment program and plan an effective portfolio assignment. Many of these questions are discussed in more detail in the remaining sections of this chapter.

- *What are the goals of the portfolio?* Why are you having students create portfolios? What learning goals should the portfolio demonstrate? As noted earlier, students should learn something important from the process of compiling a portfolio; if not, portfolios are not worthwhile.

- *Who is the portfolio's audience:* students, faculty, administrators, employers, accreditors, others? What questions does each audience group want answered by the portfolios? What decisions do they need to make?

- *How and when will students choose* what to put in the portfolio? What kinds of student work will answer audience questions? If the portfolio is program-based, do all students in the program, regardless of the program options they choose, complete these kinds of assignments?

- *How will student and faculty reflection be ensured* in the portfolio process?

- *How will the portfolios be evaluated?* What will be your evaluation criteria? Will the portfolios be graded? If not, what incentives will be provided to ensure that students put good effort into assembling and reflecting on their portfolios?

- *Who will review and evaluate the portfolios?* When?

- *How will the portfolio compilation and evaluation process be kept manageable?* How and where will portfolios be stored?

- *Who owns each portfolio?* What happens to each portfolio when the student completes the course, graduates, or leaves the program before graduating?

- *What are the benefits* of moving toward portfolio assessment? *What are the areas of concern?* Are portfolios a feasible practice in your situation?

WHAT CAN GO INTO A PORTFOLIO?

There are no rigid rules or guidelines about what might be included in a portfolio. You are limited only by your imagination! The assignments in Table 8.1 in Chapter 8 include many that might be included in a portfolio and go beyond the usual essays, term papers, and reports. Other possibilities include:

- Drafts and work logs that document the process of creating a final product.

- Self-assessments, peer assessments, attitude and interest surveys, and statements of students' learning and personal development goals.

- Notes from faculty members and supervisors, such as field experience supervisor evaluations and notes from observations, conferences, and interviews.

While students should choose at least some items for their portfolios, faculty may specify some items, and some may be chosen collaboratively by the student and a faculty member.

Whether tests or logs of test scores should be included in portfolios depends on the goals for the portfolio. As noted earlier, objective tests are often more appropriate than other portfolio items for assessing basic knowledge.

Portfolios generally focus on work completed in the latter part of a course or program. Student work completed earlier can help show growth and improvement but cannot reflect what students have learned later in the program and is therefore incomplete evidence of how well students have learned a particular goal. It's also difficult to include early work in program-based portfolios if many students transfer into the program after completing early coursework elsewhere.

WHAT GUIDELINES SHOULD STUDENTS RECEIVE ON ASSEMBLING THEIR PORTFOLIOS?

Because preparing a portfolio may be a new experience for some students, it's important to give them clear written guidelines that explain the portfolio assignment. Guidelines should explain:

- What are faculty goals for the portfolio? What will students learn by compiling it, beyond what they will learn by completing each individual item?

- What will be included in the portfolio? Which items are mandatory, and which do the students choose? When will the choices be made?

- What are key deadlines?

- How will the portfolio be stored? When and how can students access it? What will happen to it at the end of the course or program?

- How will faculty evaluate each item and the overall portfolio?

  Figure 10.1 is an example of an assignment for a portfolio.

HOW SHOULD A PORTFOLIO BE ORGANIZED?

Well-organized portfolios help students review their work and help you and your colleagues make sense of the contents. Most portfolios should include:

- A table of contents, perhaps presented as a checklist of potential items (Figure 10.2).

- A reflection page, in which students reflect on the overall contents of the completed portfolio.

- Your evaluative summary of the portfolio, perhaps in the form of a completed rubric.

- An introductory statement, if you choose to have the student write one, that will help those evaluating the portfolio understand it better (students might state, for example, why they enrolled in this course

Figure 10.1

A Portfolio Assignment From a Graduate Course for Grade School Teachers on Assessment Methods

Develop a portfolio of assessment tools that you can use in your classes. My goals for this assignment are for you:

1) To become familiar with a broad variety of assessment tools.
2) To create types of assessment tools that you are not now using.
3) To create assessment tools that are better quality (more valid) than the tools you are now using.
4) To create assessment tools that assess thinking skills.

Selection Guidelines

Include at least **eight** items in your portfolio, choosing from the list on the "Portfolio Table of Contents" (Figure 10.2). Your portfolio must also include a table of contents, a cover sheet for each portfolio item (Figure 10.3), and a completed "Reflections on the Course" form.

Other Guidelines

Your portfolio items should be in the order shown on the table of contents, with cover sheets preceding each assessment tool.

Your portfolio items need not all be tied to the same subject. You can write a test blueprint for one subject, for example, and a rubric for another.

You are welcome to submit more than the minimum number of items. Don't expect to include an example of every kind of assessment tool, however, as some may not be appropriate for what you teach.

The items you submit in your portfolio need not be your "best" work, but they should represent a serious effort to create something you can use in your classes.

Evaluation Criteria

Each item submitted—and the portfolio as a whole—will be evaluated using the following standards.

- Outstanding: Meets "good" standards below and, in addition, shows extra effort, insight, or creativity.
- Good: Reflects concepts and guidelines taught in class; shows serious effort, particularly at "stretching"—using new assessment methods—and at assessing thinking skills.
- Needs Improvement: Fails to meet "good" standards in at least one respect.

Figure 10.2

A Portfolio Table of Contents Checklist From a Graduate Course for Grade School Teachers on Assessment Methods

Check each item that you are including in your portfolio.

- ❏ This table of contents (required)
- ❏ A list of ten learning goals, including at least six for thinking skills
- ❏ A checklist rubric
- ❏ A rating scale rubric
- ❏ A descriptive rubric
- ❏ A holistic scoring guide
- ❏ A prompt for an assignment
- ❏ A prompt for self-reflection
- ❏ A prompt for a portfolio
- ❏ A test blueprint
- ❏ Six multiple-choice items
- ❏ A set of matching items
- ❏ One interpretive exercise with at least three items
- ❏ A prompt for a journal
- ❏ A cover sheet for each item in the portfolio (required)
- ❏ A completed "Reflections on the Course" form (required)

or program, their learning goals, their background before enrolling, their strengths and weaknesses, their career or life goals, etc.).

- Cover sheets for each item in the portfolio in which the student reflects upon the item (Figure 10.3).

- Your comments on or evaluation of each item in the portfolio (because of the volume of materials, your rubric or comments may be very brief and simple, perhaps included on each cover sheet).

Figure 10.3

A Cover Sheet for Individual Portfolio Items From a Graduate Course for Grade School Teachers on Assessment Methods

1) What type of assessment tool is this?

2) In what course or unit will you use this assessment tool?

3) What learning goals does this tool assess?

4) Why did you choose this item for your portfolio?

5) What does this item show me about you as a teacher?

6) What did you learn by creating this item?

7) Do you have any questions about this item?

My comments to you:

HOW CAN STUDENTS BE MOTIVATED TO PREPARE PROGRAM-BASED PORTFOLIOS?

Your students may see a program-based portfolio as simply a lot of extra work without much added benefit to them, and they therefore may give it only perfunctory attention. The following suggestions can help ensure that students give program-based portfolios their best effort and that the portfolios are the strong learning experience they are intended to be.

Make a successful portfolio a program requirement. If you decide to do this, put this requirement in writing, draw it to the attention of students entering the program, and provide interim reviews so that students with inadequate portfolios have time to make them acceptable without delaying their graduation.

As soon as students enter the program, give them written guidelines for the portfolio. Review the guidelines with them to emphasize the importance of the portfolio and answer any questions they might have.

Put procedures in place to *ensure that students review and update their portfolios regularly and that they receive regular feedback from faculty.* Perhaps each student could review his or her portfolio with a faculty advisor once each term. Portfolios may identify the need for additional study in a particular area, the need to develop further a particular skill, or an interest in further study of a particular topic, so these reviews can help students plan their studies.

Make the portfolio a project within a capstone experience such as a senior seminar. Take time during the capstone experience for students to review, reflect on, and refine their portfolios.

Recognize and honor students with outstanding portfolios.

Allow graduating students to take copies of their portfolios with them (perhaps burned onto a CD-ROM) and encourage them to use the contents in applications for jobs and programs of advanced study.

Additional strategies for motivating students to participate in program assessment projects are discussed in Chapter 6.

HOW MIGHT STUDENTS REFLECT ON THEIR PORTFOLIOS?

As noted earlier, one of the defining characteristics of portfolios is the opportunity for students to learn by reflecting holistically on their work. Students can be asked to reflect on each item in their portfolio (Figure 10.3) and on the portfolio as a whole. Questions they might reflect upon include:

- Which item is your best work? Why?
- Which item is your most important work? Why?
- Which item is your most satisfying work? Why?
- Which item is your most unsatisfying work? Why?
- In which item did you "stretch" yourself the most, taking the greatest risk in exploring new territory?
- List three things you learned by completing this portfolio.
- What does this portfolio say about you as an emerging professional or scholar in this discipline?

- What are your goals for continuing to learn about this discipline?

Table 9.1 in Chapter 9 has more examples of questions that you can ask to stimulate self-reflection. To keep things manageable and encourage students to refine their thinking, limit the number of questions you pose, and stipulate a maximum length for each response. Many reflection questions can be answered effectively in one sentence.

HOW SHOULD PORTFOLIOS BE EVALUATED?

Your goals for a portfolio assignment should determine how you will evaluate the completed portfolios. For example:

- If your goals include **assessing student progress in achieving major course or program learning goals,** use a rubric that lists those goals and criteria for acceptable performance.

- If your goals include **encouraging metacognition** (learning how to learn by reflecting on the learning process), evaluate the portfolios in terms of the effort students put into self-reflection.

- If your goals include **encouraging students to improve their performance,** have students include drafts in their portfolios, and evaluate the portfolios in terms of improvement.

- If your goals include **encouraging risk-taking and creativity,** evaluate the portfolios in terms of the reflections students provide on the risks they took in their work.

To keep the process of evaluating portfolios consistent and time-efficient, review your learning goals and expectations for the portfolio and your criteria for judging whether a portfolio is a success. Clarify what a successful portfolio would look like and how individual portfolio components will be compared or weighted in the evaluation.

Then create a rubric (Chapter 7) that reflects your goals for the portfolio and your criteria for judging whether the portfolio is a success. Figure 10.4 is an example of a simple rating scale rubric for assessing program-based portfolios, and the evaluation criteria in Figure 10.1 is a simple holistic scoring guide for assessing course-based portfolios.

If faculty are collectively reviewing portfolios, as discussed in Chapter 7 encourage faculty in the program to come to clear agreement on the meaning of each performance level in the rubric. Try using the

Figure 10.4

A Rubric for Assessing Portfolios of Business Administration Majors

Learning Goal	Outstanding	Satisfactory	Inadequate	Insufficient Information to Evaluate
1) Write articulate, persuasive, and grammatically correct business materials.	❑	❑	❑	❑
2) Use critical, flexible, and creative thinking to generate sound conclusions, ideas, and solutions to problems.	❑	❑	❑	❑
3) Use software and networking services to obtain, manage, and share information.	❑	❑	❑	❑
4) Apply understanding of domestic and international diversity concepts and issues to business situations.	❑	❑	❑	❑
5) Recognize ethical challenges and reach ethical business decisions.	❑	❑	❑	❑

rubric to score a few portfolios, compare your scores, and discuss and resolve any differences before launching into a full-scale review.

How Can Things Be Kept Manageable?

Imagine a class or program with 25 students, each of whom submits a portfolio with ten examples of their work (plus reflections on each). That's 250 items (plus reflections) to be reviewed—a daunting task. How can you keep the work of creating, managing, and evaluating portfolios from overwhelming both students and faculty? Chapters 2, 3, and 7 offer many suggestions for keeping the assessment burden manageable. Here are some other suggestions:

- Limit the number of items in each portfolio.

- Keep portfolio items short (no more than a few pages). Consider including only excerpts from lengthier items.

- Start small. Perhaps ask for only one or two items the first time you use portfolios, and then gradually increase the contents for subsequent cohorts of students.

- For program-based portfolios, ask the faculty member making each assignment to attach a rubric showing his or her evaluation of it. This may save the labor of a second review.

- For program-based portfolios in programs with many majors, consider reviewing only a sample of portfolios each year (provided that students have already received feedback on individual items in their portfolios).

Consider Electronic Portfolios

One of the more noteworthy recent developments in assessment is the use of electronic or digital portfolios, in which students store their work electronically on a secure web site, shared server, disk, or CD-ROM. Electronic portfolios are far easier to store and access than paper portfolios, and unlike paper portfolios they can easily include multimedia projects such as videos, slide shows, and web sites.

A number of commercial software packages support electronic portfolios. Their features and capabilities vary so, before you choose one, have a clear sense of what kinds of student work will go into your portfolios and how the portfolios will be accessed and used. Consider a trial run using traditional paper portfolios on a small scale; the experience will help you understand your goals and needs and make a more appropriate software choice.

If you are interested in learning more about electronic portfolios, attend an assessment conference, speak to colleagues at campuses using electronic portfolios, or do a web search for "electronic portfolios" and "digital portfolios."

TIME TO THINK, DISCUSS, AND PRACTICE

1) Share with others in your group what excites you about portfolios and what makes you skeptical about portfolios.

2) Identify someone in your group teaching a course for which a portfolio might be a worthwhile learning experience. Help that group member answer the following questions:

- What should be the learning goals of the portfolio? What should students learn through the process of assembling and reflecting on their portfolios?

- What questions should the portfolio answer?

- Who are the portfolio's audiences? What decision(s) should the portfolio help each audience make?

- What should the portfolio include? (Remember to keep the portfolios small enough to be manageable!)

- What might be the criteria for evaluating each completed portfolio?

RECOMMENDED READING

Belanoff, P., & Dickson, M. (Eds.). (1991). *Portfolios: Process and product*. Portsmouth, NH: Boynton/Cook.

Black, L., Daiker, D. A., Sommers, J., & Stygall, G. (Eds.). (1994). *New directions in portfolio assessment: Reflective practice, critical theory, and large-scale scoring*. Portsmouth, NH: Boynton/Cook.

Huba, M. E., & Freed, J. E. (2000). Using portfolios to promote, support, and evaluate learning. In *Learner-centered assessment on college campuses: Shifting the focus from teaching to learning* (pp. 233–268). Needham Heights, MA: Allyn & Bacon.

Jons, C. G. (1996). The portfolio as a course assessment tool. In T. W. Banta, J. P. Lund, K. E. Black, & F. W. Oblander (Eds.), *Assessment in practice: Putting principles to work on college campuses* (pp. 285–288). San Francisco, CA: Jossey-Bass.

Lambdin, D. V., & Walker, V. L. (1994). Planning for classroom portfolio assessment. *Arithmetic Teacher, 15*(2/3), 48–64.

Magruder, W. J., & Young, C. C. (1996). Portfolios: Assessment of liberal arts goals. In T. W. Banta, J. P. Lund, K. E. Black, & F. W. Oblander (Eds.), *Assessment in practice: Putting principles to work on college campuses* (pp. 171–174). San Francisco, CA: Jossey-Bass.

Palomba, C. A., & Banta, T. W. (1999). Using performance measures and portfolios for assessment. In *Assessment essentials: Putting principles to work on college campuses* (pp. 115–148). San Francisco, CA: Jossey-Bass.

Paulson, F. L., Paulson, P. R., & Meyer, C. A. (1991). What makes a portfolio a portfolio? *Educational Leadership, 48*(5), 60–63.

Yancey, K. B., & Weiser, I. (Eds.) (1997). *Situating portfolios: Four perspectives.* Logan, UT: Utah State University Press.

11

Writing a Traditional Objective Test

W hile performance assessments (see Chapter 6) are growing in popularity, multiple-choice and other objective tests may still have a place in some assessment programs. This chapter discusses how to plan an objective test, when and how to write effective multiple-choice, true-false, matching, and fill-in-the-blank items, and how objective tests can be used to assess some thinking skills.

WHAT IS AN OBJECTIVE TEST?

As discussed in Chapter 6, *objective* tests can be defined as those that can be scored by a competent eight-year-old armed with an answer key, while *subjective* tests and assignments require professional judgment to score.

The most common kind of objective test item is the *multiple-choice item*. It consists of two parts. The *stem* asks the question; it may be phrased either as a question or as an incomplete sentence. The remainder of the test item is a set of *responses* or *options* from which the student chooses one answer. The incorrect options are called *distracters* or *foils* because their purpose is to distract or foil students who don't know the correct answer from choosing it.

Other kinds of objective test items are really just variations on the multiple-choice theme. A *true-false* item is a multiple-choice item with only two options. *Matching* items are a set of multiple-choice items with identical options. A *completion* or *fill-in-the-blank* item is a multiple-choice item with no options.

WHY USE AN OBJECTIVE TEST?

As discussed in Chapter 6, despite years of often justified criticisms, objective tests remain widely used for three reasons:

- They are what testing experts call *efficient:* They can collect a lot of information on many learning goals in a relatively short amount of time and therefore encourage broad—but sometimes shallow—learning.

- While they are difficult and time-consuming to construct, they are fast and easy to score.

- Their results can be summarized into a single number, which is all that many busy administrators, board members, and legislators are interested in seeing.

Objective tests are especially good at assessing fundamental knowledge and understanding. They can also assess some important thinking skills, such as the ability to identify correct applications, examples, functions, causes, or effects. *Interpretive exercises*, a special kind of objective item discussed later in this chapter, can assess application, problem solving, and analysis skills.

Well-constructed multiple-choice tests can also help diagnose problem areas. Consider this simple example:

What is 2 x 0.10?

A. 20

B. 2.10

C. 0.2

D. 0.02

Each distracter gives a clue as to where the student's thinking goes wrong. Choosing B, for example, might indicate that the student confuses multiplication and addition signs. Choosing A might indicate that the student confuses multiplication with division, while choosing D might indicate a problem with decimal place value. Faculty can thus use the results of multiple-choice tests to identify areas of difficulty and help their students accordingly.

Objective tests are not always an appropriate assessment choice, however. As discussed in Chapter 6, they cannot measure many important thinking skills and they do not measure "real world" performance as well as performance assessments do. They have other shortcomings as well:

- As you'll learn in this chapter, writing good, clear items with good distracters can be difficult and time-consuming.

- Most objective tests require significant reading ability, so students who fail, say, a multiple-choice science test might truly understand the tested scientific concepts but fail because they read unusually slowly. While reading skill is essential for success in academic efforts, if we are assessing understanding of science concepts we want an assessment tool that assesses only that.

- It's possible to guess the correct answer to multiple-choice, true-false, and matching items, either through plain luck or through skill in being "test-wise." While a well-constructed test minimizes test-wise students' advantage, there is always the possibility that a student who doesn't know the material will do well on a test through chance.

How Should an Objective Test Be Planned?

You may recall from Chapter 7 that effective assignments are planned by developing a rubric: a list of the learning goals that students are to demonstrate in the completed assignment. Effective tests are similarly planned by developing a *test blueprint:* a list of the learning goals that students are to demonstrate on the test. Test blueprints are critical to creating effective tests for several reasons.

Test blueprints help ensure that the test focuses on the learning goals you think are most important. Suppose that you are writing a test for Units 8, 9, and 10 of a particular course. While you consider Unit 10 the most important of the three, you may find that it's much easier to think of test questions for Unit 8. If you write your test without a blueprint, you can easily end up with too many questions on Unit 8 and too few on Unit 10. Students taking such a test may be able to do fairly well without having mastered important concepts of Unit 10, while students who have mastered Unit 10 may nonetheless earn low scores.

Test blueprints help ensure that a test gives appropriate emphasis to thinking skills. Faculty writing test questions without a blueprint often find that questions asking for simple conceptual knowledge are easier to write than questions asking students to interpret, infer, analyze, or think in other ways. Tests written without blueprints can thus become tests of trivia rather than tests of thinking skills. Students who do well on such tests may not have mastered important skills, while students who have truly learned those important skills may nonetheless earn low scores.

Test blueprints make writing test questions much easier. Armed with a test blueprint, you'll know exactly what must be covered on the test (one question on Concept A, two on Skill B, etc.), and you'll spend less time pondering what to write.

Test blueprints help document that students have achieved major learning goals. This makes test blueprints an important part of an assessment program. As discussed in Chapter 1, test scores or grades alone give little direct information on exactly what students have learned. But if those test scores or grades are accompanied by test blueprints that describe the learning goals covered on the tests, you'll have direct evidence of exactly what students who did well on the tests have learned.

Create a Test Blueprint

Begin creating a test blueprint by using syllabi, lecture notes, readings, and other curricular materials to list the major areas to be covered by the test. A midterm exam, for example, might cover the first five chapters in the textbook. A comprehensive exam for graduating seniors might cover the six courses required of all majors.

Second, allocate fractions of the test to each of those areas, in proportion to the relative importance of each area, by assigning points or a number of test questions to each area (e.g., 20 points or four questions to Unit 1, 30 points or six questions to Unit 2, etc.).

Third, within each area, list the learning goals that you would like to assess. To make clear both to yourself and your students exactly what you want students to demonstrate on the test, phrase your learning goals using action verbs that describe what students should be able to think and do, as discussed in Chapter 5. Instead of simply listing "Hemingway" in a test blueprint on 20th century American literature, for example, state the knowledge and skills you want students to demonstrate regarding Hemingway (e.g., "Identify works written by

Hemingway," "Distinguish Hemingway's writing style from those of his peers").

Finally, spread the points or test questions within each major area among the learning goals within that area, again in proportion to their importance. For example, if you have allocated four questions to Unit 1 and you list four learning goals within that chapter, you may decide to have one question on each learning goal. But perhaps one of the learning goals is especially important. If so, you may decide to have two questions on that particular learning goal, and you'll need to eliminate one of the other Unit 1 learning goals from the test. Figure 11.1 is an example of a test blueprint.

Once your test blueprint is finalized, give copies to your students to help them focus their studies on the learning goals that you think are most important.

WHAT ARE THE KEYS TO WRITING GOOD MULTIPLE-CHOICE ITEMS?

Once your test blueprint is developed, you are ready to begin writing test questions. As with any other assessment, multiple-choice tests should yield fair and truthful information on what students have learned. There are just two basic precepts to writing fair and truthful multiple-choice items.

- *Remove all the barriers that will keep a knowledgeable student from answering the item correctly.* Students who truly understand the concept or skill being tested by a particular item should choose the correct answer.

- *Remove all clues that will help a less-than-knowledgeable student answer the item correctly.* Students who truly *don't* understand the concept or skill being tested by a particular item should answer the item *incorrectly.*

All the suggestions that follow stem from these two precepts. Figure 11.2 gives some examples of multiple-choice items that follow most of these suggestions and assess thinking skills as well as conceptual understanding.

Writing good multiple-choice items can be difficult; test publishers write, test, and discard many, many items for each one that ends up in

Figure 11.1

A Test Blueprint for an Examination in an Educational Research Methods Course

(There is one test question on each topic unless otherwise indicated.)

Sampling

- Understand the difference between a sample and a population.
- Understand how each type of sample is selected.
- Understand how to choose an appropriate sample size.

Instrumentation and Survey Research

- Understand the relative merits and limitations of published and locally developed instruments.
- Recognize examples of each of the four frames of reference for interpreting scores.
- Understand appropriate uses of each item format (e.g., multiple-choice, Likert scale).
- Understand the characteristics of a good instrument item, including how to avoid biased questions.

Descriptive Statistics

- Select the most appropriate descriptive statistic for a given research situation.
- Use percentage guidelines to interpret standard deviations.
- Identify the direction and strength of r and/or a scatterplot.
- Identify the likely direction and strength of a correlation between two given variables.

Validity and Reliability

- Identify the type of reliability or validity evidence provided by given information on an instrument. (2 questions)
- Understand the meaning and implications of measurement error.
- Recognize examples of measurement error in a given situation.
- Understand the general principles for ensuring validity.

Inferential Statistics

- Select the most appropriate inferential statistic (t, F, or X^2) for a given research situation. (2 questions)
- Know the most common "cut-off" points that statisticians use in deciding whether two means differ significantly from one another.

Continued on page 206

- Interpret the results of *t* tests as presented in research articles.

Experimental Research

- Interpret the symbolic representations of experimental designs.
- Identify the appropriate research design for a given research situation.

Correlational Research

- Understand what r^2, R, R^2, and partial correlations are and what they tell us. (2 questions)
- Understand what multiple regression analysis is used for and what it tells us.

a published test. So don't expect to be able to follow all these suggestions all the time, and don't expect your test questions to work perfectly the first time you use them. Analyze the results (see Chapter 14), revise the test accordingly, and within just a few cycles you'll have a really good test.

Keep each item as concise as possible. Avoid irrelevant material, digressions, and qualifying information unless you are specifically assessing the skill of identifying needed information. Don't repeat the same words over and over in the options; put them in the stem.

Define all terms carefully. If you ask, "Which of the following birds is largest?" make clear whether you mean largest in terms of wingspan or weight. What do you mean by "sometimes," "usually," or "regularly"?

Don't make the vocabulary unnecessarily difficult. Except for terms you are specifically assessing, keep your vocabulary simple—perhaps high school level. Otherwise, you may unfairly penalize students who know your material but don't have a strong general vocabulary.

Watch out for "interlocking" items, in which a student can discern the answer to one question from the content of another. Review carefully all items that share similar options. In a similar vein, don't ask students to use their answer to one question to answer another. If they get the first question wrong, they will automatically get the other question wrong as well, even if they understand the concept tested in the second question.

Figure 11.2

Multiple-Choice Questions on Assessment Concepts

Correct answers are in **boldface**.

1) Which statement refers to measurement as opposed to evaluation?

A) Mary got 90% correct on the math test.

B) Joe's test scores have increased satisfactorily this year.

C) John's score of 20 on this test indicates that his study habits are ineffective.

D Ellen got straight As in her history courses this year.

2) Cindy took a test on Tuesday after a big fight with her parents Monday night. She scored a 72. Her professor let her retake the same test on Thursday when things cooled off. She scored 75. The difference in her scores may be attributed to:

A) chance or luck

B) lack of discrimination

C) lack of validity

D) measurement error

3) People who score high on the Meyers Musical Aptitude Scale usually score low on the Briggs Biologists Aptitude Test. People who score low on the Meyers usually score high on the Briggs. Which of the figures below *most likely* represents the correlation between the two tests?

A) .80

B) .00

C) –.10

D) –.60

4) Choose the *most likely* correct answer to this nonsense question, based on what you know about informed guessing on tests. A drabble will coagulate under what circumstances?

A) only when pics increase

B) only when pics change color

C) by drawing itself into a circle

D) usually when pics increase, but occasionally when pics decrease

Write a Good Stem

The stem should ask a complete question, even if it is phrased as an incomplete statement. The student shouldn't have to read the options to discern the question. To check this, ask yourself if students would be able to answer the question posed in the stem correctly if no options were provided.

Avoid "Which of the following" items. These require students to read every option and can penalize slow readers in a timed-testing situation.

Don't ask questions that can be answered from common knowledge. Someone who hasn't studied the material shouldn't be able to answer the questions correctly.

Avoid negative items; in a stressful testing situation, students can miss the words "not" or "no." If you must have them, underline, capitalize, and/or boldface words like **NOT** or **EXCEPT.**

Avoid grammatical clues to the right answer by using expressions like "a/an," "is/are," or "cause(s)." Test-wise students know that grammatically incorrect options are wrong.

Write Good Options

You needn't have the same number of options for every question. Four options are usually best, as a good fifth option is often hard to come up with, takes extra reading time, and reduces the chances of guessing the correct answer only from 25% to 20%. Some questions, meanwhile, may have only three plausible options (e.g., "Increases," "Decreases," "Remains unchanged").

Order responses logically: numerically if numbers, alphabetically if single words. This helps students who know the answer find it quickly. If the options have no intuitive order, insert the correct answer into the responses randomly.

Line up the responses vertically rather than horizontally. It's much easier—and less confusing—to scan down a column than across a line to find the correct answer. If your options are so short that this seems to waste paper, arrange your test in two columns.

Make all options roughly the same length. Test-wise students know that the longest option is often the properly qualified, correct one. (For this reason, a relatively long option can make a good distracter!)

Avoid repeating words between the stem and the correct response. Test-wise students will pick up this clue. (On the other hand, verbal associations between the stem and a distracter can create an effective distracter.)

Avoid using "None of these" because a student may correctly recognize wrong answers without knowing the right answer. Use this option only when it's important that the student know what *not* to do. If you use "None of these," use it in more than one question, both as a correct answer and an incorrect answer.

Avoid using "All of the above" because it requires students to read every option, penalizing those in a timed testing situation who know the material but are slow readers. Students who recognize Option A as correct and choose it without reading further are also penalized. "All of the above" also gives full credit for incomplete understanding; some students may recognize Options A and B as correct and therefore correctly choose "All of the above" even though they don't recognize Option C as correct.

Write Good Distracters

The best distracters help diagnose where each student went wrong in his or her thinking, as discussed earlier. Identify each mental task that students need to do to answer a question correctly, and create a distracter for the answer students would arrive at if they completed each step incorrectly.

Use intrinsically true or at least plausible statements. Test-wise students recognize ridiculous statements as wrong. To see if your test has such statements, ask a friend who's never studied the subject to take the test; the score should be roughly what would be earned from guessing randomly on every item (25% for a four-option multiple-choice test).

Avoid Trick Questions

Most tests include a few difficult questions to challenge the very best students. Unfortunately, writing difficult multiple-choice questions is, well, difficult; it's very hard to come up with distracters that will foil all but the best students. Too often such questions become trick questions that focus on trivia or some finely nuanced point rather than an important concept. An example of such a question is:

On what date was the A.F.L. and C.I.O. merger agreement reached?
    A) February 8, 1955
    B) February 9, 1955
    C) February 10, 1955
    D) February 11, 1955

(It's rarely important to know the exact date in history on which an event occurred; it's usually more important to know what came before, during, and after the event and to understand how each event affected the others.)

If you want to write meaningful, challenging multiple-choice questions that assess important learning goals rather than trick questions:

- *Use a test blueprint,* as described earlier in this chapter, to make sure each item assesses an important concept or skill.

- *Make your tests open-book, open-note.* Tell students they can bring anything they like except a friend or the means to communicate with one. Using open-book, open-note tests forces you to eliminate items assessing simple knowledge that can be looked up and include only items that assess deeper comprehension and thinking skills.

- *Build items around common misconceptions.* Many people, for example, think that plants get nutrients only from soil and water, not air; this misconception can become the basis of an effective botany test question.

- *Create interpretive exercises* (discussed later in this chapter) to assess thinking skills.

- *Analyze your test results* (see Chapter 14) and revise any misleading or overly difficult items before including them in another test.

WHAT ABOUT TRUE-FALSE ITEMS?

True-false items are simply multiple-choice items with only two options. Their most common use is simple knowledge: Is a given statement correct or not? But they can also be used in other situations with just two possible answers: Is a statement fact or opinion? Is it an example of qualitative or quantitative assessment evidence? Does A cause B?

True-false items have no particular advantages beyond those of any other objective format. They are best used to assess basic conceptual understanding and, like other objective formats, they are answered and scored quickly. Because they have serious shortcomings, however, they should be used rarely, if at all:

- Students who haven't learned the material have a high probability (50%) of guessing the correct answer.

- Unlike multiple-choice and matching items, true-false items give no diagnostic information; they give no clues about where students who answered incorrectly went wrong in their thinking.

- It's difficult to write true-false items assessing thinking skills, although they can be used in interpretive exercises, discussed later in this chapter.

- For classic true-false items—those giving true or false statements—it can be very difficult to write unambiguous, unqualified statements that are either definitely true or definitely false.

- Students may correctly recognize a false statement without knowing its true counterpart.

Writing Good True-False Items

If true-false items appear to be appropriate for your situation, the following suggestions will help make the best of them.

- *Keep them simple.* Avoid lengthy qualifiers and broad generalizations, which can be confusing and hard to make plausible as true or false statements.

- *Use them only to assess important learning goals.* It's especially easy for true-false items to descend into trivia.

- *Avoid negative and double-negative statements.*

- *Keep the proportion of true statements close to but not exactly 50%.* Test-wise students will scan the number of true statements they've marked and use that to decide how to guess on the items they don't know.

WHAT ABOUT MATCHING ITEMS?

Matching items are a set of multiple-choice items with a common set of responses. If, as you write a multiple-choice test, you find yourself writing several items with similar options, consider converting them into a matching set.

Matching items are even more efficient than multiple-choice questions. Because students need to read only one set of options to answer several items, students can often answer eight well-written matching items more quickly than eight multiple-choice items, giving you more assessment information in a given amount of testing time. They are also faster to write, as you don't have to come up with a fresh set of distracters for each item.

Matching items can be a good way to assess certain kinds of basic knowledge. Students can match terms and definitions, causes and effects, authors and titles of their works, people and their achievements, foreign words and their English translations, or tools and their uses. Matching items need not be entirely verbal; students can match symbols with the concepts they represent, pictures of objects with their names, or labeled parts of a pictured entity (say, a microscope or a cell) with their functions.

Matching items can also assess some thinking skills, especially the ability to apply what has been learned to new situations and the ability to analyze interrelationships. Students can match concepts with examples of them, causes with likely effects, and hypothetical problems with the tools, concepts, or approaches needed to solve them.

Writing Good Matching Items

The following suggestions will help you create good sets of matching items, possibly quite different from those you may have used or seen in the past. Figure 11.3 gives an example of a matching set that follows these suggestions and assesses application skills as well as conceptual understanding.

A matching set should consist of homogeneous items. In other words, every option in the answer key should be a plausible answer for every item or question. Otherwise, test-wise students will quickly eliminate implausible answers, while students who are less test-wise will read the full set of responses over and over.

Figure 11.3

Matching Items From a Nursing Research Methods Test

In this set of matching items, some options may be used more than once or not at all. Correct answers are in **boldface**.

Match each measurement with its level of measurement.

    A) Interval

    B) Ordinal

    C) Nominal

    D) Ratio

D   1) Fluid intake, in ounces, of a post-surgical patient

C   2) Religious affiliation

D   3) Medication dosage

C   4) Type of adjuvant therapy (chemotherapy, hormonal therapy, or radiation therapy)

B   5) Level of patient advocate support for a patient (very supportive, moderately supportive, somewhat supportive, not supportive)

Adapted with permission from test questions written by Dr. Christina Barrick, associate professor of nursing at Towson University.

Make an imperfect match between the two columns: Allow each option to be used more than once or not at all. A perfect match (in which each option is the answer for exactly one item) gives an unfair advantage to test-wise students, who will cross out each option as it's chosen and then guess among the few options that are left. A perfect match also gives an unfair disadvantage to students who misunderstand one item but truly know all the other answers; if they choose one incorrect answer, they must also, by process of elimination, choose a second incorrect answer, because it's the only option left.

Make it easy for students who know the material to find the correct answer. Make the longer statements the "questions" and limit the answer key to single words or short phrases. For example, list definitions as the "questions" and the terms they define as the options, or list accomplishments as the "questions" and the persons achieving them as the options. Otherwise students will need to continually scan through a list of lengthy options to find the correct answers, penalizing those who have learned the material but are slow readers. Limit the number of matching items in a set to no more than 10 to 15, and keep the entire exercise on one page. Arrange the options in a logical order (usually alphabetically).

Give clear directions. In an introductory sentence, explain how the two columns are related (e.g., "Match each theory with the person who conceived it"). Point out that some options may be used more than once and others not at all; your students may never have seen this kind of matching set before. Give each column an explanatory title (e.g., "Theory" and "Originator") if that would be helpful.

Be inventive! As noted earlier, the answer key need not be words or phrases in a column; it can be lettered parts of a diagram, drawing, map, chart, and so on.

WHAT ABOUT COMPLETION OR FILL-IN-THE-BLANK ITEMS?

Completion items are multiple-choice items with no options provided. A *completion* or *short-answer* item poses a question that students answer with a word, number, or symbol. A *fill-in-the-blank* item is a completion item posed as a sentence with a missing word, number, or symbol.

To be true objective items, completion items should have *only one correct answer*. Recall the definition of an objective test given earlier in this chapter: A test is objective if a reasonably competent eight-year-old armed with an answer key can score it accurately. True completion items can be scored in this fashion. Many "short-answer" items are really *subjective*, with a number of acceptable answers that require professional judgement to score. While such subjective items may be an appropriate part of an assessment program, considering the time they take to score and the limited information they provide, performance assessments (see Chapter 8) may be a better choice, as they assess thinking skills and give students more opportunities to acquire and demonstrate deep, lasting learning.

Completion items are a good choice to assess those essential facts that must be memorized and should not be guessed from multiple-choice items. They are also appropriate when the correct answer would be easy to recognize in a multiple-choice format. Completion items are widely used in mathematics, especially when a test-wise student might deduce the correct multiple-choice answer by working backwards from each option. They can be a good way to develop multiple-choice distracters for future tests: simply choose the most common incorrect answers as item foils.

Truly objective completion items rarely assess thinking skills except in mathematics. Because scoring is difficult to automate, this format is not a good choice for large-scale assessment programs.

Writing Good Completion Items

The key to writing truly objective completion items is designing them so that *one specific word, number, or symbol* is the *only* correct answer. The following suggestions will help make completion items effective.

Keep all blanks or spaces for recording answers of uniform length, or they will give test-wise students clues. To facilitate scoring, have students record all their answers in a column on one side of the page. If you are using fill-in-the-blank items, make the blanks in the sentences very short placeholders and have students write their answers in a column of longer blanks.

If you are using fill-in-the-blank items, **structure the sentences so the blanks are toward the ends of the sentences;** they will be easier for your students to understand than if the blanks are at the beginning.

Avoid lifting sentences out of a textbook; too often the resulting items are ambiguous or focus on trivia.

WHAT ARE INTERPRETIVE EXERCISES?

Interpretive exercises, sometimes referred to as *context-dependent* or *enhanced multiple-choice* items or *scenario testing,* consist of a stimulus, such as a reading passage or a chart, that students haven't seen before, followed by a set of objective items. If you've ever looked at the SAT–Verbal or most published achievement tests, you've seen interpretive exercises.

Interpretive exercises have three defining characteristics.

First, **the stimulus material must be new to the students;** they must never have seen it before. This requires students to apply what they've learned to a new situation, making interpretive exercises a good way to assess application skills.

Second, **students must have to read or examine the material** in order to answer the objective items that follow. They should not be able to answer any of the items simply from their general understanding of what they've learned in your course or program. Again, this makes the exercise an assessment of application skill rather than simple conceptual understanding.

Third, **the items must be objective,** with one and only one correct answer for each item. If you ask students to write or otherwise create something in response to the stimulus, you have a performance assessment, not an interpretive exercise. Chapter 8 discusses how to create effective performance assessments.

While all interpretive exercises, by definition, assess skill in applying knowledge and skills to new situations, interpretive exercises can also assess skill in generalizing, inferring, concluding, problem solving, and analysis. Performance assessments can also assess these skills, but interpretive exercises are more efficient: Given the same amount of work time, students will give you information on a broader range of skills than they can through performance assessments, and you can score interpretive exercises more quickly.

Interpretive exercises are not always appropriate, however. As with other objective items, they can be difficult and time-consuming to write. If the stimuli are reading passages, interpretive exercises may unfairly penalize students who have the knowledge and skills you are assessing but are slow readers. And, while interpretive exercises are very good for assessing some thinking skills, they cannot assess many other important thinking skills such as the abilities to organize, define problems, and create.

Writing Good Interpretive Exercises

The key to writing good interpretive exercises is to keep in mind their three defining characteristics: 1) They have a stimulus that the students haven't seen before, 2) the students must read or study the stimulus in order to answer the items that follow, and 3) the items must be objective. The following suggestions will help you create effective interpretive exercises. Figure 11.4 is an example of an interpretive exercise that follows most of these suggestions.

Keep the size of stimulus in proportion to the questions asked. Having students read a full page of text in order to answer only three questions is hardly an efficient use of their time. Generally, aim to ask at least three questions about any stimulus, and ask more about longer stimuli.

Be on the lookout for interlocking items, which seem to crop up more often in this format.

Give students realistic scenarios, such as:

- A description of a real or imaginary scenario, such as a scientific experiment or a business situation.

- A brief statement written by a scholar, researcher, or other significant individual.

- A passage from a novel, short story, or poem.

- A chart, diagram, map, or drawing with real or hypothetical information.

- For foreign language courses and programs, any of the above written in a foreign language.

Be creative! Remember that the stimulus need not be a reading passage; it can be a diagram, or picture, or chart, as shown in Figure 11.4

HOW SHOULD AN OBJECTIVE TEST BE ASSEMBLED?

Before assembling items into a test, review them in terms of the following:

- **Do the items follow the test blueprint?** Do they each assess an important learning outcome, or are any of them trick questions that ask about trivia? Are the formats and content appropriate for the learning goals you're assessing?

- **Are the items at an appropriate reading level?** Other than vocabulary terms that you're specifically assessing, are the items simple, clear and straightforward? Are they free of excessive verbiage?

- **Would experts agree on the answers?**

- **Are the items of appropriate difficulty?** Ideally, there should be a few easy items on fundamental concepts that virtually everyone

Figure 11.4

An Interpretive Exercise on Assessment Concepts

Correct answers are in **boldface**. (Item analysis is discussed in Chapter 14.)

Items 1–5 refer to the item analysis information given below. The correct options are marked with an *.

Item 1	A	B*	C	D
Top third		10		
Bottom third	1	4	3	2

Item 2	A*	B	C	D
Top third	8			2
Bottom third		7	3	

Item 3	A	B	C*	D
Top third	5		1	4
Bottom third	2		4	4

Item 4	A*	B	C	D
Top third	10			
Bottom third	9	1		

Write the item number (1, 2, 3, or 4) in the space provided.

1) **4** Which item is easiest?
2) **3** Which item shows negative (i.e., very bad) discrimination?
3) **2** Which item discriminates best between high and low scores?

For the remaining items, write the option letter (A, B, C, or D) in the space provided.

4) **B** In Item 2, which distracter is most effective?
5) **A** In Item 3, which distracter must be changed?

answers correctly, and perhaps a few items that challenge the most knowledgeable students. An excessively difficult test, no matter how you curve the scores, is frustrating and demoralizing. See Chapter 14 for further discussion of item difficulty.

- **Are there any interlocking items** or items with any other clues for test-wise students?

Next, order your items. The first items should be the easiest ones, to reassure the test-anxious, and quickly answered, to help those who aren't test-wise. The last items should be the most difficult and the most complex (requiring the most thinking time). Interpretive exercises often go toward the end.

Next, write directions that explain:

- The purpose of the test.

- How the answers will be scored.

- How to answer (Can they choose more than one answer? Should they choose the one *best* answer? Is guessing encouraged?).

- How to record answers.

- Any time limits (if the test is lengthy and timed—a two-hour final exam, for example—you may want to suggest time limits for each section).

Finally, let the test sit for 24 hours, and then proofread it one last time. Prepare the scoring key *before* the test is duplicated, as the process of preparing the key can identify typos and unclear items missed in earlier readings.

SHOULD STUDENTS EXPLAIN THEIR ANSWERS TO OBJECTIVE ITEMS?

As noted earlier, a major concern with objective items, especially true-false items, is the possibility that students who haven't learned the material can still guess the correct answer. One way to solve this problem is to ask students to write brief explanations of why they chose their answer. For true-false items, students can be asked to correct any statements they mark as false.

While this does eliminate the possibility of students blind-guessing the correct answer, it also removes one of the primary advantages of objective items: their efficiency. Students won't be able to answer as many questions in a given amount of testing time, so the test will assess a narrower range of goals. And, rather than having a scanner or a competent eight-year-old score the tests, you must read every answer and use your professional judgment to decide which are correct and which are not, which takes far more of your time.

If you want students to explain their answers, consider instead giving them an assignment or essay question (see Chapter 8) for which they must compose a more complete written response. This will elicit deeper thought, give you richer assessment information, and give your students a better learning experience.

SHOULD STUDENTS BE ENCOURAGED TO GUESS?

In a word, yes. The "correction for guessing" used on some published tests tries to equate the scores of students who answer questions randomly and those who leave questions blank. Test-wise students readily guess on items they're not sure of, knowing that if they can eliminate even one option as implausible, they raise their odds of guessing correctly beyond random chance. If students who aren't test-wise aren't encouraged to guess, they're being unfairly penalized for not being sufficiently test-savvy.

TIME TO THINK, DISCUSS, AND PRACTICE

Write each of the following for a unit or concept that you teach or have studied, following as many of the guidelines in this chapter as you can. Share your drafts with group members for comments and suggestions.

1) Six multiple-choice items

2) A set of matching items

3) An interpretive exercise

RECOMMENDED READING

Carey, L. M. (1994). *Measuring and evaluating school learning* (2nd ed.). Boston, MA: Allyn & Bacon.

Clegg, V. L., & Cashin, W. E. (1995). *Improving multiple choice tests* (IDEA Paper No. 16). Manhattan, KS: Kansas State University, Center for Faculty Evaluation and Development.

Frary, R. B. (1995). More multiple-choice item writing do's and don'ts. *Practical Assessment, Research & Evaluation, 4*(11). Retrieved February 15, 2004, from http://www.pareonline.net/getvn.asp?v=4&n=11

Gronlund, N. E. (2002). *Assessment of student achievement* (7th ed.). Boston, MA: Allyn & Bacon.

Haladyna, T. M. (1997). *Writing test items to evaluate higher order thinking.* Boston, MA: Allyn & Bacon.

Haladyna, T. M. (1999). *Developing and validating multiple choice items.* Boston, MA: Allyn & Bacon.

Jacobs, L. C., & Chase, C. I. (1992). *Developing and using tests effectively: A guide for faculty.* San Francisco, CA: Jossey-Bass.

Kehoe, J. (1995). Writing multiple-choice items. *Practical Assessment, Research & Evaluation, 4*(9). Retrieved February 15, 2004, from http://www.pareonline.net/getvn.asp?v=4&n=9

Kubiszyn, T., & Borich, G. D. (2002). *Educational testing and measurement: Classroom application and management* (7th ed.). San Francisco, CA: Jossey-Bass.

Linn, R. L., & Gronlund, N. E. (2000). *Measurement and assessment in teaching* (8th ed.). New York, NY: Macmillan.

Mehrens, W. A., & Lehman, I. J. (1991). *Measurement and evaluation in education and psychology* (4th ed.). Fort Worth, TX: Harcourt Brace.

12

Conducting Surveys, Focus Groups, and Interviews

As discussed in Chapter 6, collecting examples of the student work addressed in Chapters 7–11—hands-on assignments and tests—can give an incomplete picture of student learning. These kinds of assessments help us learn what students have or haven't learned, but they may not tell us *why* students are or aren't successful. To understand better how we are helping students learn and how we might improve what we do, we need to understand learning inputs and processes. Surveys, focus groups, and individual interviews—all discussed in this chapter—can help us understand student backgrounds, experiences, and attitudes and thereby draw a richer picture of the learning experience.

WHAT ARE SURVEYS, INTERVIEWS, AND FOCUS GROUPS?

Surveys are systematic efforts to collect information about people by asking them to respond to specific questions. While *tests* collect information on what students have learned, surveys collect information on other things, such as students' backgrounds, experiences, plans, opinions and attitudes. Survey participants can respond by completing a paper or web-based questionnaire or by answering questions asked over the telephone or in person by an interviewer who records their answers.

Questionnaire surveys usually ask for very brief responses, such as a rating or a number; participants are rarely asked to provide more than a word or two in response to any one question. Because questionnaires are usually structured to yield predetermined responses, such as ratings on an established scale, their results are usually quantitative (see Chapter 6) and can be easily tabulated and sometimes analyzed statistically (see Chapter 14).

Interviews usually consist of open-ended questions asked by an interviewer over the telephone or in person, although people can be asked short, questionnaire-type questions in these settings as well. *Focus groups* are in-person interviews of small, often homogeneous groups of people. Because interview and focus-group responses can be wide-ranging and generally do not yield numeric results, qualitative techniques (see Chapter 9) are typically used to look for response patterns and themes.

HOW MIGHT SURVEYS AND INTERVIEWS BE PART OF AN ASSESSMENT PROGRAM?

People who might contribute useful information related to student learning through surveys or interviews include the following.

- **Current students** can describe their backgrounds, opinions, attitudes, experiences, and plans. Student self-ratings are discussed in Chapter 9, and student evaluations of peers are discussed in Chapter 7.

- **Graduating students** can describe their overall experiences with a program or institution and their opinions regarding it.

- **Alumni** can describe their post-graduation experiences and their sense of their program from the perspective of their current activities, such as how well the program prepared them for their current position.

- **Current and prospective employers** of alumni can provide valuable information about employer needs and how well a program or institution prepares students for careers in their businesses. Because of liability issues, employers will generally refuse to give information about individual employees, so ask them instead for general perceptions of a program or institution and its graduates (e.g., "How well does Jamesville College prepare students in terms of analytical skills?").

- **Supervisors of students in field experiences** can be a fountain of information on how well students are demonstrating their knowledge and skills in real-life work. A carefully constructed evaluation form can provide direct and compelling evidence of how well students have achieved critical program goals.

What About Students Who Leave Before Graduating?

While it's tempting to try to survey or interview students in the process of dropping out of your institution or shortly thereafter, researchers have found that these can be the worst times to try to collect information. Because many of these students are disenfranchised from your institution by the time they decide to leave, they will say they're leaving because of "financial difficulties" or "personal reasons"—pat answers that are often only the symptoms of underlying problems. Furthermore, once students have left, they can be difficult to track down, resulting in a poor participation rate. You'll get far better information if you survey appropriate cohorts of currently enrolled students (such as first-year students or high-risk groups), hold the results for a term or year, find out who's still enrolled and who has left, and compare the two groups for differences in responses.

WHICH SURVEY FORMAT SHOULD YOU USE?

Surveys can be conducted as mailed questionnaires, web-based and other electronic questionnaires, questionnaires administered in person (such as in a class or at a meeting), telephone interviews, in-person interviews, and focus groups. Which format you choose depends on several factors.

What Do You Need?

Because questionnaire surveys often yield quantitative information and are designed to draw inferences about a larger group of students, they are a good choice if:

- You want to learn about the experiences, views, or plans of a large group of students.

- You want participants to make simple ratings or provide other very short responses.

- The audience for your results will have more confidence in rigorous, quantitative research.

- Your assessment has the potential to lead to major decisions or is likely to be controversial and therefore needs the credibility of hundreds of responses.

Telephone surveys are a good choice if you have only a few questions and the questions and responses are short and simple. If your questions are lengthy and/or you have a complex rating scale (with five or more potential responses), the survey will be difficult to administer over the telephone and you should consider a paper or web-based survey.

While interviews and focus groups are not the best choice for making inferences about a large group of students, they can nonetheless have an important role in an assessment program as they can help:

- Plan an assessment, by identifying goals, issues, and questions that your assessment efforts should address.

- Corroborate the results of quantitative assessments. If a questionnaire survey, for example, yields a finding that your audience is likely to dispute, corroborating your finding with some focus groups strengthens the credibility of your results.

- Understand the results of quantitative assessments. If your students' academic performance is disappointing, for example, some focus groups can help you understand why your students didn't meet your expectations.

How Sensitive Are Your Questions?

While you will, of course, keep participants' responses absolutely confidential, participants may be more reluctant to provide information on sensitive topics through some formats. Confidentiality in focus groups is a particular concern because you cannot guarantee that other participants will keep responses confidential. While anonymous paper questionnaires offer participants the most convincing assurances of absolute confidentiality, if they are mailed they can suffer from low participation rates because targeted follow-up contacts aren't possible.

Who Are Your Participants?

Not all groups are equally accessible through all formats. Questionnaires administered in person to a "trapped audience" such as a class have a higher participation rate than other formats, but this format isn't suitable if the students you want to survey aren't in one place at one time.

Another consideration is how comfortable your participants are with each format. Web-based surveys might be very successful with first-year students, less so with older alumni. If you are considering a telephone survey, think about how likely your participants are to be home when you call and to use voicemail to screen all incoming calls.

The success of mailed, web-based, and telephone surveys also depends in part on the completeness and accuracy of participants' contact information. Sometimes email addresses are more up-to-date than telephone numbers and mailing addresses, but sometimes not.

What Is the Cost?

The costs of surveys and interviews vary by format and can include the following.

Technological support. Web-based questionnaire surveys require special software or programming expertise. Focus groups sometimes require audio- or videotaping and transcription. Telephone surveys require access to telephones and low long-distance rates (if you are calling people off campus), and they're more effective if they're "computer assisted," with software that lists questions on a computer screen and lets interviewers immediately enter responses into a database. Paper questionnaire surveys do not require special software, but data entry and analysis is faster and smoother if the surveys are created using "bubble" fonts or software that let them be processed with a high-speed scanner.

Staff time. All surveys and interviews take time to plan and administer. Telephone surveys, in-person interviews, and focus groups can be the most expensive because of the staff time required to conduct them; using volunteers can reduce the cost but may affect quality. Web-based surveys and computer-assisted telephone surveys don't require staff time to enter the results into a database (see Chapter 14); other formats do.

Printing and postage. Paper questionnaires must be duplicated; mailed paper questionnaires also require envelopes and postage (unless the questionnaires are distributed and returned via campus mail).

How Much Time Do You Have?

Mailed questionnaire surveys cannot be conducted quickly because of the time it takes for mail to be delivered, both going and coming. Other survey and interview formats can often be undertaken more quickly, especially if you have sufficient staff and technological support.

WHAT MIGHT SURVEY QUESTIONS LOOK LIKE?

Survey and interview questions can follow several formats.

Multiple-Choice Questions

Multiple-choice survey questions, just like multiple-choice test questions (Chapter 11), consist of a question or stem followed by a set of answers from which participants choose. Their main advantages are that they can be answered quickly and the responses tallied easily; their main disadvantage is that respondents can choose only from the responses provided. To create effective multiple-choice survey questions, follow the suggestions for multiple-choice test questions in Chapter 11.

Rankings

In ranking items, participants are asked to number all responses, or perhaps the top three, according to specified criteria. Alumni might be asked, for example, to rank a list of thinking skills according to their importance in their career.

Rankings have serious weaknesses. First, they can be tedious to complete; participants must reread the list repeatedly as they are ranking it. Second, the format does not allow ties; it incorrectly assumes that participants feel differently about every item on the list when this is often not true. Third, the format doesn't provide information on the size of the gaps between rankings; does Todd have a big difference in his opinion of what he ranked first and second, or is the difference negligible?

Because of these limitations, avoid rankings. Rating scales, discussed below, are just as easy to create and will provide far more useful information.

Rating Scales

Likert (pronounced Lick-ert) scales are probably the best-known rating scales, usually characterized by the descriptors "strongly agree," "agree," "disagree," and "strongly disagree." Rating scales can use any other descriptors that span a spectrum (e.g., excellent to poor, frequently to never, very positive to very negative, very comfortable to very uncomfortable, strongly approve to strongly disapprove, much better to much worse). Letter grades (A, B, C, D, and E or F) can be a good choice when asking for evaluations because they are universally understood. Figure 12.1 is an example of a rating scale survey of graduating students.

Rating scales are a good choice for many questionnaires because they are efficient (a great deal of information can be obtained quickly and compactly) and permit comparisons among answers within the scale. Faculty using the survey in Figure 12.1, for example, can compare graduates' opinions of their ability to work in teams against their ability to communicate effectively. If you use a rating scale in your survey, follow the suggestions for rating scale rubrics in Chapter 7 plus the following tips.

Label each response category with names, not just numbers. Don't ask, for example, for a rating of 1 through 5, with 1 being most and 5 being least. People will have different conceptions of 2, 3, and 4 unless you spell them out.

Don't use more than seven response categories; people often can't distinguish consistently among more than seven points. Usually four or five are plenty.

Take care to write unambiguous items for Likert scales. Think of the very different people who might disagree with "My math course requires as much time and effort as other courses."

Include some statements presenting a negative or opposing view. This will help prevent the "yeasayer/naysayer" effect, in which some people with generally positive feelings toward your topic may check all the "strongly agree" responses without reading each item and those with generally negative feelings may do the opposite.

Use a "Neutral" or "Neither agree nor disagree" column in the center of a Likert scale if it's inappropriate to force your participants to agree or disagree. If you are surveying students on whether "The instructor spoke clearly," for example, it could be argued that the instructor either spoke clearly or didn't, and every student should be able to either agree or disagree with this statement. But for other statements, such as "The library facilities are conducive to study," it could be argued that some students might be truly neutral.

Ecosystem Rating Scales

An *ecosystem* rating scale (also known as *goal attainment scaling* or *gap analysis*) asks for two ratings, with the second rating giving information on the environment in which the first rating was made and thus helping us interpret the first rating. In Figure 12.2, students are asked to rate each goal twice: first on the growth *obtained* and second on the growth *desired*. In Figure 9.2 in Chapter 9, students are asked to rate each goal first on their skill level and second on how much library sessions have helped them develop each skill.

As these examples show, ecosystems can be a very good way to evaluate the attainment of goals and objectives, as responses in the second column greatly improve interpretation of the first. Suppose, for example, that the first two goals in Figure 12.2 both receive low "growth obtained" ratings, but the "limitations of our current knowledge" item receives a high "growth desired" rating, while "nature of science" item receives a low "growth desired" rating. The second ratings help us understand that the two low "growth obtained" ratings represent very different situations. The results for the first item are of concern because students view this as an important goal but feel they did not learn much. The results for the second item, meanwhile, are also of concern but for a different reason: Students have apparently also failed to develop an appreciation of the importance of this goal.

Ecosystems can ask for many kinds of information. The first rating might ask, for example, for the participant's satisfaction with various aspects of a program and the second for the relative importance or value of each aspect or how much the participant participated in each aspect.

Open-Ended Questions

Open-ended questions allow participants to compose their own answers. While open-ended questions are critical elements of interviews and focus groups, they are usually not very popular with ques-tionnaire recipients, because they lengthen the time required to complete the questionnaire and require more mental energy to respond. Very often participants will

Figure 12.1

An Exit Survey for Students Completing a B.S. in Computer Information Systems

Please tell us how well each CIS program learning goal was met for you personally. For each objective, please check the one response that best reflects your feelings, opinions, and/or experiences.

SA = Strongly Agree

A = Agree

U = Unsure

D = Disagree

SD = Strongly Disagree

This objective was met for me:	SA	A	U	D	SD
Graduates will:					
1) Have a thorough grounding in key IS principles and practices and the quantitative analysis principles that underpin them.	❑	❑	❑	❑	❑
a) Demonstrate proficiency with IS tools, IS analysis and design, and the role of IS in organizations.	❑	❑	❑	❑	❑
b) Demonstrate proficiency in relevant aspects of quantitative analysis.	❑	❑	❑	❑	❑
2) Understand the quantitative and business principles that underlie IS principles and practices.	❑	❑	❑	❑	❑
a) Understand calculus and statistics.	❑	❑	❑	❑	❑
b) Understand basic principles of accounting and economics.	❑	❑	❑	❑	❑
3) Be informed and involved members of their communities and responsible IS professionals.	❑	❑	❑	❑	❑
a) Be familiar with basic concepts and contemporary issues in the social sciences and humanities.	❑	❑	❑	❑	❑
b) Understand global, social, professional, and ethical considerations related to IS.	❑	❑	❑	❑	❑

This objective was met for me:	SA	A	U	D	SD
Graduates will:					
4) Have appropriate social and organizational skills.	❑	❑	❑	❑	❑
a) Be able to work effectively in teams.	❑	❑	❑	❑	❑
b) Be able to communicate effectively.	❑	❑	❑	❑	❑
5) Be able to acquire new knowledge in the information systems discipline and engage in lifelong learning.	❑	❑	❑	❑	❑

Adapted with permission from a survey developed by the faculty of the Department of Computer and Information Sciences at Towson University.

Figure 12.2

An Ecosystem Assessing General Education Growth

For each goal statement, please make **two** ratings: the first on how much you **grew** in terms of this goal during the program, and the second on how much you **wanted to grow** in terms of this goal during the program. For both ratings, enter the appropriate number:

4 = a great deal

3 = somewhat

2 = a little

1 = not at all

	Growth Obtained	Growth Desired
1) An appreciation of the limitations of our current knowledge	❑	❑
2) An understanding of the nature of science and scientific research	❑	❑
3) An awareness of the value of pursuing lifelong education	❑	❑
4) Skill in writing effectively	❑	❑

simply leave them blank! Open-ended items are therefore best used sparingly in questionnaires, specifically when:

- Many answers (more than six or seven) are possible.

- You are asking for occupation.

- A structured questionnaire item (multiple-choice or rating scale) might bias responses by steering participants in a particular direction.

- Your question is interesting enough that people will want to answer it. For example, people enjoy being asked, "How would you improve . . . ?"

If you find that a questionnaire survey you are developing is largely composed of open-ended questions, consider switching your survey format to focus groups or interviews.

WHAT ARE THE KEYS TO WRITING GOOD QUESTIONS?

The fundamental characteristic of a good survey or interview question is that it is *clearly understood*. If participants find your question difficult to understand or answer, they may answer what they think is the spirit of the question rather than the question itself, and their interpretation may not match your intent. The following strategies will help participants interpret questions as intended.

Keep questions short. Short, straightforward items are usually easier to understand than complex statements. They also mean a shorter survey and therefore, as discussed later, an increased participation rate.

Make sure each item asks only one question. A "double-barreled" item such as, "Is this job a step toward your career goal or related to your major?" asks two questions that might each be answered differently. To avoid double-barreled questions, check your use of the words "and" and "or" and limit your questions to one adjective or adverb each.

Keep questions understandable. Keep your vocabulary simple. Avoid the jargon of your field or of higher education (e.g., "attrition," "articulation"). Avoid negative words like "not," as participants may overlook them. If you must use negative words, underline them and/or put them in all capital letters or boldface (**NOT, EXCEPT**) to draw attention to them.

Make definitions, assumptions, and qualifiers clearly understood. Terms like "adequate," "minority," "value," "usually," "access," "convenient," "most," "quality," "diversity," "acceptable," "often," and "now" are full of ambiguities.

Avoid making significant memory demands. Asking, "How many times did you visit the library last week?" will give you more accurate information than asking, "How many times did you visit the library last year?"

Avoid asking for very precise responses. Questions asking annual salary to the exact dollar or grade point average to two decimal places will probably not be answered accurately. Rather than ask for precise amounts, use a multiple-choice format that asks participants to choose from ranges of responses.

Avoid asking for broad generalizations about attitudes or opinions. It's easier for people to describe concrete actions accurately than to make accurate generalizations, especially about their feelings or opinions. Instead of asking, "Do you consider yourself a hard-working student?" ask, "How many hours per day do you usually study?" or "How many hours did you study yesterday?"

Avoid biased, loaded, leading, or sensitive questions. While no ethical researcher purposely writes biased questions, it's easy to write them inadvertently. To avoid such questions:

- *Imagine you're writing questions from the opposite point of view.* If you're trying to collect information to support the need for increased funding for library materials, for example, imagine you're trying to cut back on funding (difficult though this may be for you!). Would you still ask the same questions and phrase them the same way?

- *Ask about both the pros and cons of an issue.* Don't ask participants to make criticisms without giving them a chance to praise as well. Don't ask participants if they favor extending the hours that an office is open (who wouldn't?) without noting the costs and liabilities.

- *Avoid questions that people are uncomfortable answering honestly.* People tend to be comfortable with the status quo, to deceive themselves about their propensities in sensitive areas, and to be reluctant to admit inferiority or wrongdoing. Researchers have found that many people will not answer honestly when asked if they smoke, watch TV, go to art museums or religious services, or vote. Many will also not report accurately their salary, their age, their job, their grade point average, or whether they failed a particular course.

- *If appropriate, let people admit that they don't know or can't remember.* Forcing an opinion from people who don't have one or a memory from people who can't remember one is tantamount to forcing them to lie.

- *Use multiple assessments with a variety of formats,* as discussed in Chapter 2, to corroborate survey results.

WHAT ARE THE KEYS TO CREATING AN EFFECTIVE QUESTIONNAIRE OR INTERVIEW SCRIPT?

Once individual questions and rating scales have been created, they must be pulled together into a complete questionnaire or interview script that spurs active, engaged responses.

Keep the questionnaire or script short. The shorter the questionnaire or interview, the less formidable it appears and the higher the participation rate. Try to keep any questionnaire to no more than *one piece of paper,* a telephone interview to no more than five or ten minutes, and a focus group or in-person interview to no more than thirty minutes (at most, an hour). If your survey or interview is longer, you're probably trying to cover too much ground at one time. Review the questions posed in Chapter 4 about the purpose of your assessment and make sure the survey or interview focuses only on essential issues.

Make the first questions interesting. The first questions should hook participants into the survey or interview and should therefore be *intriguing,* the kind of questions that make participants think, "I'm glad they asked me that! I've always wanted to tell someone what I thought about that!" Perhaps you could ask for an opinion on an interesting (but, at this point, relatively benign) topic, such as why participants chose to enroll in a particular course, program, or institution. The first questions should also be *easy to answer.* They should not require a lot of deep thought and, if you are using a questionnaire, should be answerable with something like a simple check mark or mouse click.

The last questions should be the ones your participants will be least enthused about answering. We hope that by this point they are indeed hooked and willing to answer these last few questions, which may include:

- *Boring questions,* including demographic items (make sure you really need each piece of demographic information, as your participants will find them irritants at best).

- *Complex questions* that take time to read or a lot of thought to answer.

- *Delicate, intimate, or sensitive questions* such as those on age, salary, personal habits such as whether the participant smokes, and sensitive or controversial subjects.

- If you are using a questionnaire, *open-ended questions* since these take time to answer.

Use survey software. Commercial survey software can help create scannable paper questionnaires, web-based questionnaires, and online scripts and response entry forms for computer-assisted telephone interviews. Chapter 4 gives suggestions for identifying and evaluating software.

WHAT IS AN ACCEPTABLE PARTICIPATION RATE?

There are both simple and complex answers to this question. The simple answer is that most survey experts aim to have 70% to 80% of those contacted participate in a survey or interview and consider a 50% participation rate minimally adequate. (Professional pollsters get well over 95%.)

The complex answer is that the *quality* of responses is more important than the *quantity*. Having participants who are representative of the group from which you're sampling can be more important evidence of your survey's credibility than its participation rate. Imagine that faculty at two very large universities, each graduating about 8,000 students annually, want to learn about their seniors' self-perceptions of their thinking skills. Faculty at Eastern State University send a survey to all 8,000 seniors, of which 400 are returned. Faculty at Western State University choose a random sample of 600 seniors and not only send them a survey but also make strong efforts to convince them to complete and return the survey and, as a result, 360 are returned.

Which is the better approach? While more students completed Eastern State's survey, its response rate is only 5%. This makes it unlikely that the respondents represent all seniors. Some cohorts may be underrepresented (perhaps students in certain majors or students with certain experiences), which calls the value of the survey into question. Western State's survey, on the other hand, yields a more respectable 60% response rate, which gives us more confidence that the respondents are a good cross-section of all seniors, even though the number of returned surveys is smaller. Western State's approach may, furthermore, be more cost effective; it may be less expensive to survey 600 students intensively than 8,000 scattershot.

Relatively small-scale assessments with high participation rates may thus yield more credible results than larger assessments with low participation rates. No matter what your participation rate is, collect demographic information on your participants and, when you share your results, provide your participation rate and describe how representative your participants are of the group you're surveying (see Chapter 14), so audience members can judge for themselves how credible the survey results are.

How Can You Maximize Your Participation Rate?

Four factors probably have the most effect on participation rates:

- **The nature of your questions.** A survey asking for simple, non-threatening opinions will generally get a higher participation rate than one asking for opinions on a sensitive issue.

- **The people you are surveying.** Students who have been dismissed from your institution will be less likely to participate in a survey, for example, than students in good standing.

- **How professional and important the survey appears.** If the survey appears professional and important, your participants' contribution will seem much more worthwhile and they'll be more likely to participate.

- **How considerate you are of your participants.** Recognize that you have no right to expect anyone to go to the trouble of filling out a form or spending time in a focus group and that your participants are doing you a great favor when they do. If you show your appreciation by doing all you can to minimize their trouble and make their job as easy as possible, they will be much more likely to participate and give you sound, useful information.

There's usually not much that can be done about the first two factors; you probably cannot change the basic subject of the survey or the students who must be contacted. But you can do many things about the last two factors—*being professional and considerate of your participants*—and thereby maximize your participation rate. Tables 12.1 and 12.2 list questions you can ask to check how considerate you are and how professional you appear.

Of all the strategies noted in Tables 12.1 and 12.2, *follow-up contacts are more effective than any other single technique for increasing participation*. Each follow-up contact will typically yield an additional 50% beyond the previous contact. Thus, if you get a 30% response to your first contact, you can expect an additional 15% from your second contact and another 7% if you do a third—a total participation rate of over 50%. Follow-up contacts can thus almost double your participation rate. Another important reason to send follow-up contacts is that late participants sometimes differ significantly from early ones, and including them gives a more complete picture.

WHAT ABOUT CONDUCTING AN IN-PERSON QUESTIONNAIRE SURVEY?

Here are some tips that will help an in-person administration yield good-quality results.

Prepare a statement to read to the group explaining the nature and purpose of the survey and soliciting the group's help.

If you are administering the survey to two or more groups, **keep your directions identical** from one group to the next. If several people are administering the survey, make sure they all administer the survey

Table 12.1

How Considerate Are You of Your Participants?

- **How long is your questionnaire or interview?** The shorter it is, the more considerate you are of your participants' time.
- **How long does your questionnaire appear to be?** A cluttered page of minuscule type looks long and complicated.
- **How clear are the questions?** Must participants spend time trying to figure out what you really mean?
- **Was the questionnaire or interview pre-tested?** If it wasn't, you can't be sure your questions are truly clear.
- **When is the survey mailed or the interview scheduled?** Is it at a time when participants are busy with other matters, such as before a holiday or during finals week?
- **Is a postage-paid, addressed return envelope enclosed with a mailed questionnaire?** If it isn't, you're telling participants that you really don't care whether you hear from them or not.
- **Do you offer a summary of the findings,** so participants can see the impact of their efforts?
- **Have you brainstormed all possible reasons** for people not to participate? Have you done all you can to overcome those obstacles?

in the same way. Try to anticipate questions so everyone will give roughly the same answers.

Repeat key parts of your spoken statement at the top of the questionnaire.

Establish an atmosphere in which participants feel comfortable. Don't let anyone feel obliged to complete the survey unless doing so is a stated requirement.

WHAT ABOUT CONDUCTING A TELEPHONE SURVEY?

Here are some tips that will help a telephone survey yield good-quality results.

- Keep the survey to no more than ten minutes, preferably five.

Table 12.2

How Professional Will Your Survey Appear to Your Participants?

• *Does the invitation convince the reader* that it's worth taking the time to participate? The invitation should:

    – *Make the survey look important* by explaining how participation will make an impact on something significant that participants understand and appreciate. Date the invitation and set a response deadline (two weeks is usually adequate) to give a sense of urgency.

    – *Appeal to participants' self-interest.* Answer their unspoken question, "What's in this for me?" Explain how the results will benefit either participants directly or some cause or issue about which they are concerned.

    – *Address the issue of confidentiality.* Guarantee unconditional confidentiality. If you're using surveys with code numbers or other identifying information, explain why. Stress that you're interested only in aggregate responses.

    – *Be signed by someone meaningful to your participants.* Sad to say, this may not be you! For some alumni surveys, a highly regarded retired faculty member may be perfect. For students, perhaps a popular professor or student life administrator may be best. Having the invitations co-signed by the leader of a respected student organization may also help.

    – *Include someone's name and contact information* should your participants have questions about the survey.

• *Does your invitation to participate note the survey's sponsor?*

• *Does your questionnaire or interview ask interesting, important-sounding questions?*

• *If you are using a questionnaire, is it laid out carefully and grammatically flawless?*

• *Are all written materials cleanly reproduced on quality paper?*

• *If you are using a mailed or web-based questionnaire, will you send follow-up mailings or emails to non-respondents?*

• Keep question formats simple, so directions can be easily understood over the phone. Use simple rating scales, seek one-word responses, and use just a few question formats.

- Avoid many open-ended questions unless you are only seeking a word or two in response; they take too long to record.

- Pre-test the interview by reading it to a few people without looking at them.

- Train interviewers carefully and have them rehearse.

- Send an advance postcard advising participants of the upcoming call.

- Try scheduling an appointment to call.

- Document attempts to reach participants. If you reach an answering machine, leave a message explaining the purpose of your call and saying you'll try again later.

- Make the interviewer's introduction convincing.

- Document the participant's consent to participate.

WHAT ABOUT CONDUCTING FOCUS GROUPS OR INTERVIEWS?

Here are a few tips that will help focus groups and interviews yield good-quality results.

Plan focus group sessions and interviews as carefully as you would any other assessment. Have a clear purpose for the sessions and know how you will use the results; don't let them turn into unfocused gripe sessions.

If you are using focus groups, *plan on conducting several,* not just one or two, because of the possibility that participants' comments in any one group may be dominated by one "opinion driver." Professionals continue conducting focus groups until they begin to hear the same themes expressed repeatedly across groups.

Select a site in a conducive environment that participants find comfortable.

Make sure participants are a representative sample of the group whose thoughts you want to assess.

Offer an inducement to attend. Only rarely will the research topic alone be a sufficient enticement to come. You may need to offer a meal or a gift certificate, reimburse participants for travel expenses, and/or pay them outright.

Select and train interviewers and focus group moderators care-fully. Focusing questions is an art. Focus group moderators must be trained to elicit responses from all participants and keep the talkative few from dominating the session. Write out the moderators' introduction and questions beforehand so sessions stay on track, and arrange to have participants' comments recorded.

Plan questions carefully. They should be broad enough to elicit discussion, yet focused enough to make the replies useful. Some examples:

- "What did you think was the best part of this program?"

- "Tell me one way you would improve this program."

- "How has Bellefonte College helped you be successful here?"

- "What do you think will be the biggest barrier to your finishing your degree?"

SHOULD YOU USE A PUBLISHED SURVEY OR DESIGN YOUR OWN?

A number of published questionnaires are available on subjects such as first-year students' attitudes, student retention, faculty views, alumni satisfaction, and campus climate. Should you participate in these surveys or conduct your own? Chapter 13 discusses the pros and cons of using published assessment instruments, including surveys, and offers advice on how to choose one.

TIME TO THINK, DISCUSS, AND PRACTICE

Faculty in your department would like to survey recent alumni to assess their satisfaction with your program and identify areas for improvement.

1) Decide on the *critical* questions to be answered by the survey. What decisions will the survey results help you make?

2) Draft an ecosystem that could be used in the questionnaire.

3) Draft a question or rating scale that could go at the *beginning* of the questionnaire.

4) Assume the survey will be mailed to a random sample of alumni. Brainstorm *three* feasible strategies to maximize the participation rate.

ACKNOWLEDGMENT

Some of the material in this chapter is adapted from my earlier book, *Questionnaire Survey Research: What Works*, published by the Association for Institutional Research. I am grateful to the association for permission to adapt this material.

RECOMMENDED READING

Couper, M. P. (2000). Web surveys: A review of issues and approaches. *Public Opinion Quarterly, 64,* 464–494.

Cox, J. (1996). *Your opinion please! How to build the best questionnaires in the field of education.* Thousand Oaks, CA: Corwin.

Dillman, D. A. (1999). *Mail and internet surveys: The tailored design method.* New York, NY: John Wiley & Sons.

Ehrmann, S. C. (2003, March 19). *Increasing student response rates by making the study more valuable: A dozen principles of good practice.* Takoma Park, MD: The TLT Group, The Flashlight Program. Retrieved June 2, 2003, from http://www.tltgroup.org/resources/Flashlight/Participation.html

Fowler, F. J., Jr. (2001). *Survey research methods* (3rd ed.). Thousand Oaks, CA: Sage.

Krueger, R. A., & Casey, M. A. (2000). *Focus groups: A practical guide for applied research* (3rd ed.). Thousand Oaks, CA: Sage.

Lavrakas, P. J. (1993). *Telephone survey methods: Sampling, selection, and supervision.* Thousand Oaks, CA: Sage.

Morgan, D. L., & Krueger, R. A. (Eds). (1997). *The focus group kit.* Thousand Oaks, CA: Sage.

Oishi, S. M. (2002). *How to conduct in-person interviews for surveys.* Thousand Oaks, CA: Sage.

Patten, M. L. (2001). *Questionnaire research* (2nd ed.). Los Angeles, CA: Pyrczak.

Rea, L. M., & Parker, R. A. (1997). *Designing and conducting survey research: A comprehensive guide* (2nd ed.). San Francisco, CA: Jossey-Bass.

Salant, P., & Dillman, D. A. (1994). *How to conduct your own survey.* New York, NY: John Wiley & Sons.

Sudman, S., & Bradburn, N. M. (1982). *Asking questions: A practical guide to questionnaire design.* San Francisco, CA: Jossey-Bass.

Suskie, L. A. (1996). *Questionnaire survey research: What works* (2nd ed., Resources for Institutional Research No. 6). Tallahassee, FL: Association for Institutional Research.

13

Selecting a Published Instrument

Published tests and surveys play an important role in many assessment programs. This chapter discusses why published instruments might be useful, how to find potential instruments, and how to evaluate them to determine if they're appropriate for your situation. (Specific instruments mentioned are offered as examples, not necessarily as endorsements.)

WHAT IS A PUBLISHED INSTRUMENT?

Published instruments are those published by an organization and used by a number of institutions. Often, they are copyrighted and a fee must be paid to use them.

A common misconception is that published instruments consist exclusively of multiple-choice or rating-scale questions. While multiple-choice and other "bubble" formats predominate, a number of published instruments ask students to "show their work" or provide writing samples that are evaluated by trained scorers.

Table 13.1 describes four categories of published instruments that may be useful in higher education assessment programs.

WHAT IS A STANDARDIZED INSTRUMENT?

Standardized instruments are those published instruments that are administered and scored under comparable ("standardized") conditions to ensure that scores are comparable across institutions and across time. All students receive exactly the same instructions on how to complete the

Table 13.1

Types of Published Instruments Available for Higher Education Assessment Programs

- Instruments designed to assess the **knowledge and skills acquired in general education curricula**, including the:
  - *Academic Profile*, published by Educational Testing Service.
  - *Collegiate Assessment of Academic Proficiency* (CAAP), published by ACT.
  - *College-Base Examination* (C-Base), published by the University of Missouri.
- Instruments designed to assess the **knowledge and skills acquired in major fields of study**, including:
  - *Major Field Tests* in a variety of subjects, published by Educational Testing Service.
  - *Graduate Record Examinations* in a variety of subjects, also published by Educational Testing Service.
  - Tests published by disciplinary associations and other organizations to assess or certify student learning in specific fields, such as the *National Council Licensure Examination for Registered Nurses* (NCLEX-RN), published by the National Council of State Boards of Nursing.
- Surveys of **student goals, experiences, satisfaction, and plans**, including the:
  - *National Survey of Student Engagement*, published by Indiana University.
  - *Community College Survey of Student Engagement*, published by the Community College Leadership Program of the University of Texas–Austin.
  - *Student Satisfaction Survey*, published by Noel-Levitz.
  - Cooperative Institutional Research Program (CIRP) *Freshman Survey, College Student Survey* (CSS), and *Your First College Year* (YFCY) Survey, published by the Higher Education Research Institute at the University of California at Los Angeles.
  - *First-Year Initiative* survey, published by Educational Benchmarking.
- Instruments **not specifically designed for higher education** that may be nonetheless useful. Examples include:
  - Tests of basic skills such as the *Nelson-Denny Reading Test*, published by Riverside.

Continued on page 246

> – Instruments to identify learning styles such as the *Myers-Briggs Type Indicator,* published by Consulting Psychologists.
>
> – Career interest inventories such as the *Vocational Preference Inventory,* published by Psychological Assessment Resources.

instrument. If there is a time limit for completing the instrument, it is enforced at all administration sites. If there are writing samples that are scored using rubrics, the scorers are trained so that scoring is consistent.

WHY USE A PUBLISHED INSTRUMENT?

Published instruments can add some important dimensions to an assessment program.

They get us out of the ivory tower. Published instruments let us compare our students against those at other institutions. As discussed in Chapter 6, this benchmarking can give a valuable perspective on what students are learning. Without benchmarking, we may think our students are learning a great deal when in fact they are learning less than their peers. Or we may think our findings are disappointing, only to learn that our results are better than those at many peer institutions. The availability of peer information is probably the strongest argument for using a published instrument.

They can have greater perceived legitimacy than locally designed assessments. Board members, legislators, donors, and other external audiences are often more impressed by student performance on a published examination than they are by locally designed tests and rubrics.

They can have good-quality questions. Many publishers design questions in consultation with experts in the field and test them extensively before including them in the published instrument. Yes, there have been many publicized examples of poorly written questions on published instruments, but far more could be found on most locally designed instruments.

They can provide good breadth of coverage. A published chemistry test, for example, may include a broader range of chemical concepts than we might think to include in our own test.

They sometimes enable us to see growth over time. If a published instrument is carefully normed and scored, its information on student growth is more definitive than that obtained through local assessments. A local assessment of student writing at Lancaster University might show, for example, that average rubric scores have grown from 3.7 to 4.2, on a five-point scale, between first and senior years. This looks like good news, but it's difficult to tell if this degree of change is "good enough." A published writing assessment, on the other hand, might show that, while Lancaster first-year students scored at the 40th percentile of first-year students nationally, as seniors they scored at the 75th percentile of seniors nationally. This is more convincing evidence that Lancaster's writing program is successful.

They sometimes have evidence of their quality. Some publishers have made serious efforts to evaluate and document instrument quality. Because publishers may be able to invest more resources in time-consuming and expensive validation studies than an individual campus, their research may be more rigorous and extensive than what might be accomplished locally.

They sometimes allow us to identify strengths and weaknesses. Some instruments provide subscores that can be compared against one another. The *Academic Profile*, for example, provides seven subscores including reading, writing, critical thinking, and mathematics, making it easy to identify relative strengths and weaknesses in student performance.

They require less time to implement. It can take many months of hard work by many people to draft, refine, and pre-test a locally designed survey or test before it is good enough to be usable. Then, once the instrument is developed, scoring, processing, and reporting all need to be handled by campus staff each time the instrument is administered. Published tests and surveys can be researched, adopted, and implemented more quickly and with less work by fewer people.

When Is a Locally Designed Assessment a Better Choice?

While published instruments have definite advantages, a locally designed assessment tool may be a more appropriate choice under the following circumstances.

Your goals and interests don't match the goals and content of available published instruments. If your institution defines critical thinking as the ability to think creatively and the willingness to take risks, most published "critical thinking tests" won't give you the information you're looking for. If a chemistry program focuses on preparing students for entry-level work in medical laboratories, a chemistry test designed to assess preparation for graduate study isn't appropriate. If your institution is primarily or exclusively in the distance-learning business, a survey asking students about their satisfaction with parking, residence halls, and other campus facilities won't be helpful. *A mismatch between an institution's or program's goals and interests and the goals and content of available published instruments is probably the most important reason not to use a published instrument.*

Your students are so atypical that comparing them against other students isn't helpful. Suppose that Roslyn College has many students for whom English is a second language, and who therefore do relatively poorly on typical writing assessments, while many students at Woodwyn College never studied algebra in high school, leaving them far behind typical college students in quantitative skills. In such cases, a locally designed assessment, interpreted using a value-added or longitudinal perspective (see Chapter 6), may be more useful.

You're cash-poor. A single administration of a published instrument can cost thousands of dollars. Some institutions simply don't have this kind of hard cash available, but they do have faculty and staff willing to spend the time developing and administering a locally designed instrument.

HOW CAN POTENTIAL PUBLISHED INSTRUMENTS BE IDENTIFIED?

If you think that a published instrument might be a useful component of an assessment program, collaborate with faculty and staff in the review and decision process. Collaboration contributes to:

- *The quality of your decision,* because faculty and staff are familiar with program goals and curricula.

- *The successful deployment of the instrument,* because this usually requires faculty and staff support.

- (Most important) *the effective use of the results,* because uninvolved faculty and staff may characterize a published instrument as poor quality and inappropriate for their programs. The ensuing debate can make it impossible to use the results to improve student learning experiences.

The first step in identifying potential published instruments is to clarify the instrument's purpose. What learning goals are you trying to assess? What information do you need? How will you use the results? What key decisions will the results inform? How might the results be used to improve student learning or the environment for it? There's no point in surveying students about, say, satisfaction with tutoring services if institutional leaders aren't interested in taking steps to address any shortcomings that the survey identifies.

Once your assessment purpose is clarified, your next step is to identify potential published instruments. The following resources can help.

The **Mental Measurements Yearbook (MMY),** published by the Buros Institute and available in many college libraries, is an excellent source of information on instruments assessing all kinds of mental traits. It includes instrument information, contact information, research citations, and critical reviews by scholars. The Buros web site (http://www.unl.edu/buros/) gives tips on using the MMY and an index of all instruments reviewed by the MMY since 1985.

Tests in Print (TIP), also published by the Buros Institute and available in many college libraries, is another excellent source for identifying potential instruments. It provides information on "all known commercially available tests that are currently in print in the English language," so it is more comprehensive than the Mental Measurements Yearbook, but it lacks MMY's critical reviews and citations.

The NPEC Sourcebook on Assessment, Volume 1: Definitions and Assessment Methods for Critical Thinking, Problem Solving, and Writing (http://nces.ed.gov/pubs2000/2000195.pdf) has descriptions and analyses of many published tests and rubrics assessing critical thinking, problem solving, and writing skills.

The *Assessment Instrument Resource Page* of the Policy Center on the First Year of College (http://www.brevard.edu/fyc/resources/index.htm) has information on many tests and surveys that can be used to assess first-year learning goals.

Web search engines such as Google can also help identify potential instruments.

Professional journals, conferences, and colleagues at other institutions can also be sources of information on potential instruments. A query posted to a disciplinary discussion list can yield useful suggestions. Keep in mind, though, that an instrument used successfully at another institution may not be suitable for your own circumstances.

HOW CAN INFORMATION ON POTENTIAL INSTRUMENTS BE OBTAINED?

Once you have identified potential instruments, the next step is to obtain more information on them from their publishers. Ideally, you should be able to view:

- *A copy of the instrument itself.* Sometimes instruments are available in multiple versions (perhaps a paper version, an online version, a version on CD-ROM, and an abbreviated version). Because of test security or copyright concerns, some publishers will not let you view the actual instrument before purchasing it. Such publishers should, however, let you see enough examples of items—perhaps on an outdated edition of the instrument—to make an informed decision about whether to adopt the instrument.

- *Instructions for administering the instrument.*

- *Ordering information and prices.*

- *How the completed instruments are scored.* Some instruments must be self-scored; others must be sent to the publisher for processing, tabulation, and analysis; and still others give you the option of either approach.

- *How the results are reported to you and prices for each option.* Some publishers offer a variety of report options, with more detailed reports costing more. Some offer reports or even full data sets on disk or CD-ROM as well as on paper, allowing you to manipulate the results yourself, perhaps comparing residential and commuter students or looking only at business majors.

- *Technical information,* including how the instrument was designed, how it was normed, and evidence of its quality (reliability and validity). This information may be posted on the publisher's web site or provided in a manual or as a series of reports.

HOW SHOULD POTENTIAL INSTRUMENTS BE EVALUATED?

Once you have obtained information on each potential instrument, review the information in terms of the following questions.

Does the Instrument's Stated Purpose Match Your Philosophy?

The instrument's publisher should have a statement on the instrument's philosophy and purpose, and that philosophy and purpose should match your own. Some faculty believe, for example, that general education courses in mathematics should emphasize the development of analytical reasoning skills through the study of pure mathematics, while others believe that such courses should emphasize the development of skills for solving real-life problems. The quantitative reasoning test that you choose should match your faculty's philosophy.

Do the Instrument's Objectives Match Your Goals and What You Teach?

Some undergraduate biology programs focus on preparing students for doctoral programs in biology, some are largely pre-med programs, some focus on educating high school biology teachers, some focus on preparing students for entry-level positions in medical laboratories, and some emphasize preparing students for environmental careers. There is probably no one published biology test that is equally appropriate for all these emphases.

It's thus important to compare the knowledge and skills assessed by any published instrument against the learning goals of your curriculum. *The degree of congruence between your learning goals and those covered by the published instrument is the most important consideration in deciding whether to adopt it.* The publisher should provide information on the specific kinds of knowledge and skills assessed by the published instrument. Some publishers provide a test blueprint or table of specifications (see Chapter 11) that lists the content and skills covered by the test. Some publishers go further, identifying the individual test items that assess each learning goal. Review this information carefully and see how well the instrument's goals and content correspond to your goals and curriculum.

Do Suggested Uses of Results Match Your Needs?

The publisher should offer suggested uses of the instrument results and also describe *inappropriate* uses. A quantitative reasoning test designed to assess students' problem solving skills may, for example, be inappropriate for deciding whether to place students into calculus.

Some publishers, recognizing that neither students nor faculty want to spend a great deal of time on tests and surveys, design very short instruments. While these instruments can give good information on how students are doing in general, they usually have too little information to make sound decisions about individual students. Thus, a writing test designed to assess only the overall effectiveness of a writing program may not be appropriate to determine which students need remediation.

Are the Subtests and Subscores What You Need?

As noted earlier in this chapter, some instruments provide subscores on specific skills or content areas being assessed. There's no point in paying for subtests and subscores that you don't need, and there's no point in investing in a test that doesn't provide the subscores that you do need to help decide how to improve student learning. A critical thinking test that provides only a single "critical thinking" score for each student won't help you identify strengths and weaknesses in students' thinking skills or how to improve them.

When Was the Instrument Published? Is It Current?

All instruments should be periodically reviewed and updated to ensure that they reflect current research and theories and don't have obsolete material. How frequently an instrument should be revised depends in part on its subject; a test of technological fluency would obviously have to be updated very frequently, for example.

Is the Instrument Practical to Administer?

Consider the following.

- **Cost:** There may be separate charges for purchasing copies of the instrument, getting them processed, and receiving the results in the format you need.

- *Time required to administer the instrument:* Instruments that take longer than a standard class meeting time require special administration periods that may be difficult for both students and faculty to attend.

- *Administration requirements:* Instruments administered electronically may be inappropriate if a significant number of your students don't have easy access to a computer.

Does the Instrument Have an Appropriate Emphasis on Reading Skills?

Reading skills are essential for success in college and beyond, so it may be appropriate that a test of academic achievement include a lot of reading material to which students must respond. An assessment of English literature majors, for example, should certainly ask students to read and respond to literature passages.

If a test's reading level is too difficult, however, it becomes more a general reading comprehension test than a test of its purported subject. If students do poorly on a sociology test with a difficult reading level, for example, we can't tell if they did poorly because they don't understand sociology concepts or if they understand sociology concepts but are simply slow readers. Highly verbal tests are particularly likely to underrepresent the achievements of students who are not native English speakers and students from disadvantaged backgrounds. Tests that minimize text and maximize the use of charts, diagrams, pictures, numbers, and other nonverbal material may be more fair to these students but give less complete pictures of their performance.

If you're looking for a published survey rather than a test, it's equally important to consider the reading skills required by the instrument. If the survey's reading level is too difficult, some students may misinterpret questions and give erroneous information.

It's therefore important to evaluate the reading skill required to complete an instrument and decide whether the expected skill level is appropriate.

Is the Instrument Biased?

An instrument's technical materials often include information on steps the publisher has taken to reduce bias (see Chapter 2 for a more extensive discussion of fairness and bias in assessment). Some publishers ask people from diverse backgrounds to review items for possible bias, and some discard items on which students from particular backgrounds do unusually poorly. Beyond examining such information, it's also helpful to ask people of diverse backgrounds to review potential instruments and advise you of any concerns they identify.

Does the Instrument Have Convincing Evidence of Its Quality?

As discussed in Chapter 2, a good-quality assessment instrument yields accurate, truthful information regarding whatever the instrument purports to measure. Psychometricians refer to this attribute as *validity*. While technical materials should provide evidence of an instrument's validity, keep in mind that the most important evidence of an instrument's validity is how well the instrument's content matches your learning goals. You may find that an instrument widely regarded as well validated may be nonetheless inappropriate for your situation because it doesn't assess what you consider important. A writing test that focuses on grammar, for example, would be inappropriate if your writing courses focus more on developing well-reasoned arguments than on syntax.

Perhaps the second most important evidence of an instrument's quality is simply how it looks to you and your colleagues. Examine the individual items. Are they clear? Do they appear to measure what they purport to measure?

Other validity evidence can be quite technical, and you may wish to ask a psychology or education faculty member to help interpret the information. Validity evidence may include:

- Correlations of instrument scores with scores on other, similar instruments.

- Correlations of instrument scores with grades in appropriate courses.

- Correlations among subscores (scores on related subtests, such as reading and writing, should have some degree of correlation, while scores on dissimilar subtests, such as writing and quantitative skills, should be less strongly correlated).

- Increases in scores after participation in an appropriate program (graduating students, for example, should generally score higher on many tests than entering students).

Another characteristic of a good-quality instrument is that the results are consistent or *reliable*. Instruments can be consistent in several ways. Students should answer similar items within an instrument similarly; this is called *internal consistency*. Students who retake the instrument after a period of time without any intervening instruction should score about the same as they did the first time; this is called *test-retest reliability*. Publishers should provide statistical evidence that instrument results are consistent in these ways.

Are the Norms Adequate and Appropriate?

Because many published instruments are used for benchmarking one's students against students in peer programs or institutions (see Chapter 6), their value can depend on the quality and completeness of the groups used to establish the instrument's *norms* (averages, percentiles, etc.). An instrument normed on college seniors, for example, would be inappropriate for benchmarking the performance of first-year students. An instrument "normed" on only 125 students at two colleges wouldn't be useful for benchmarking any performance anywhere.

An instrument's technical information should include information on how its norms were developed. Find out:

- *How many colleges and students are included in the norms?* Obviously you can have greater confidence in norms developed from thousands of students at dozens of colleges than in norms developed from a few hundred students at a handful of colleges.

- *Do the norms represent your institution?* Do the norms include an adequate number of students from institutions of your mission type?

- *Do the norms represent your students?* Do the norms include an adequate number of students similar to those at your institution? If your institution attracts commuters, part-time students, non-traditionally aged students, students of color, or students in particular majors, are such students well represented in the norms?

- **When did the norming take place?** Students today are different from students 15 years ago, so norms created then and not updated since may not be useful.

How Are Results Made Available?

Some publishers provide reams of information on test or survey results, while others provide little more than a tally of final scores. Review information on available score formats to find out:

- Will the results give you useful feedback on your students?
- Will they tell you what you're doing right and wrong?
- Will they identify problem areas that you need to address?

If your answers to these questions are "No," there's probably little point in using the instrument.

WHAT IF THERE IS LITTLE OR NO INFORMATION ON A POTENTIAL INSTRUMENT?

Because interest in assessment at the higher education level is relatively recent, many published instruments aimed at the higher education market have been developed only recently, and their publishers may not yet have answers to all of the questions listed here. Lack of information on an instrument does not automatically mean that it's of poor quality and should be removed from consideration. It simply means that the instrument is unproven, and an unproven instrument may nonetheless be a worthwhile, useful addition to an assessment program. Some learning style inventories, for example, have few or no published validation studies, but faculty and students have still found them helpful. And locally developed instruments usually lack evidence of their psychometric properties yet can be very useful nonetheless.

If you are considering an instrument whose quality is largely undocumented, you and your colleagues must rely on your own appraisals rather than the work of others to determine if the instrument is of sufficient quality to be useful. Review the instrument itself and whatever information you do have about it and ask the following questions.

- **Overall, does the instrument make sense?** Does it appear to measure what it purports to measure?

- *Does the instrument look as if it would give us useful information?* Does its content appear to match our learning goals?

- *Are the individual items clearly written?* Will students have any difficulty answering them?

- *Does the instrument appear to be unbiased and fair?* Does it have any stereotyped or offensive material?

- *What is the potential for harm if it turns out that the instrument is of poor quality and doesn't give accurate information?* Any assessment tool—validated or not—should never be the sole basis for any important decision. It should simply add to the picture of student learning and growth that you're drawing from multiple sources.

You can also try the instrument on a small scale, essentially conducting your own validation study. If you are considering a writing test, for example, you could give the test to some students completing a first-year composition course and compare their scores against rubric scores of essays they've written in class and/or their grades in the course. If the scores correlate reasonably well, you may decide that the test is a worthwhile addition to your assessment program.

HOW SHOULD YOU DECIDE IF AN INSTRUMENT IS RIGHT FOR YOU?

Just as homebuyers quickly learn that the perfect house does not exist (at least not within their budget), neither does the perfect published instrument. Probably no publisher will be able to answer all the questions posed in this chapter to your satisfaction and that of your colleagues. As you assimilate all the information you've collected and perused, ask these fundamental questions about each potential instrument:

- Does this instrument assess what you think is important?

- Will this instrument help you understand what and/or why students are learning?

- Will the results help you decide how to improve students' learning experiences?

- Will you have enough confidence in the results to use them to help make decisions?

If your answers to these questions are a resounding "No," the instrument does not meet your needs and should not be considered further. If you answer "No" to these questions for all the instruments you've reviewed, it's likely that no published instrument meets your needs and you should turn your attention to designing and implementing a local assessment strategy.

DO PUBLISHED INSTRUMENTS HAVE A PLACE IN AN ASSESSMENT PROGRAM?

Published instruments may have value in an assessment program under *some* circumstances, and an instrument that's effective at one institution may not be effective at another. Published instruments may have value:

- *If* they match your learning goals or other important goals.

- *If* you are reasonably convinced that they indeed measure what they purport to measure.

- *If* they are part of a multiple measures approach to assessing student learning.

- *If* you give students compelling reasons to complete them and take them seriously (see Chapter 6).

- *If* they give you useful information that will help improve students' learning experiences.

TIME TO THINK, DISCUSS, AND PRACTICE

1) One of Kingsway College's learning goals is that graduating students can write effectively. Brainstorm three arguments for assessing this goal using a locally designed assessment tool and three arguments for assessing it using a published assessment tool.

2) Exercise 1 in Chapter 5 asked you to write a learning goal that describes more clearly a local community college's aim that all its students graduate with "quantitative problem solving skills."

- Use the resources described in this chapter to identify three possible published instruments for assessing these skills as you clarified them in that exercise.

- Find whatever information you can on each instrument and evaluate it. Which instrument would you most want to use? Why?

RECOMMENDED READING

American Association for Higher Education. (n.d.). *9 Principles of good practice for assessing student learning.* Washington, DC: Author. Retrieved June 2, 2003, from http://www.aahe.org/assessment/prin cipl.htm

American Educational Research Association. (Ed.). (2000). *Standards for educational and psychological testing 1999.* Washington, DC: Author.

Borden, V. M. H., & Zak, J. L. (2001). *Measuring quality: Choosing among surveys and other assessments of college quality.* Tallahassee, FL: Association for Institutional Research.

Christensen, D. D. (2001, December). Building state assessment from the classroom up. *School Administrator Web Edition.* Retrieved June 2, 2003, from http://www.aasa.org/publications/sa/2001_12/chris tensen.htm

Ewell, P. (2001). Statewide testing in higher education. *Change*, *33*(2), 21–27.

Gardiner, L. F., Anderson, C., & Cambridge, B. L. (Eds.). (1997). *Learning through assessment: A resource guide for higher education.* Washington, DC: American Association for Higher Education.

Hopkins, K. D. (1997). *Educational and psychological measurement and evaluation.* Boston, MA: Allyn & Bacon.

Kubiszyn, T., & Borich, G. D. (2002). *Educational testing and measurement: Classroom application and management* (7th ed.). San Francisco, CA: Jossey-Bass.

Mehrens, W. A., & Lehmann, I J. (1987). *Using standardized tests in education* (4th ed.). Harlow, United Kingdom: Longman Group United Kingdom.

Mehrens, W. A., & Lehmann, I. J. (1991). *Measurement and evaluation in education and psychology.* Belmont, CA: Wadsworth.

Palomba, C. A., & Banta, T. W. (1999). *Assessment essentials: Planning, implementing, and improving assessment in higher education.* San Francisco, CA: Jossey-Bass.

Rudner, L. M. (1994). Questions to ask when evaluating tests. *Practical Assessment, Research & Evaluation*, *4*(2). Retrieved June 2, 2003, from http://www.pareonline.net/getvn.asp?v=4&n=2

PART IV
Putting Assessment Results to Good and Appropriate Use

14

Summarizing and Analyzing Assessment Results

A fter weeks or months of careful planning, your assessments have finally been conducted. Your students have finished tests, assignments, or surveys; faculty have scored student work with rubrics. The completed rubrics, surveys, and test scores are piled up on your desk or saved in a computer. Now what?

Before you can share your results with others (Chapter 15) and use them to launch conversations about their implications (Chapter 16), you'll need to aggregate and *summarize your results*. You should also *evaluate the quality of your assessment strategies*, looking for evidence that they're yielding reasonably accurate information. Depending on the kind of results you have and what you would like to learn, you may also wish to *analyze the results* in some way, in addition to summarizing them. And, before you begin any of this, you must first *plan* how your results will be summarized, evaluated, and analyzed and do a little "housekeeping" to prepare the results for analysis. This chapter reviews all these steps.

PLAN YOUR ANALYSIS

How you summarize and analyze your assessment results depends on the kinds of questions you'd like your assessments to answer and the kinds of results you have.

What Questions Would You Like Answered?

Begin by reconsidering why you conducted this assessment, your audience for the results, and your audience's needs (see Chapter 4). Many assessments are conducted simply to *describe* student learning, which can be done by tallying results. Other assessments, however, are intended to *explain, predict,* or *explore,* considering questions such as "What kinds of students are most likely to drop out?" or "What instructional strategies most help students learn to think critically?"

What Kinds of Results Do You Have?

Assessment results fall into five categories.

Qualitative results are open-ended text-based results, such as reflective writing (Chapter 9) and responses to focus groups, interviews, and open-ended survey questions (Chapter 12). Chapter 9 discusses strategies to summarize and analyze qualitative results.

Categorical (or *nominal*) results break students into discrete categories. Students' majors, hometowns, and responses to multiple-choice questions are examples of categorical information. Responses can be tallied but means or medians cannot be calculated and, because of this, categorical results can be used only in a very limited way in statistical analyses designed to explain, predict, or explore.

Ordered (or *ranked* or *ordinal*) results can be put in a meaningful order. Many survey rating scales (see Chapter 12) yield ordered results. Medians can be calculated, and results can be analyzed using *non-parametric* statistical analyses (analyses that do not examine variation from a mean). If you or someone you know has expertise in non-parametric statistics, you can use ordered results to explain, predict, or explore.

Scaled (*interval* and *ratio*) results are numerical and the difference between, say, a 1 and a 2 is the same as the difference between a 4 and a 5. Grade point averages, earned credits, starting salaries, and retention, graduation, and employment rates are examples of scaled results. Means can be calculated, and results can be analyzed using a wide variety of powerful statistical techniques.

A topic of hot debate among social science researchers is whether results from Likert and other rating scales can be treated as scaled rather than ordered results, as doing so makes possible a far broader range of statistical analyses. Some researchers assert that we can't be sure that the degree of difference between "strongly agree" and "somewhat agree" is the same as the difference between "somewhat agree" and "slightly agree," so rating scale results should be considered ordered, not scaled. Other researchers, however, argue that statistical analyses designed for scaled results are sufficiently "robust" that they can be used to analyze ordered results. These researchers point to the multitude of published journal articles using such analyses with ordered results as evidence that this approach is widely accepted.

Dichotomous results are results that have only two possible values. Gender and full-time/part-time status are examples of dichotomous results. Although such results are technically categorical, because there are only two values with only one interval between them, some researchers assert that they can be treated as scaled results and used to explain, predict, and explore.

Take Care of Housekeeping Details

If your assessment results are on paper, a few housekeeping details may need to be addressed before the results can be summarized and analyzed.

Editing

If you are using surveys or rubrics, some may have ambiguous or inappropriate responses that need editing (web-based surveys can be designed to prevent such responses).

Inapplicable responses: Suppose that only business majors were to answer Question 4, but some students in other majors answered it as well. In this kind of situation, delete inapplicable responses.

Multiple responses: Sometimes, even though you clearly ask students to check the one best response to each survey question, some students will check two or more answers to some questions. There are three ways to handle this:

- **Include all the student's responses to the question.** This is not advisable because it gives unfair weight (in essence, counting two answers instead of one) to students who followed directions incorrectly. Had everyone been given this opportunity, other students might also have checked more than one response and thereby changed the overall results.

- **Choose one response at random and delete the others.** Some prefer this approach because it salvages at least some of the student's responses. Just make sure to choose one response randomly; don't always choose the first response checked.

- **Disregard all the student's responses to the question.** Some think this is the most valid approach, because we have no way of knowing which one response the student would have selected had he or she followed directions correctly, but some potentially useful results will be lost.

Responses outside given categories: Suppose a rubric's categories are Excellent, Good, Fair, and Poor, and one faculty member checks midway between Excellent and Good. The choices here are either to disregard this particular rating or to recategorize the response randomly to either Excellent or Good.

"Other" responses that really aren't: Some students will check an "Other—please specify" survey response when in fact one of the given responses suits them. Read all the "Other—please specify" comments and recategorize if necessary.

Coding and Data Entry

Unless you have just a handful of assessment results, you will probably want to enter the results into a computer to make them easier to summarize and analyze. Today many software programs facilitate data entry. Software with data entry screens include database software, some statistical analysis packages, and special survey and testing software. As noted in Chapter 4, a scanner or optical mark reader can be used to enter results from paper tests and forms with "bubbles" created with special software or fonts.

Results may be easier to summarize and analyze if you code the results before entering them, changing every rating or response into a number or character. A rating of excellent, for example, might be coded 4, good as 3, fair as 2, and poor as 1. Some data entry software will handle this task for you.

Discuss your coding and data entry plans with your institution's technical support staff *before* you finalize your forms and conduct your assessment, or it may not be possible to enter and analyze your results as you hope.

Coding qualitative results is discussed in Chapter 9.

Documenting and Storage

Once your results are entered into a computer, make sure they are securely saved. Then document the results by creating, reviewing, and saving the following.

A listing of the raw data (each individual response or rating for each student). This will help you find and correct data entry errors. Once the results have been thoroughly checked and edited, you may want to delete identifying information, such as student names or ID numbers, to ensure confidentiality. If you want to preserve identifying information, store this list very securely. Don't leave it on a hard drive or server if there is any chance of an unauthorized person accessing it. If you keep the list on paper or a disk, store it in a locked drawer or cabinet.

Tallies of every result or response (for example, the number of student papers rated excellent in terms of organization, very good, etc.). This will give you a quick picture of your results and also help identify data entry errors.

Notes on coding. Keep careful notes explaining every piece of information in your computer files and the meaning of each code. The notes will minimize confusion and will be invaluable if anyone decides to repeat the assessment later.

You may wish to keep the completed rubrics, surveys, tests, and so forth, on file in case they are needed to answer questions from people who discuss your results. If these documents have identifying information (e.g., faculty name or student ID number), remove such information or store these documents *very* securely.

SUMMARIZE YOUR RESULTS

Tallies, tables, graphs, and averages can all be used to summarize assessment results.

Tallies are straightforward counts of how many students earned each rating, chose each option, and so forth. They're the simplest way to summarize assessment results. If you don't have many results, you can make these simple tallies by hand. Your audience will grasp tallies more quickly if the results are presented as percentages rather than as raw numbers. If there are many possible results (e.g., scores on a 100-point test), you may want to group the results, showing, say, the percent scoring 90–100, 80–89, etc. This makes it easier for your audience to visualize the results.

Tables can summarize tallies succinctly. Table 14.2, shown later in the chapter, and the table in Figure 15.1 in Chapter 15 are examples.

Graphs are another effective way to summarize assessment results, and they can be created quickly using spreadsheet or presentation software. Line graphs can summarize ordered or scaled results and show trends over time, while bar graphs can summarize virtually any type of assessment results. The graph in Figure 15.1 in Chapter 15 is an example.

Averages are single numbers that summarize the central tendency of the results. The best known such statistic is the mean: the arithmetic average we learned in grade school. It's an appropriate statistic for scaled results.

If your results are ordered, a more appropriate statistic is the *median*: the midpoint of all results when listed from highest to lowest. Medians are also a good choice when a few very high or very low results distort the mean. Suppose, for example, that 20 students take a national certification exam whose passing score is 80. Eighteen students score 85 and pass comfortably, but two students fail miserably, scoring 10. The mean of these 20 students is 77.5, which gives the incorrect impression that the "average" student failed the test. The median of 85 better reflects the performance of the "typical" student in this group.

If your results are categorical, the appropriate statistic is the *mode*: the most frequent result.

Creating Effective Tables and Graphs

A picture is worth a thousand words only if it is a good one! In effective tables and graphs, key points almost jump out at the reader. Here are some tips for creating good tables and graphs.

Give each table and graph a meaningful, self-explanatory title. "Student Responses" won't do it; "Freshman Self-Ratings of Critical Thinking Skills" will.

Label every part of a table or graph clearly. Label each table column and each graph axis, avoiding abbreviations.

Make each table or graph self-explanatory, since some readers won't read any accompanying text. Use footnotes to provide definitions, assumptions, and notes needed to interpret the table or graph properly.

Convert counts into percentages, which are more meaningful. Few readers will care that 125 students passed a test; more will care that only 23% did.

Make it easy for readers to see differences and trends. If a table is presenting results from this year's and last year's assessments, add a third column showing the amount of change. If your table is comparing male and female students, add a third column showing the differences between their results.

Avoid putting too much information into one table or graph. Round percentages to the nearest whole number. If you find that you must insert vertical lines into a table to make it clear, you have too many columns or figures. Break your results into two or more tables or simply delete some information.

Present your results in an order that makes sense to the reader and helps convey your point. Listing results in their order on the original assessment instrument is neither interesting nor enlightening. Present your results with the most frequently chosen responses or highest scores at the top, so readers can quickly discern relative successes and areas of concern. Because people expect scales to increase from left to right, when presenting trends over time, put the oldest information on the left and the most recent on the right.

Draw attention to the point you want your table or graph to make. Use boldface, italics, borders, colors, and fonts to draw attention to your most important figures. Put totals in boldface. If you are comparing your institution against peer institutions, put your institution's results in boldface. In a graph of student responses about proposed changes to current policies, use a different color for the bar representing current policy.

Don't assume a software-generated table or graph is readable. Some software packages' default settings generate distorted tables or graphs or provide poor labels if any. Use software options to make your table or graph readable and distortion-free.

Date each graph and table and note its source. Readers may share tables and graphs with colleagues without accompanying text.

Table 14.1 is an example of a table of one (fictitious) school's results for a portion of the Cooperative Institutional Research Program freshman survey. The table's flaws?

- *There are too many columns*—so many that vertical lines must be inserted to make them readable.
- *The table presents too much information.* One can use this table to compare men against women, the entire class against two sets of national averages, men against two sets of national averages for men, and women against two sets of national averages for women.
- *The percentages are not rounded,* so some readers will focus on trivial differences, such as that 42.4% of St. Stephens freshmen and 42.2% of freshmen at all public universities expect to make a B average.
- *The table doesn't point out any meaningful differences.* The reader must do the math to decide which differences are big and which aren't.
- *The items aren't arranged in any particular order* (other than, perhaps, the order on the survey).

As a consequence of these flaws, the table tells no story and has no apparent point. Few readers will easily derive anything meaningful from it.

Now compare Table 14.1 with the revision in Table 14.2. This table has a number of improvements:

- *All the gender results have been eliminated,* simplifying the table. (If the author wants to make a point of gender differences, those results can be put in a separate table.)
- *Only one set of national norms is presented*—the set that the author feels is of greatest interest.
- *The first column has been right-justified,* so it is easier for the reader to read the correct figures for each item.

Table 14.1

A Table of Results of a First-Year Student Survey

Percent of first-year students saying chances are very good that they will:

	St. Stephens University			All Universities			All Private Universities		
	Men	Women	All	Men	Women	All	Men	Women	All
Change major field.	13.4%	13.2%	13.3%	11.7%	12.7%	12.2%	13.0%	13.4%	13.3%
Change career choice.	10.9%	11.9%	11.5%	10.8%	12.8%	11.9%	11.4%	12.6%	12.1%
Get a job to help pay for college expenses.	32.5%	42.1%	38.3%	35.2%	41.9%	38.8%	33.0%	41.1%	37.5%
Make at least a "B" average.	48.3%	53.5%	51.4%	42.3%	44.3%	43.3%	40.8%	43.3%	42.2%
Need extra time to complete your degree requirements.	7.9%	8.3%	8.1%	8.3%	9.7%	9.0%	9.6%	10.3%	10.0%
Get a bachelor's degree.	72.5%	81.1%	77.7%	63.7%	69.0%	66.6%	70.5%	76.1%	73.6%
Be satisfied with your college.	61.2%	75.2%	69.7%	44.2%	55.6%	50.4%	43.1%	53.2%	48.8%

Table 14.2

An Improved Version of Table 14.1

Percent of first-year students saying chances are very good that they will:	St. Stephens University	All Private Universities	Difference
Get a bachelor's degree.	78%	74%	+4%
Be satisfied with your college.	70%	49%	+21%
Make at least a "B" average.	51%	42%	+9%
Get a job to help pay for college expenses.	38%	38%	—
Change major field.	13%	13%	—
Change career choice.	12%	12%	—
Need extra time to complete your degree requirements.	8%	10%	-2%

- *All figures have been rounded* to the nearest whole percent, simplifying the table and encouraging readers to focus on only sizable differences.

- *Differences from national norms have been added* in a new column.

- *The items have been ordered* from greatest agreement to least agreement among St. Stephens students.

All these changes make it much easier for readers to discern the major story the table is trying to tell: St. Stephens' first-year students are more optimistic about college than their peers at other private universities.

EVALUATE THE QUALITY OF YOUR ASSESSMENT STRATEGIES

Chapter 2 defines "good quality" assessments as those that yield truthful information about what students have *truly* learned. There are several questions you can consider to see if your assessments are indeed "good quality."

How Well Does Your Sample Reflect All Your Students?

Sometimes, when assessing program- or institution-wide student learning, it isn't practical to assess what *every* student has learned, especially in a program or institution with hundreds or thousands of students. In such cases, we can assess a sample of student work, as discussed in Chapter 6.

The conclusions we draw from a sample of students are valid only if we can assume that the students in the sample mirror the group from which they were taken. If 55% of all students are female, for example, roughly 55% of the students being assessed should be female. Similarly, the students in the sample should be similar to all students in terms of their grades, class level, major, full-time/part-time status, or any other factor considered important.

But how similar is good enough? If 55% of all students are female, for example, is it good enough that 54% of the sample is female? What if the sample is 52% female? 50% female? Fortunately, statistical analyses such as chi-squared tests and t-tests can help make these decisions. Consult someone knowledgeable about statistics for help conducting these analyses.

How Precise Are Your Sample Results?

Suppose that faculty assess a sample of 200 essays and find that 84% of them are at least "satisfactory" in terms of overall writing skill. You would like to be able to say that 84% of all students at your college write satisfactorily. Assuming you assess a random sample of essays and that the students in your sample mirror all students, can you say this? No! It's very unlikely that *exactly* 84% of all students write satisfactorily. It's possible that the real overall percentage may be 83%, 82%, even 91%. The discrepancy between your 84% and the true percentage is called an *error margin* and is discussed in Chapter 6. It's not really an "error," just a phenomenon that exists because even a good random sample is unlikely to mirror all students *precisely*.

When reporting results, you will be much more credible if you mention the error margin of your findings. Instead of simply saying that "84% of students write satisfactorily," you could say, "84% of students write satisfactorily *with an error margin of plus or minus 7%*." This means that you are 95% sure that between 77% and 91% of all students (84% plus and minus 7%) write satisfactorily.

Table 6.6 in Chapter 6 provides the error margins for some sample sizes. The error margin for other sample sizes can be estimated with this formula:

$$\sqrt{\frac{1}{n}} \times 100\% \text{ where n = your sample size}$$

If faculty evaluate 200 essays, the approximate error margin is:

$$\sqrt{\frac{1}{200}} \times 100\% = \sqrt{.005} \times 100\% = 7\%$$

If you want a more accurate error margin, consult someone knowledgeable about statistics or look in any basic statistics textbook for a discussion of confidence intervals.

Is Your Test or Rubric Working the Way You Intended?

Scores from objective tests (Chapter 11) and rubrics (Chapter 7) can be reviewed to see if these assessment tools are "working" the way they should. Some software for processing bubble-sheet or web-based instruments can generate these types of analyses. If software isn't available, these analyses aren't difficult to compute, although they may be time-consuming with large volumes of results.

Difficulty: What percentage of students answered each test item correctly or earned an acceptable score on each rubric criterion? For objective tests, count the number of students answering each item *incorrectly* (which is usually faster than counting the number answering each item *correctly*). For rubrics, count the number of students earning *unacceptable* scores on each criterion (which is usually faster than counting the number earning *acceptable* scores). Then compare the results against your standards: how difficult you intended the item or criterion to be. Take a close look at objective test items that more than half your students got wrong. Often such items are flawed in some way, causing the better students to misinterpret them, or they assess some relatively trivial concept that most students missed.

Discrimination: How well does each test item or rubric criterion discriminate between high and low scorers? The idea is that students who do well on a test overall should be more likely to answer any one test item correctly than students who do poorly on the test overall. Similarly, students who do well on an assignment overall should be more likely to do well on any one rubric criterion, such as syntax, than students who do poorly overall. To calculate the discrimination of objective test items:

1) Sort the scored tests from highest to lowest total score.

2) Choose a manageable number of tests with high and low scores for further analysis. Depending on how many tests you have, you might choose the top and bottom thirds, the top and bottom fifths, or the ten tests at the top and bottom. Make sure you have exactly the same number of tests in the top and bottom groups.

3) For each group, count the number answering each item *incorrectly* (which is usually faster than counting the number answering each item *correctly*).

4) For each item, subtract the number of incorrect answers in the top group from the number of incorrect answers in the bottom group.

Table 14.3 presents some examples of item discrimination results for an objective test. Item 5 is an example of a question with *very good discrimination*. Only two students in the top group got this question wrong, while eight students in the bottom group got it wrong. This is an item that clearly distinguishes the top students (as defined by this particular test) from the bottom ones. Item 4 is another example of a test question with good discrimination, although not quite as strong as for Item 5.

Item 2, meanwhile, is an example of a question with *no discrimination;* in each group four students got it wrong. Test experts would say that this is not an effective item, because it doesn't help us distinguish between the students who have learned a lot and the students who learned comparatively little.

Item 6 is an example of a question with *negative discrimination;* more top students got it wrong than bottom students. This is an item that is simply not working correctly; the top students are reading something into the item that the test writer didn't intend. Items with nega-

Table 14.3

Examples of Item Discrimination Results

Item Number	Number Incorrect in Top Group (10 students)	Number Incorrect in Bottom Group (10 students)	Difference (bottom–top)
1	0	0	0
2	4	4	0
3	0	1	1
4	2	5	3
5	2	8	6
6	6	2	-4

tive discrimination should generally be thrown out and the tests rescored, as they unfairly penalize top students. They should definitely be discarded or revised when future editions of the test are prepared.

Note that, in order to interpret discrimination information correctly, the difficulty of each item must be taken into consideration. Item 1 is very easy (everyone in both groups got it correct), so of course there's no discrimination. Everyone in the top group got Item 3 correct and only one person in the bottom group got it wrong, so while the discrimination of 1 may not seem high, the item is so easy that this is the highest possible discrimination.

Rubric scores can also be analyzed for discrimination. If essays have been scored for organization, focus, and mechanics, for example, you can compare the papers with the highest overall scores against the papers with the lowest overall scores in terms of the ratings they earned on each criterion. If bottom-scoring papers generally score higher than top-scoring papers on, say, organization, you have an important clue that something isn't right with the assignment or with how faculty scored the essays.

Is Your Assessment Tool of Good Quality?

Chapter 2 gives many examples of strategies that you can use to evaluate the quality (truthfulness) of assessment tools, including the following:

Compare the results against other evidence of what students have learned. (This is called corroboration or triangulation.) Test scores, for example, might be compared against course grades and faculty and student ratings of students' skill levels.

If faculty are scoring student work using a rubric, *have two faculty members score each paper or project* and compare their scores for consistency.

See if the results fall in expected patterns. Graduating students, for example, should generally have higher scores than first-year students.

SHOULD YOU ANALYZE YOUR RESULTS?

Using assessment results to *explain, predict, or explore* may be more interesting and useful than simply summarizing them. Some of the questions that can be answered through statistical analyses are:

- Why did students learn X but not Y?

- Why did some students master Z but others didn't?

- What high school courses best prepare students to do well in this program?

- Do students at this college learn more than students at peer colleges? Do students perform better or worse on the ABC Test than students nationally?

- Do subgroups of students differ from each other? Is there a difference, for example, between students who live on and off campus?

- Do assessment "sub-results" differ? Is the organization of student papers significantly better than their grammar?

- Have students' knowledge and skills increased over time?

- Are current students' knowledge and skills different from those of past students?

- Are there any relationships among results? Is there, for example, a relation between students' survey responses and their grades? Is there a relation between students' test scores and whether they graduate or drop out?

Analyzing results to answer these kinds of questions requires 1) a background in inferential statistics or access to someone with such a background, 2) a statistical software package, and 3) a computer powerful enough to handle the software and your database. You may also need scaled or at least ordered results. If you're comfortable with inferential statistics (the kind of statistical analyses needed to answer these questions), Chapter 6 of Suskie's (1996) *Questionnaire Survey Research: What Works* provides a series of charts to help choose an appropriate analysis. Keep in mind, however, that even statistical experts may disagree on the most appropriate analysis for given results.

If you're not knowledgeable about inferential statistics, find people on your campus who can help you. Ask your computer center, institutional research office, or faculty with backgrounds in educational or social science research methods for referrals to people with expertise in inferential statistics and appropriate software.

TIME TO THINK, DISCUSS, AND PRACTICE

1) The Business Administration faculty have decided to use the rubric in Figure 7.2 in Chapter 7 to assess the oral presentation skills of students in the program's senior seminar.

- Have one member of your group play the role of a faculty member in this department. Ask this person to describe the questions that the faculty want the rubric scores to answer and the decisions the faculty need to make.

- Decide if the results will be qualitative, categorical, ordered, scaled, or dichotomous.

- Decide on the best format(s) for sharing the results and answering the faculty's questions: a tally, table, graph, average, or perhaps some further statistical analysis designed to explain, predict, or explore.

2) Faculty teaching first-year composition scored 200 student essays and obtained the following results: for Language Use, 100 essays scored Excellent, 50 scored Adequate, and the rest scored Unacceptable; for Content, 75 scored Excellent, 75 scored Adequate, and the rest scored Unacceptable; and for Organization, 25 scored Excellent, 50 scored Adequate, and the rest scored Unacceptable.

- What are the major conclusions you would draw about these students' writing performance?

- Create a table or graph that conveys your conclusions clearly.

3) Of 300 Jameson College alumni responding to a survey, 74% said they were satisfied with the quality of their Jameson education. Calculate the error margin of this result and write a sentence explaining the result and the error margin.

ACKNOWLEDGMENT

Some of the material in this chapter is adapted from my earlier book, *Questionnaire Survey Research: What Works*, published by the Association for Institutional Research. I am grateful to the association for permission to adapt this material.

RECOMMENDED READING

Carroll, S. R., & Carroll, D. J. (2002). *Statistics made simple for school leaders: Data-driven decision making*. Lanham, MD: Scarecrow Press.

Coughlin, M. A., & Pagano, M. (1997). *Case study applications of statistics in institutional research*. Tallahassee, FL: Association for Institutional Research.

Fraenkel, J. R., Wallen, N. E., & Sawin, E. I. (1999). *Visual statistics: A conceptual primer*. Boston, MA: Allyn & Bacon.

Gonick, L., & Smith, W. (1994). *The cartoon guide to statistics*. New York, NY: HarperCollins.

Ravid, R. (2000). *Practical statistics for educators* (2nd ed.). Lanham, MD: University Press of America.

Statistical Services Centre. (2001, March). *Informative presentation of tables, graphs and statistics*. Reading, United Kingdom: University of Reading. Retrieved June 2, 2003, from http://www.rdg.ac.uk/ssc/develop/dfid/booklets/toptgs.html

Urdan, T. C. (2001). *Statistics in plain English*. Mahwah, NJ: Lawrence Erlbaum Associates.

Wainer, H. (1992, January/February). Understanding graphs and tables. *Educational Researcher, 21*(1), 14–23.

Wainer, H. (2000). *Visual revelations: Graphical tales of fate and deception from Napoleon Bonaparte to Ross Perot*. Mahwah, NJ: Lawrence Erlbaum Associates.

Wallgren, A., Wallgren, B., Persson, R., Jorner, U., & Haaland, J. (1996). *Graphing statistics and data: Creating better charts*. Newbury Park, CA: Sage.

15

Sharing Assessment Results

A ssessments are worthwhile only if they're used to improve teaching and learning, and those improvements can take place only after careful consideration and discussion. That consideration and discussion, in turn, can take place only if assessment results are communicated clearly, accurately, and usefully. How you share assessment results should therefore be planned as carefully as any other part of the assessment process. You'll need to consider how to reach your particular audience and which communication formats will best meet both your needs and your audience's. This chapter addresses these considerations.

WHO IS YOUR AUDIENCE?
WHAT DOES YOUR AUDIENCE NEED?

As discussed in Chapter 4, planning an assessment begins with considering its audiences and their needs. Review your assessment plans to remind yourself who your audiences are; what their perspectives, needs, and priorities are; what decisions they need to make; and what information they need from your assessment in order to make those decisions. When in doubt, plan to share your results widely rather than narrowly. As Gangopadhyay (2002) notes, "Remember the wider the outreach, the greater the impact" (p. 3). Also consider:

How much information does your audience need? Are audience members already familiar with the assessment, or will they need a complete description of what was done? Will they want only your findings and recommendations, or will they want to know how you arrived at your conclusions? Are they knowledgeable about empirical research methodology, or will you need to explain what you did in everyday language?

Do your audience members have any preferences for how they receive assessment information? Would they rather absorb information through text, numbers, or graphs? Would they rather receive information on paper, electronically, or at a meeting? Do they favor brevity or abundant information? Do they have time to study an extensive report?

Might your audience feel threatened by your results and therefore criticize the study?

Are others likely to question your audience about the study? Will your audience need enough details to respond to others' concerns?

WHY ARE YOU SHARING YOUR ASSESSMENT RESULTS?

Chapter 4 notes that planning an assessment begins with clarifying its purposes. Remind yourself why you undertook this assessment, and then think about what you want to accomplish by sharing the results. Perhaps you have positive results that you want to use to convince others of the quality of your program or institution. Perhaps you've identified areas of concern that you want to use to initiate conversations on how best to improve the program or institution. Whatever your purpose, choose formats and venues for sharing your results that will help achieve those ends.

HOW CAN YOU REACH YOUR AUDIENCE AND FULFILL YOUR PURPOSE?

Options for sharing assessment results include the following:

At-a-glance tables, graphs, and bulleted lists. If your audience is already familiar with your assessment, it may be sufficient to share a few tables and graphs highlighting your principal findings. A couple of brief explanatory paragraphs accompanying your tables may help those who have difficulty understanding tables and graphs. Chapter 14 offers suggestions for creating effective tables and graphs.

Print materials. Results can be shared not only through the usual reports but through articles in an employee newsletter or alumni magazine, articles or advertisements in the student newspaper, department memos, press releases, or brochures.

Slides and posters. An increasingly popular means of sharing assessment results is through slides or posters created with presentation software. Slides and posters can accompany oral presentations or be shared electronically. Suggestions for creating effective slides are offered later in this chapter.

Electronic media. Assessment results can be posted on a web site, burned onto a CD-ROM, or attached to email messages. These approaches let you present your results in a variety of formats—text, tables, graphs, slides, even video.

Presentations allow audience members to receive information through multiple formats: reading, listening, viewing visuals such as graphs and slides, and interaction. Suggestions for making effective presentations are offered later in this chapter.

As you consider communication formats and venues, think about how people tend to communicate on your campus. People on some campuses use email extensively, while those on other campuses continue to rely on paper materials delivered through campus mail. On some campuses the employee newsletter is read avidly, while on others it's largely ignored. Observe which formats get the most attention on your campus and take advantage of them.

You may need to use different communication formats with different audiences. If you are assessing student learning in an academic program, for example, you may want to prepare a detailed report for the department faculty, an executive summary for the dean, a web page for students in the program, a short summary for the college public relations office to use in press releases, and a slide presentation for the department assessment committee. If you have multiple audiences, consider developing a dissemination plan listing who will receive information, what information will be shared with each group, in what format, and when. This helps ensure that no one is inadvertently left out of the loop.

How Can You Engage Your Audience in Your Assessment Results?

Regardless of the presentation format you choose, you'll need to help your audience pay attention to your results and not simply file or discard them. Take your cues from the messages that you absorb each day in newspapers, magazines, on television and the web, and in other media. What catches your eye? What convinces you to read an article or an advertisement? Emulate those approaches to engage your audience in *your* message.

Tell a Story With a Meaningful Point

Assessment results should tell an important, coherent, interesting story. To give your results the most impact, try the following.

Use an engaging, meaningful title and headings that help convince your audience to read, view, or listen to your results. Headings should describe the point of an analysis ("Factors Affecting Grade Point Average") rather than the analysis itself ("Results of Multiple Regression Analysis"). Questions ("Why Do Students Drop Out?") can pique readers' curiosity. Try writing your title and headlines like newspaper headlines that condense your principal findings. "Women Are Generally More Satisfied than Men" conveys more than "Differences Between Men and Women."

Open with something intriguing. Make your very first statement or visual interesting and intriguing, like the lead sentence in a newspaper article.

Orient your audience. Explain very briefly why the assessment was done and what it was designed to find out. See Chapter 2 for information that should be provided to help readers determine the quality and usefulness of the results. Explain how anyone interested in more details can obtain them.

Cascade from major points to details. Begin with an overall descriptive summary of the results. A simple table may be more effective than text. Include the error margin (see Chapter 14), which will help readers judge which differences are truly meaningful.

Make sure everything you include tells an important, interesting part of your story. Consider this paragraph from a report on one fictitious college's participation in the Cooperative Institutional Research Program Freshman Survey:

> *Between 78% and 80% of Lawndale College first-year students rely on family financial support. Lawndale first-year students are more likely to have student loans (48%) than first-year students nationally. Only 57% were dependent on grants, compared to 62% nationally.*

What's the point of this paragraph? I don't know, and if I don't, the report's readers probably don't either, and they aren't going to spend time puzzling it out. On the other hand, consider these paragraphs on different results from the same survey at another fictitious institution.

> *First-year women at Kensington College have a stronger preparation for college than do men. First-year women have, on average, earned higher grades in high school and have spent more time volunteering, studying, and participating in student clubs and groups. They are more likely attending college to "gain a general education," "learn more about things that interest me," "become a more cultured person," and "prepare for graduate study." It is more important to them to help others in difficulty, influence social values, and promote racial understanding.*
>
> *First-year men, on the other hand, are less likely than women to have completed high school homework on time and to have come to class on time. They have spent more time in high school playing sports, watching television, and working. Men are more likely attending to "make more money" and it is more important to men to "be very well off financially." Despite their weaker preparation for college, men rate themselves higher in intellectual self-confidence, mathematics ability, competitiveness, originality, popularity, social self-confidence, physical health, and emotional health.*
>
> *First-year men and women at this school both need help adjusting to college, but of vastly different kinds. Women need more self-confidence, while men need more help building academic skills and an appreciation of the broader benefits of a college education.*

Because the Kensington report has a clearer point, people will probably pay more attention to it than to the Lawndale one.

Provide a context for your results. Summarize other information related to your assessment that's available from your campus or in research literature. If you are sharing results of a survey related to student retention, for example, give a brief summary of the research literature on student retention. If you are repeating an assessment conducted three years ago, compare past and present results. Explain how and why the contextual information supports—or doesn't support—your results.

Offer informed commentary. Make clear the implications of your results, as shown in the concluding paragraph above on Kensington College students. Explain how the results answer the questions that formed the purpose of the assessment and how the results relate to institutional or programmatic priorities. Spur conversation by offering possible discussion questions suggested by the results.

You may even wish to suggest possible implications of the results for institutional and program policies and practices. Suggest possible conclusions and implications only if you don't mind being wrong about them! Before you offer them, discuss them with appropriate colleagues to make sure they seem logical and apropos. If you decide to offer recommendations, make them clear, well reasoned, practical, constructive, and concrete.

Make Your Information Relevant to Your Audience

Connect your results to your audience's interests. Your audience will probably be most interested in:

Matters your audience can do something about. If you are sharing results with faculty, point out results related to teaching and learning. If you are sharing results with student life staff, point out results related to out-of-class activities and personal development. If you are sharing results with admissions staff, point out results that could be used to market the institution or program to prospective students.

Meaningful differences. Don't emphasize, for example, that 15% of your program's students are African American when 16% of all students at your institution are African American. Keep in mind that a *statistically* significant difference may not be great enough to have practical, *meaningful* significance. In a survey of 1,500 students, for example, a 4% difference may be *statistically* significant but not large enough to merit special attention. It might be more appropriate to point out only differences of, say, 10% or more and thus focus your audience on the *major* differences that warrant their attention.

Interesting and unanticipated findings. Don't bother telling your readers that your Catholic students largely have Catholic parents, but do tell them that growing proportions of students are from upper-income households or that interest in extracurricular activities is well below the national average.

Keep It Short

In today's busy world, few of us have time to wade through a lengthy report, sit through an extensive presentation, or click through endless web pages. Most people want *very* brief summaries highlighting only key results. The shorter your communication of assessment results, the more likely that people will read, listen to, or view it, and the more likely that your results will be put to good use.

Avoid the temptation, therefore, to report every result and every statistical analysis. While you may have found each detail of your assessment project fascinating, your audience probably won't. If a particular result doesn't make a meaningful contribution to your conclusions and will not help decision-makers, leave it out. As Harris and Muchin (2002) note, "Most information is useless. Give yourself permission to dismiss it" (p. 4). Aim to give your audience just a quick overview of your principal findings and implications—no more than one or two pages, if you are conveying your results in writing. Figure 15.1 is an example of a brief but complete assessment report.

Sometimes, of course, one brief report won't meet all your audiences' needs. In that case, you may need to prepare a series of brief reports, each targeted to a particular audience. If you have surveyed a sample of graduating seniors, for example, you might share their opinions of library resources only with the library staff.

Keep Things Simple and Clear

While your audience members are probably intelligent and well educated, they may not have time or inclination to scrutinize a scholarly missive filled with dense prose. Make it easy for your audience to discern your key points by following these suggestions:

Keep your sentences and paragraphs short. If one sentence runs four or five lines or one paragraph fills half a page, your report is too difficult to read.

Avoid jargon. Some members of your audience may have a limited assessment vocabulary, so use language that everyone will easily under-

Figure 15.1

A Brief Assessment Report:
The Effect of Learning Community Participation on First-Year Grade Point Averages

The Office of Assessment compared the grade point averages (GPAs) of 177 learning-community students against those of a random sample of 199 other first-year students. As shown in the graph below, the mean GPAs for **men** were 2.85 for those in learning communities and 2.30 for those not in learning communities, a statistically significant difference. The mean GPAs for **women** were 3.04 for those in learning communities and 3.01 for those not in learning communities, an insignificant difference.

Because students self-selected into the learning communities, we looked at their high school grade point averages, SAT scores, and majors to see if any of these factors might explain the difference in GPA. (See the table on the next page.) While an analysis of covariance to examine the effects of these factors on GPA was originally planned, the large number of factors and relatively small numbers of students made such an analysis impractical. When we accounted for differences in high school GPA, our findings remained the same. SAT Verbal and Math scores didn't contribute significantly to our analysis, so we eliminated them as possible factors. Other statistical tests led us to conclude that variations in student major also did not significantly affect our overall conclusions. Please let us know if you would like any details on these analyses.

Our overall conclusions are that, on average, 1) participating in a learning community improves the grade point averages of men and 2) women do well academically regardless of whether or not they're in a learning community.

Grade Point Averages of Men and Women In and Out of Learning Communities

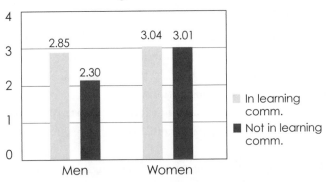

Profile of Men and Women
In and Out of Learning Communities

	Men		Women	
	In LC*	Not in LC**	In LC*	Not in LC**
Total no. of students	58	75	119	124
Average GPA	2.85	2.30	3.04	3.01
Undecided major	31%	41%	22%	29%
Average HS GPA	3.28	3.20	3.49	3.49
Average SAT-Verbal	574	524	559	534
Average SAT-Math	582	564	536	541

Note: Percentages may not sum to 100% due to rounding.
* In learning communities
** Not in learning communities (random sample)

stand. Avoid technical terms, formulas, statistical symbols, and research jargon such as "aggregate," "variable," "subject," or "population." (If you absolutely cannot avoid jargon, provide a glossary.) Spell out every abbreviation the first time it is used. Explain statistical analyses in lay terms. For example, the following paragraph describes a discriminant analysis without using that term:

> The analysis split the students responding to the survey into three groups: 462 students who returned or graduated, 50 students who were dismissed from the college for poor academic performance, and 92 students who voluntarily left without graduating. The three groups were then compared to identify distinguishing characteristics of each group.

Use numbers sparingly, only when they're necessary or inherently interesting. "Mathephobes" will glaze over a paragraph like the following:

> A greater percentage of Cape Anne College students are first generation college students than nationally. Exactly 40% of fathers and 48% of mothers have never attended college, compared to 37% of fathers and 40% of mothers nationally. Over

36% of fathers of Cape Anne freshmen are college graduates, while nearly 27% of mothers have college degrees.

Now consider this rewrite:

The parents of Cape Anne College students are not quite as well educated as those of students nationally; they are less likely to have attended college or earned a college degree.

The second paragraph, with no figures, communicates its point far more clearly than the first. Often it's sufficient to say something is more or less, or above or below average, without getting into figures. The rewritten paragraph is also more effective because it is more succinct; it tells in one sentence what the original paragraph said in three.

Round your figures to the nearest whole number. Stating that 10.3% said X and 10.4% said Y encourages readers to focus on trivial, statistically insignificant differences and unnecessarily increases the number of digits that "mathephobes" must try to absorb.

Give Your Most Important Points Visual Impact

Make your message graphically interesting and engaging:

Make liberal use of headings, bulleted lists, and simple tables and graphs. Many of your audience members will only scan your results. Help them quickly find what interests them by providing plenty of headings. Put your main points into bulleted lists and simple, well-constructed tables and graphs so your audience can quickly and easily see and understand your results. Chapter 14 includes suggestions for creating effective tables and graphs.

Use different fonts for headings and subheadings to draw attention to them.

Use "pull quotes": important statements taken from your text and repeated in a margin or sidebar. They ensure that your major points aren't missed.

Have a Friend Review Your Draft

Even if he or she knows nothing about assessment, empirical research methods, or statistics, a friend should be able to understand the purpose of your assessment, your basic findings, and your conclusions and why you drew them.

What Else Should Be Included in Any Communication of Assessment Results?

Include the following whenever you share assessment results.

Author, Originating Office, and Date

It's amazing how useless a report is if no one can remember who did it or when. For the sake of those pulling your results from a file or bringing up your web site five years from now, note the author, the originating office, and the date of release. Consider carefully whom to list as author. While you may have done the actual work (and you should receive an acknowledgement of that), it may be more prudent to show the results as being released by, say, a task force or a dean's office. If these entities are more visible than you are, the results may be given more attention. If the results are likely to be controversial, it may be wise to associate others with them.

Acknowledgments

If anyone provided financial support for your assessment, helped with the mechanics, assisted with data entry and analysis, or helped in any other way, it's only courteous to acknowledge that assistance and express appreciation for it—especially if you'd ever like help again!

An Offer to Make Additional Information Available

A short, effective communication will engage your audience in your findings but may not answer everyone's questions. Include information on whom to contact for additional information. (But don't be disappointed by how few people take you up on your offer!)

What Are the Keys to Making an Effective Presentation?

A presentation allows you to share results through multiple formats—oral remarks, slides or posters, handouts, and discussion. These media collectively create a more complete learning experience for your audience than any of them would alone, if you design them so they build upon rather than replicate each other. The following suggestions will maximize the impact of your presentation.

Make Effective Oral Remarks

Keep your remarks short and informal and concentrate on your findings. Rather than read from a prepared text, keep your presentation fresh by using a bulleted list to remind you of what to say.

You may wish to consider asking someone else to make the presentation or co-present it with you. Having someone viewed as important (say, a dean or senior faculty member) make the presentation may help your assessment be taken more seriously. If you are uncomfortable with public speaking, having a dynamic speaker help with the presentation may make it more effective.

Create Effective Slides or Posters

A set of slides or posters should open with the presentation's title and an overview of major points, continue with content information that constitutes the substance of the presentation, and conclude with a reiteration of major points. These tips will help you create effective slides:

Use presentation software rather than word processing or spreadsheet software to create slides and posters. Presentation software has greater flexibility, including a wide selection of fonts, colors, and graphics, to help reinforce key points.

Use a data projector connected to a computer to present your slides rather than an overhead projector and transparencies. Projecting directly from a computer allows you to use fades, dissolves, and other animation effects to emphasize your main points and prevents the awkwardness of shuffling among a pile of transparencies. You can also make last-minute changes to your presentation should you need to correct a typo or clarify a point.

Keep slides and posters simple, uncluttered, and readable. If a slide has more than a few words, your audience will focus on reading it rather than listening to you. Keep the text to just a few key words that emphasize your major points rather than longer phrases or sentences that compete with or duplicate your remarks. Use bulleted lists rather than paragraphs, limiting the number of bullets per slide to five or six. Use animation effects such as fades and dissolves sparingly, only when they clarify your main points. (If you use them frequently, your audience will be so dazzled by the effects that they'll be distracted by them, and your points will be lost.)

Use a large font. For slides, use at least 36-point for major headings and 24-point for text. Make sure that those in the farthest seats can easily read your projected slides. If your list, spreadsheet, or chart is too detailed to present on a slide using a large font, share it through a handout instead.

Prepare Effective Handouts

There are two kinds of handouts: those to which you'll be referring during the presentation and those that you'll want your audience to read afterwards. Those to which you'll be referring during your presentation should be very simple tables, graphs, and bulleted lists, so readers can quickly digest them and grasp your point. Follow the suggestions in Chapter 14 for creating effective tables and graphs. If you have several handouts, considering duplicating them on paper in a variety of colors to help audience members locate them quickly ("Now please turn to the chart on green paper").

"Take away" materials can include complete reports and other more detailed materials. Follow the suggestions given earlier in this chapter to maximize the impact of written materials.

Stimulate Discussion

We have all sat through lectures and presentations that, while interesting and informative, didn't inspire us to change our thinking or actions. You want to do more than entertain; you want your audience to think about your findings and leave with a sense of commitment to act upon them. The key to getting audience members to do this is to engage them in a structured discussion that will lead to action. To achieve this end:

Plan to speak for no more than half to two-thirds of the time that you've been allotted, allowing the rest of the time for questions and discussion.

While it's fine to allow questions and comments during the presentation portion of your allotted time, *remain in charge* and don't let such remarks eat up your time and derail your presentation. Don't be shy about saying, "These are great questions, but I'm afraid I have time for only one more" or "This is a great discussion and I hate to interrupt it, but I have several more points that I want to share with you."

When you conclude your remarks, **launch a structured conversation** by listing a few discussion questions on your last slide, such as:

- What was the most important thing you learned today?

- What one thing most surprised you?

- How can we use this information to help our students?

To make the discussion even more effective, **consider asking each member of your audience for a contribution.** If your group is too large for you to call on everyone, use Minute Papers (see Chapter 9) or break your audience into small groups to discuss your questions. Each small group can then share its most common responses with the entire group.

Next, **record the answers** to your discussion questions on a flipchart, white board, or other medium visible to everyone in the audience. (If you can't write legibly, ask someone else to do this for you.) After your presentation, **transcribe the answers and send them to the participants,** who can use them as the starting point for an action plan.

WHAT IF YOUR AUDIENCE WON'T BE HAPPY WITH YOUR FINDINGS?

As discussed in Chapter 3, no one likes to hear bad news. It's easy to feel threatened by bad news and to want to "kill the messenger" by blaming the bad news on flaws in the assessment. If your assessment unearths a problem, how can you get your audience to focus on addressing the problem rather than attacking you or the assessment process?

Be prepared. Try to learn about opposing views in advance, and address those views when you share your results.

Avoid surprising people. People will be less inclined to criticize something in which they've been involved so, as discussed in Chapter 4, include your audiences in planning your assessment. When you do so, discuss the possibility of disappointing results and how they might be shared. Then, as soon as you suspect that your assessment may indeed yield disappointing results, talk to those audience members with a stake in those results. (If students' general education quantitative skills are disappointing, for example, talk to faculty teaching those courses.) You may gain insight that helps explain your findings and modifies your conclusions. At the very least, you will have forewarned your colleagues so they can begin planning a response. If your colleagues have enough lead time, your reports can include not only your findings but also their plans to address those findings, giving the reports a very positive "problem solved" spin.

Provide corroborating information. As suggested earlier in this chapter, include information gathered either on campus or through a review of research literature that adds credibility to your findings.

Acknowledge possible flaws in your assessment strategy. Remember that all assessment methods are inherently imperfect and may not yield accurate information. Perhaps, through plain chance, you happened to sample the 50 worst student writing samples of the year. Assessments only provide *indications* of a problem, not *proof* of it. Often it's appropriate to repeat an assessment before concluding that changes are warranted, especially if the changes would be expensive or time-consuming.

Balance negatives with positives. Bad news is easier to digest if it's balanced with good news. Try sandwiching bad news between two positive outcomes, even if they're relatively minor.

Be gentle and sensitive. Your stakeholders may bristle if you announce "bad news," a "serious problem," or a "failure." They may be more receptive if you present bad news as an "area of concern" or a "suggestion for further improvement." Rather than say, "The faculty is doing a poor job advising students," say, "Consider strengthening professional development opportunities for faculty on advising." Avoid pinning blame on individuals.

Help stakeholders identify possible solutions. Stakeholders may find bad news especially threatening if they see it as an insurmountable problem. Draw upon research, your own experiences, and those of your colleagues to come up with practical suggestions for addressing problem areas. If you don't feel qualified to do this, sponsor a meeting to brainstorm possible solutions.

TIME TO THINK, DISCUSS, AND PRACTICE

1) Table 15.1 presents part of the results of the National Survey of Student Engagement for seniors at a fictitious college. You have been asked to prepare a short summary of these results for the college's senior administrators. Develop a summary that presents these results effectively. You may want to develop tables, graphs, bulleted lists, slides, and/or a few paragraphs of text.

2) The writing skills of students completing the first-year composition course at your college have been assessed using the ABC Writing Test. The results have come back and they're very disappointing; on average, students score well below the national mean on every characteristic of effective writing assessed by the test. Discuss how you might constructively communicate this information to the faculty who teach first-year composition.

Table 15.1

Selected Results From the 2002 National Survey of Student Engagement: How Often Students at Rodney College Report Engaging in Various Learning Activities During Their Senior Year

	Average Frequency [1]	
	At Rodney College	At All institutions [2]
• Asked questions in class or contributed to class discussions	3.02	3.10
• Made a class presentation	2.91	2.81
• Prepared two or more drafts of a paper or assignment before turning it in	2.46	2.50
• Worked on a paper or project that required integrating ideas or information from various sources	3.33	3.33

	Average Frequency [1]	
	At Rodney College	At All Institutions [2]
• Worked with other students on projects **during class**	2.65*	2.45
• Worked with classmates **outside of class** to prepare class assignments	2.70	2.72
• Put together ideas or concepts from different courses when completing assignments or during class discussions	2.77	2.82
• Participated in a community-based project as part of a regular course	1.53	1.59
• Used an electronic medium (listserv, chat group, Internet, etc.) to discuss or complete an assignment	2.92*	2.76
• Used email to communicate with an instructor	3.13	3.07
• Discussed grades or assignments with an instructor	2.85	2.81
• Discussed ideas from your readings or classes with faculty members outside of class	1.97	2.09
• Received prompt feedback from faculty on your academic performance (written or oral)	2.75	2.81

*Difference between Rodney and national averages is statistically significant (p<.05)

[1] 4 = Very often, 3 = Often, 2 = Sometimes, 1 = Never

[2] Participating in the survey

ACKNOWLEDGMENT

Some of the material in this chapter is adapted from my earlier book, *Questionnaire Survey Research: What Works*, published by the Association for Institutional Research. I am grateful to the association for permission to adapt this material.

REFERENCES

Gangopadhyay, P. (2002, September). *Making evaluation meaningful to all education stakeholders.* Kalamazoo, MI: Western Michigan University, The Evaluation Center. Retrieved June 2, 2003, from http://www.wmich.edu/evalctr/checklists/makingevalmeaningful.pdf

Harris, E., & Muchin, S. (2002). Promising practices: Using information architecture to improve communication. *The Evaluation Exchange*, 8(3), 4–5. Retrieved June 2, 2003, from http://www.gse.harvard.edu/hfrp/content/eval/issue20/winter2002.pdf

RECOMMENDED READING

Bers, T. H., with Seybert, J. A. (1999). *Effective reporting* (Resources in Institutional Research No. 12). Tallahassee, FL: Association for Institutional Research.

Eline, L. (Ed.). (1997). *How to prepare and use effective visual aids.* Alexandria, VA: American Society for Training and Development.

Hendricks, M. (1994). Making a splash: Reporting evaluation results effectively. In J. S. Wholey, H. P. Hatry, & K. E. Newcomer (Eds.), *Handbook of practical program evaluation* (pp. 575–571). San Francisco, CA: Jossey-Bass.

Lilley, S. (2002, June). *How to deliver negative evaluation results constructively: Ten tips for evaluators.* Retrieved June 2, 2003, from http://www.chebucto.ns.ca/~LilleyS/tips.html

MacGregor, J., Tinto, V., & Lindblad, J. H. (2001). Assessment of innovative efforts: Lessons from the learning community movement. In L. Suskie (Ed.), *Assessment to promote deep learning: Insight from AAHE's 2000 and 1999 assessment conferences* (pp. 41–48). Washington, DC: American Association for Higher Education.

Morris, L. L., Fitz-Gibbon, C. T., & Freeman, M. E. (1987). *How to communicate evaluation findings*. Newbury Park, CA: Sage.

Palomba, C. A., & Banta, T. W. (1999). Reporting and using results. In *Assessment essentials: Putting principles to work on college campuses* (pp. 297–330). San Francisco, CA: Jossey-Bass.

Wainer, H. (Ed.). (1993). Making readable overhead displays. *Chance: New Directions for Statistics and Computing, 6*(2), 46–49.

16

Using Assessment Findings Effectively and Appropriately

A ssessment reports that end up briefly perused and then filed with-out further action are, to be blunt, a waste of time. In Chapter 1, assessment was defined as a four-step cycle: 1) defining student learning goals, 2) providing students with learning opportunities to achieve those goals, 3) assessing how well students have achieved those goals, and 4) using assessment results to improve the other three steps, primarily learning opportunities. All the time and effort that goes into assessment is worthwhile only if that work eventually leads to improved teaching and learning. This makes the fourth step, the one that closes the loop in Figure 1.1 in Chapter 1, the most important.

Making good use of assessment findings can also be the most diffi-cult of the four steps. Recall one of the principles of good assessment (Chapter 2): Assessment results should never dictate decisions to us; we should always use our professional judgment to interpret assessment results and make appropriate decisions. This is not easy! Getting faculty and staff to agree on what the results mean and what changes, if any, are indicated can be daunting.

This chapter provides some frameworks and considerations to guide your thinking on clarifying what you're looking for, setting stan-dards, addressing both positive and disappointing results, and review-ing your assessment plans and efforts.

KNOW WHAT YOU ARE LOOKING FOR

It's all too easy to plunge into assessment without a clear sense of what you're trying to find out or how the assessment you're undertaking relates to what you're trying to teach. Imagine a college deciding, without much discussion, to administer the XYZ Critical Thinking Test to its students. The tests are scored and the college community learns that its students average 145, far lower than the national average of 175. The community is plunged into a quandary and questions fly:

- Why did our students do so badly?

- Why are we testing critical thinking?

- Why did we choose this particular test?

- What is critical thinking, anyway?

- Whose fault is this? Who is supposed to be teaching critical thinking, and in what courses?

- How are we supposed to teach critical thinking?

- How can we possibly boost critical thinking scores in all our students when there's no one course emphasizing critical thinking that all students take?

Most of these questions could have been avoided if the college had begun its assessment work with clear answers to at least the following questions, all addressed earlier in this book:

- Why are we assessing? What decisions will this assessment help us make (see Chapter 4)?

- What are our most important student learning goals (Chapter 5)? Do we have a common understanding of what fuzzy terms like "critical thinking" mean?

- Do we have a clear strategy in place to ensure that every student has adequate opportunity to achieve each of our major goals (see Chapter 4)?

- Do the assessment tools and techniques that we're considering clearly correspond to our student learning goals as we define them (see Part III)?

Much of the difficulty that campuses face in closing the loop could thus be prevented by focusing more on the kind of planning described in Chapter 4. Often the major outcome of an ill-conceived assessment strategy is to bring attention back to the need for careful planning, yielding a more useful assessment strategy on the second try.

WHAT LEVEL OF STUDENT PERFORMANCE IS GOOD ENOUGH?

One of the toughest questions facing faculty and staff when they review assessment findings is whether the results are "good enough": Is student performance satisfactory? Do we have a problem or not?

Unless your performance standards are mandated by some external source, such as a licensure board, deciding what performance level is "good enough" is essentially a subjective decision. Some assessment practitioners advocate setting standards as part of the assessment planning process, before assessments are undertaken. You might set a standard that at least:

- 80% of students should pass this test.

- 75% of students' writing samples should be scored "outstanding."

- 65% of students should score above the national average.

- Student scores on this rubric should improve an average of five points between the beginning of the year and the end.

But setting standards before an assessment is undertaken may lead to arbitrary and perhaps unrealistic standards. It may be more feasible to first implement the assessment on a small scale and then use the results to discuss with colleagues what standards are appropriate, using the following questions as a springboard for conversation:

- From what perspective(s) do we want to interpret these results (see Chapter 6): standards-based, benchmarking, best practice, value-added, longitudinal, and/or potential?

- Which samples of student work represent at least minimally acceptable work for a graduate of our program or institution? Which samples are unacceptably inadequate?

- How do the acceptable and inadequate samples differ? What characteristics define minimally acceptable work?

- Which samples represent exemplary work? Would it be realistic to establish these as the standards we aim for in all students?

To help inform this discussion, find out if colleagues in peer programs have established standards that might be adapted to your situation. Perhaps appropriate disciplinary associations have issued statements on expectations for graduates of your program. A simple web search may turn up examples of rubrics and grading standards, particularly for fairly common learning goals such as writing, science laboratory skills, and information literacy. If your professional colleagues have a discussion list, post a query asking for examples of standards they use.

WHAT SHOULD YOU DO WHEN ASSESSMENT FINDINGS ARE POSITIVE?

Suppose that, in blind reviews, faculty score 85% of anthropology senior theses "outstanding" in terms of clarity, organization, comprehensiveness of review of scholarly literature, and soundness of analysis and conclusions. Five percent are scored "very good," 5% "adequate," and 5% "inadequate." What might the anthropology faculty do with this information?

Celebrate!

Because the purpose of assessment is usually to improve teaching and learning, it's easy to focus on problem areas and not celebrate positive findings. Obviously these results are, on the whole, very good and should be celebrated as such, perhaps by:

- Providing a public forum for students to present their work, such as a student research conference.
- Awarding prizes to students for outstanding work.
- Hosting a party for students and faculty.
- Making outstanding papers available to other students as models (first obtaining written permission from the papers' authors).

Publicize!

Positive assessment results are good news for everyone with an interest in your program or institution: faculty, students, administrators, alumni, prospective students, donors, and so on. Let all these people know that your program or institution is worthy of attendance, investment, and support.

- Post a summary of the results on a departmental or institutional web site or in department or employee newsletters.

- Send students a brief email or paper newsletter or brochure summarizing results.

- Present a summary of results at an appropriate student meeting. For institution-wide assessments, this might be a student government meeting; for program assessments, this might be a disciplinary club meeting.

- Ask faculty to announce results in appropriate courses.

- Ask faculty advisors to share results with their advisees.

- Send a press release announcing the results to the student newspaper.

- Include the results in brochures for prospective students, who will be attracted to your program when they see solid evidence that they will learn important things.

- Send a brief summary to major prospective employers of your graduates, who will be more likely to hire your graduates when they see convincing evidence of their knowledge and skills.

- Ask institutional leaders, such as the dean of your division or the chief academic officer, to help share the results both on and off campus.

- Send a brief summary to your fundraising staff and office. They will be delighted to have solid evidence to share with prospective donors that your program or institution is worthy of investment!

- For really major or exceptional results, ask the campus public relations office to send a press release to local media.

- If your campus has an assessment office, share your results with it; the staff may be able to help publicize the results.

All these suggestions refer to sharing *aggregated* results for *all* students participating in the assessment. As discussed in Chapter 2, *individual* results must be kept confidential, shared only with the student and the faculty involved in his or her education.

What About the "Inadequate" 5%?

Should we aim for every student to do acceptable work on every assignment? No, for two reasons. First, while it's appropriate to expect every student who *successfully completes* a program to have achieved every major learning goal, failing students will, appropriately, not achieve some learning goals. Second, as noted in Chapter 2, every assessment is an imperfect, incomplete sample of what students have learned, and it's entirely possible that a few students who have truly mastered important learning goals may do poorly on one particular assignment or test.

So should you be concerned about the "inadequate" 5%? Here are some questions to help you decide.

Are you certain that these papers are inadequate? Score the inadequate papers twice, using two separate scorers, to confirm the scores before taking any further action.

Are these results corroborated by other evidence? Look at other work these students have produced before finalizing conclusions about their performance level.

How many students are you talking about? If a program graduates 20 students a year, you are only talking about one student—hardly enough to warrant wholesale revisions in curriculum or teaching methods. Repeat the assessment next year, and possible the year after, before deciding that this is an ongoing problem.

Is this problem big enough to be a real worry? Despite our best efforts, occasionally a student with inadequate skills may slip through the cracks. If we are talking about very fundamental skills, such as the ability to write in complete sentences, any student who graduates with inadequate levels of such skills is indeed a concern. Similarly, if students are preparing for careers in which errors can have serious consequences, such as nursing or civil engineering, it's vital to ensure that every student graduates with a certain base of knowledge and skills. But the consequences may not be quite so dire if, for example, an occasional economics student slips through with, say, less-than-desired public speaking skills. Weigh the costs of perfection against the benefits.

Can Results Be Too Positive?

Some faculty might be more concerned about the large proportion of students in this example who earned high scores than the few students who performed unacceptably. If 85% of senior theses are scored outstanding, are the standards too low? If the scores are based on clear, challenging criteria, high scores simply reflect a very successful teaching/learning experience. But it may be worthwhile to review those standards and discuss whether they should be ratcheted up a bit.

WHAT SHOULD YOU DO WHEN ASSESSMENT FINDINGS ARE DISAPPOINTING?

First, don't try to brush disappointing results under the carpet. Remember that the primary purpose of assessment is to improve student learning, and disappointing results can help achieve this aim.

Second, don't be punitive. The fastest way to kill an assessment effort is to use less-than-positive results to deny tenure, promotion, or merit pay to individual faculty members or to cut a department's budget or program. Even the vaguest rumor of such a possibility will seriously impede assessment efforts. Never mandate the use of assessment results in faculty evaluations. Faculty must be confident that assessment results will not be used against them.

Does this contradict the suggestion made in Chapter 3 to recognize and reward assessment efforts through tenure, promotion, and merit processes? Not if the inclusion of assessment results is *voluntary*. Faculty should be *encouraged* to include positive assessment results in tenure, promotion, and merit applications along with other evidence of teaching effectiveness but never *compelled* to include specific results.

Finally, try to identify what caused the disappointing results and what needs to be addressed to improve them. As the example of the XYZ Critical Thinking Test that opened this chapter demonstrated, it can be very difficult to do this! Examine four general areas—learning goals, curriculum, teaching methods, and assessment strategy—as any of them may be contributing to the disappointing results.

Consider Your Learning Goals

As you consider your learning goals, ask the following questions.

Do you have too many goals? Can a typical student truly be expected to achieve all the goals that have been identified for a course or program? Research is showing that "time on task" is one of the biggest contributors to deep, lasting learning. Students will learn and remember more if you focus on just a few key learning goals than if you address many superficially. If you have too many goals, you and your colleagues must decide which ones to emphasize and which to deemphasize. These discussions go to the heart of what faculty value, and discussions can easily become contentious. Chapter 5 gives suggestions for refining goals collaboratively.

Are your goals appropriate? It's unrealistic, for example, to expect to turn an incompetent writer into one capable of writing a senior thesis in just one semester. Similarly, faculty can't prepare a student who's only taken high school business mathematics for calculus in one semester— or even two. Student life staff can't expect students to become outstanding leaders in a one-week leadership program. Librarians can't expect students to master a full array of information literacy skills in a one-hour bibliographic instruction class. Consider whether your goals need to be scaled back to levels that still challenge students but are more realistic.

Should you clarify or refine your goals? Suppose that Ashford College biology majors scored poorly on the botany section of the ABC Biology Test. Some biology faculty feel this is not a concern, because virtually all Ashford biology graduates go on to careers in health fields, where they don't need a strong background in botany. Other faculty feel, however, that a grounding in botany is essential to being a well-rounded biologist. How might the faculty resolve this? Here are some strategies.

- ***Collect information to inform the discussion.*** Survey students to determine how many are planning careers that require an understanding of botany. Survey alumni to determine if they need or use botany in their careers.

- ***Investigate other tests and assessments*** that might be viewed as more relevant by a majority of the faculty.

- **Vote** on whether to keep the goal of giving students a grounding in botany and whether to continue using the test. Because important work can be stalled indefinitely by endless efforts to seek unanimous consensus, sometimes it's simply time to take a vote, let the majority rule, and move on.

Consider Your Curriculum

Sometimes students perform poorly on an assessment because relevant learning goals are given insufficient attention in a course or program's curriculum. Students may have poor research skills, for example, because they've had few opportunities to develop and practice those skills. If a particular learning goal is truly a major priority, faculty should ensure that students have ample opportunity to study and practice it repeatedly and intensively.

Take a hard look, therefore, at how well your curriculum addresses each major learning goal. If you are assessing student learning in a course, examine its content and requirements, especially how much time students must spend achieving the course's major learning goals. If you are assessing student learning throughout a program, examine your course offerings (both required and elective), course content and requirements, course sequencing and prerequisites, admissions criteria, placement criteria, support services such as tutoring, and cocurricular activities. If you're not sure exactly where the problem lies, review the transcripts of your best- and worst-performing students. Are there any patterns in the order in which your best- and worst-performing students took required courses? In the grades they earned in those courses? In the elective courses they chose?

Most curricula are already packed to the gills, so how can faculty add more intensive study of a particular goal? Here are some suggestions.

Make some tough choices regarding your priorities for student learning goals, as discussed earlier. Reduce attention to some less important goals to make room for more coverage for this one, either by dropping a less-critical course requirement or by scaling back coverage of less important concepts in some courses.

Increase the credit value of a key course, or spread a curriculum over two courses. Some students may be more successful in Calculus I, for example, if they can study it in two three-credit courses rather than in one four-credit course.

Replace a program elective with a required capstone course that reteaches this learning goal.

Require students in their last semester to complete an independent project that emphasizes this goal. If you want to help students learn how to make oral presentations, for example, consider requiring graduating students to make oral presentations on their projects at a department research conference.

Ask faculty to review the skill or concept in several courses.

If the goal is a fairly generic skill, such as conducting statistical analyses or making oral presentations, *require students to take an appropriate course in another department as a cognate or general education requirement.* (If you elect this approach, you still need to build attention to these skills within your own curriculum, so students learn the nuances of applying the skill to your discipline.)

Give students more responsibility for learning on their own. Have students learn basic content knowledge outside class, perhaps by reading the textbook or working with peers, freeing up class time to focus on key learning goals. Or, if students need to strengthen their information literacy skills, see if online lessons are available. If students need to strengthen their writing skills but you don't have the time to read every draft, periodically ask students to read and comment on each other's drafts. Or have students strengthen their writing skills by composing summaries of concepts that the class can use as supplemental reading or study guides.

Look for ways to use class time more effectively. If students need to strengthen their oral presentation skills, but you don't have time to hear individual oral presentations, have students enhance their skills by teaching key topics to the class so your curriculum doesn't fall behind. Or have students make group rather than individual presentations.

As you examine your curriculum, ask yourself if students adequately understand its whys and wherefores. Students learn more effectively when they understand the goals, rationale, and structure of courses and programs. Ewell (1997) has noted that we often operate with four curricula—designed, delivered, expectational, and experienced—that may not be congruent. You may need to improve your students' under-standing of your curriculum by revising catalog descriptions, program brochures, course syllabi, and the like.

Consider Your Teaching Methods

Sometimes we have to own up to a cruel fact: Despite our best efforts, we simply didn't teach a particular skill or concept well. Improving one's teaching methods can be difficult because few faculty have received formal instruction in teaching methods. Consequently, many haven't a clue on how to teach more effectively.

Fortunately, increasing research evidence on how students learn offers clues on teaching strategies that are likely to be effective. Table 16.1 offers many research-based ideas on ways to approach teaching and learn-ing.

Colleges and universities that want to help faculty learn how to teach more effectively see assessment as a vehicle to promote profes-sional development. They offer professional development resources such as teaching/learning centers, instructional technology centers, workshops, readings, and sponsored attendance at conferences on teaching and learning.

One principle in Table 16.1 that's especially important to assess-ment efforts is giving students prompt, concrete feedback on their work. Assessment activities can be valuable learning opportunities for students *if* they receive prompt feedback on their performance. To require students to participate in an assessment activity and *not* give them feedback on their performance diminishes the overall value of the assessment experience and is inconsiderate of their contributions to an assessment effort.

Sometimes, however, it's not practical to give students feedback on their individual performances. Graduating seniors, for example, might provide writing samples that can't be scored until after they have grad-uated. In these situations, consider making an overall summary of the results available to current students.

If you give students feedback *and* engage them in evaluating assess-ment results, you'll not only help them learn but also improve your assessment strategies. If you're not sure why students performed poorly, ask them! In an appropriate class or other setting, tell them honestly,

Table 16.1

Strategies That Promote Deep, Lasting Learning

A growing body of research evidence indicates that students learn most effectively when:

- They understand course and program goals and the characteristics of excellent work.
- They are academically challenged and given high but attainable expectations.
- They spend more time actively involved in learning and less time listening to lectures.
- They engage in multidimensional real-world tasks in which they explore, analyze, justify, evaluate, use other thinking skills, and arrive at multiple solutions. Such tasks may include realistic class assignments, field experiences, and service-learning opportunities.
- The diversity of their learning styles is respected; they are given a variety of ways to learn and to demonstrate what they've learned.
- They have positive interactions with faculty and work collaboratively with fellow students.
- They spend significant time studying and practicing.
- They receive prompt, concrete feedback on their work.
- They have opportunities to revise their work.
- They participate in co-curricular activities that build on what they are learning in the classroom.
- They reflect on what and how they have learned and see coherence in their learning.
- They have a synthesizing experience such as a capstone course, independent study, or research project.
- Assessments focus on the most important course and program goals and are learning activities in their own right.

"A lot of you got that test question wrong/did poorly on that assignment. We didn't think it would be that hard; why it was so difficult?" Your students will likely give you surprisingly perceptive and useful replies.

Consider Your Assessment Strategies and Tools

Sometimes poor performance is due to the assessment itself. Sometimes test questions and assignments are so poorly written that students misinterpret them; sometimes they're a poor match with major learning goals; and sometimes they're simply too difficult. If any of these is the case, students may actually have achieved key learning goals more completely than is evidenced by their performance. This is especially likely the first time a new, untested test or assignment is given. Chapter 14 discusses ways to analyze the results of a test or rubric and identify poorly written or overly difficult assessments. Revise such assessments before using them again.

Isn't Poor Performance Sometimes the Student's Fault?

Yes. As the adage goes, you can lead a horse to water, but you can't make it drink. Despite our best efforts, some students will not make an adequate effort to learn and deserve to fail. But these students are usually in the minority; most students generally want to do whatever's necessary to pass their courses and graduate.

One way to identify whether responsibility for poor performance lies with the student or elsewhere is the "50% rule" mentioned in Chapter 14: If more than half the students get a particular test question wrong or fail a particular part of an assignment, the problem probably lies not with the students but with one of the other reasons discussed in this chapter: goals, curriculum (including placement), teaching methods, or assessment strategies and tools. If this is the case, students shouldn't be penalized. Give everyone credit for that part of the assessment.

REVIEW YOUR ASSESSMENT PLAN AND EFFORTS

A final, important aspect of closing the loop is periodically reviewing and updating the overall assessment plan and program developed in Chapter 4. Keep in mind that every aspect of assessment is an ongoing work in progress. As the needs of your students evolve in a rapidly changing world, so will your goals, curricula, teaching methods, and assessment practices. As you review your assessment program, examine the following.

Goals and outcomes: How well has assessment in practice matched your intentions? Is everything working the way you intended?

Unexpected results: What have been your major success stories? What have been your biggest disappointments? What went smoothly, and what was more difficult than you'd anticipated?

Quality: Are your assessment results generally of sufficient quality that you can have confidence in them and use them for improvements?

Cost and benefits: What has been the cost of your assessment program in terms of faculty and staff time, hard dollars, and other resources? What have been the program's benefits, and how do the costs measure up against the benefits? Is any part of the assessment program less useful or more burdensome than envisioned?

Changes in context and culture: How has the campus culture evolved since the plan was developed? How have students changed? How has current thinking on the nature and practice of assessment changed? How might these changes impact assessment policies and practices?

Possible modifications: Is the plan still appropriate? How might you improve your assessment efforts?

Just as you should celebrate positive assessment *results*, you should also celebrate superior and improved assessment *efforts*, as discussed in Chapter 3. On a regular basis, take time to recognize and honor those who have made significant contributions to creating an assessment culture on your campus. They are laying the groundwork for even stronger assessment efforts in the years to come.

TIME TO THINK, DISCUSS, AND PRACTICE

1) For each of these scenarios, first discussed in Chapter 6, discuss whether the department should conclude that it is achieving its goal. Can you decide this? If not, what more do you need to know to make a decision? Be specific!

- One of the foreign language department's goals is for its French seniors to surpass seniors nationally on the Major Field Test in French. This year 55% of seniors scored above the national average on the test.

- One of the social work department's goals is for its graduates to succeed in graduate study. A survey of alumni who graduated five years ago shows that 40% have earned an M.S.W.

2) Faculty at Mountaintop Community College agree that graduating students should be able to think critically (which they define as analyzing, evaluating, and synthesizing), but they aren't satisfied with the critical thinking skills of their graduating students. Unfortunately, they can't find a place in the curriculum for students to practice these skills. All the faculty agree that they have so much content to cover in their courses that they don't have time to teach students how to think critically and then grade critical thinking assignments. How might the faculty reconcile the need for content coverage with the need to help students learn critical thinking skills? Brainstorm very practical, concrete advice!

3) One of the goals of the International Business program is for students to be able to "write clearly and effectively." Although International Business majors are asked to write term papers in at least four courses, their writing quality is nonetheless generally still inadequate by the time they're seniors. Faculty are quick to point to the woefully poor writing skills of entering first-year students and equally quick to blame the English department for not bringing writing skills up to par in first-year composition classes.

- Who should have lead responsibility for helping International Business majors develop their writing skills? Why?

- Brainstorm what might be done to improve students' writing skills by the time they graduate.

REFERENCE

Ewell, P. T. (1997). Identifying indicators of curricular quality. In J. G. Gaff & J. L. Ratcliff (Eds.), *Handbook of the undergraduate curriculum: A comprehensive guide to purposes, structures, practices, and change* (pp. 609–631). San Francisco, CA: Jossey-Bass.

RECOMMENDED READING

American Association for Higher Education, American College Personnel Association, & National Association of Student Personnel Administrators. (1998, June 2). *Powerful partnerships: A shared responsibility for learning.* Washington, DC: Authors. Retrieved June 2, 2003, from http://www.aahe.org/teaching/tsk_frce.htm

Angelo, T. A. (1993, April). A "teacher's dozen": Fourteen general, research-based principles for improving higher learning in our classrooms. *AAHE Bulletin, 45*(8), 3–7, 13.

Association of American Colleges and Universities. (2002). *Greater expectations: A new vision for learning as a nation goes to college.* Washington, DC: Author. Retrieved June 2, 2003, from http://www.greaterexpectations.org

Astin, A. W. (1993). *What matters in college: Four critical years revisited.* San Francisco, CA: Jossey-Bass.

Barr, R. B., & Tagg, J. (1995). From teaching to learning: A new paradigm for undergraduate education. *Change, 27*(6), 12–25.

Bonwell, C. C., & Eison, J. A. (1991). *Active learning: Creating excitement in the classroom* (ASHE-ERIC Higher Education Report No. 1). Washington, DC: George Washington University, School of Education and Human Development.

Chickering, A. W., & Gamson, Z. (1987). Seven principles for good practice in undergraduate education. *AAHE Bulletin, 39*(7), 5–10.

Chickering, A. W., & Gamson, Z. (1991). New directions for teaching and learning: No. 47. *Applying the seven principles for good practice in undergraduate education.* San Francisco, CA: Jossey-Bass.

Coalition of Essential Schools. (2002). *How to analyze a curriculum unit or project and provide the scaffolding students need to succeed.* Oakland, CA: Author. Retrieved June 2, 2003, from http://www.essen tialschools.org/cs/resources/view/ces_res/85

Ewell, P. T., & Jones, D. P. (1996). *Indicators of "good practice" in undergraduate education: A handbook for development and implementation.* Boulder, CO: National Center for Higher Education Management Systems.

Huba, M. E., & Freed, J. E. (2000). Understanding hallmarks of learner-centered teaching and assessment. In *Learner-centered assessment on college campuses: Shifting the focus from teaching to learning* (pp. 32–64). Needham Heights, MA: Allyn & Bacon.

Kuh, G. (2001). Assessing what really matters to student learning: Inside the National Survey of Student Engagement. *Change, 33*(3), 10–17, 66.

Kuh, G. D., Schuh, J. H., Whitt, E. J., & Associates. (1991). *Involving colleges: Successful approaches to fostering student learning and development outside the classroom.* San Francisco, CA: Jossey-Bass.

Light, R. (2001). *Making the most of college: Students speak their minds.* Cambridge, MA: Harvard University Press.

McKeachie, W. J. (2002). *Teaching tips: Strategies, research, and theory for college and university teachers* (11th ed.). Boston, MA: Houghton Mifflin.

Mentkowski, M., & Associates. (2000). *Learning that lasts: Integrating learning, development, and performance in college and beyond.* San Francisco, CA: Jossey-Bass.

Palmer, P. J. (1998). *The courage to teach: Exploring the inner landscape of a teacher's life.* San Francisco, CA: Jossey-Bass.

Pascarella, E. T. (2001). Identifying excellence in undergraduate education: Are we even close? *Change, 33*(3), 19–23.

Pascarella, E. T., & Terenzini, P. T. (1991). *How college affects students: Findings and insights from twenty years of research.* San Francisco, CA: Jossey-Bass.

Plater, W. M. (1998). So . . . why aren't we taking learning seriously? *About Campus, 3*(5), 9–14.

Romer, R., & Education Commission of the States. (1996, April). What research says about improving undergraduate education. *AAHE Bulletin, 48*(8), 5–8.

Shepard, L. A. (1977). *A checklist for evaluating large-scale assessment programs* (Occasional Paper Series #9). Kalamazoo, MI: Western Michigan University, The Evaluation Center. Retrieved June 2, 2003, from http://www.wmich.edu/evalctr/checklists/assessment _eval_header.htm

Strange, C. C., & Banning, J. H. (2000). *Educating by design: Creating campus learning environments that work.* San Francisco, CA: Jossey-Bass.

KEY RESOURCES ON ASSESSING STUDENT LEARNING

The following are some important resources on assessing student learning. The bibliographies of these resources will lead you to additional readings.

Allen, M. J. (2004). *Assessing academic programs in higher education*. Bolton, MA: Anker.

Anderson, R. S., & Speck, B. W. (Eds.). (1998). *New directions for teaching and learning: No. 74: Changing the way we grade student performance: Classroom assessment and the new learning paradigm*. San Francisco, CA: Jossey-Bass.

Angelo, T. A., & Cross, K. P. (1993). *Classroom assessment techniques: A handbook for college teachers* (2nd ed.). San Francisco, CA: Jossey-Bass.

Astin, A. W. (1996). *Assessment for excellence: The philosophy and practice of assessment and evaluation in higher education*. Portland, OR: Oryx and American Council on Education.

Banta, T. W., Lund, J. P., Black, K. E., & Oblander, F. W. (1996). *Assessment in practice: Putting principles to work on college campuses*. San Francisco, CA: Jossey-Bass.

Bauer, K. W. (2003). Assessment for institutional research: Guidelines and resources. In W. E. Knight (Ed.), *The primer for institutional research* (pp. 9–23). Tallahassee, FL: Association for Institutional Research.

Chun, M. (2002). Looking where the light is better: A review of the literature on assessing higher education quality. *Peer Review, 4*(2/3), 16–25.

Diamond, R. M. (1997). *Designing and assessing courses and curricula: A practical guide*. San Francisco, CA: Jossey-Bass.

Erwin, T. D. (1991). *Assessing student learning and development: A guide to the principles, goals, and methods of determining college outcomes*. San Francisco, CA: Jossey-Bass.

Erwin, T. D. (2000). *The NPEC sourcebook on assessment, volume 1: Definitions and assessment methods for critical thinking, problem solving, and writing* [Electronic version]. Washington, DC: National Center for Education Statistics. Retrieved June 2, 2003, from http://nces.ed.gov/pubs2000/2000195.pdf

Ewell, P. T. (2003). Assessment (again). *Change, 35*(1), 4–5.

Gardiner, L. F., Anderson, C., & Cambridge, B. L. (Eds.). (1997). *Learning through assessment: A resource guide for higher education.* Washington, DC: American Association for Higher Education.

Gates, S., Augustine, C., Benjamin, R., Bikson, T., Kaganoff, T., Levy, D., et al. (2002). *Ensuring quality and productivity in higher education: An analysis of assessment practices.* San Francisco, CA: Jossey-Bass.

Gray, P. J., & Banta, T. W. (Eds.). (1997). *New directions for higher education: No. 100. The campus-level impact of assessment: Progress, problems, and possibilities.* San Francisco, CA: Jossey-Bass.

Huba, M. E., & Freed, J. E. (2000). *Learner-centered assessment on college campuses: Shifting the focus from teaching to learning.* Boston, MA: Allyn & Bacon.

Jacobi, M., Astin, A., & Ayala, F., Jr. (1987). *College student outcomes assessment: A talent development perspective* (ASHE-ERIC Higher Education Report No. 7). Washington, DC: Association for the Study of Higher Education.

Linn, R. L., & Gronlund, N. E. (2000). *Measurement and assessment in teaching* (8th ed.). New York, NY: Macmillan.

Mehrens, W. A., & Lehman, I. J. (1991). *Measurement and evaluation in education and psychology* (4th ed.). Fort Worth, TX: Harcourt Brace.

Mentkowski, M., & Associates. (2000). *Learning that lasts: Integrating learning, development, and performance in college and beyond.* San Francisco, CA: Jossey-Bass.

Middle States Commission on Higher Education. (2003). *Student learning assessment: Options and resources.* Philadelphia, PA: Author.

Nichols, J. O. (1995). *A practitioner's handbook for institutional effectiveness and student outcomes assessment implementation* (3rd ed.). New York, NY: Agathon.

Nichols, J. O., & Nichols, K. W. (2001). *General education assessment for improvement of student academic achievement: Guidance for academic departments and committees.* New York, NY: Agathon.

Palomba, C. A., & Banta, T. W. (1999). *Assessment essentials: Putting principles to work on college campuses.* San Francisco, CA: Jossey-Bass.

Pellegrino, J. W., Chudowsky, N., & Glaser, R. (Eds.). (2001). *Knowing what students know: The science and design of educational assessment.* Washington, DC: National Academy Press. Retrieved June 2, 2003, from http://www.nap.edu/books/0309072727.html/

Phye, G. (Ed.). (1996). *Handbook of classroom assessment: Learning, adjustment, and achievement.* London, United Kingdom: Academic Press.

Popham, W. J. (2000). *Modern educational measurement: Practical guidelines for educational leaders* (3rd ed.). Boston, MA: Allyn & Bacon.

Schuh, J. H., & Upcraft, M. L. (2001). *Assessment in practice in student affairs: An applications manual.* San Francisco, CA: Jossey-Bass.

Steen, L. A. (1999). Assessing assessment. In B. Gold, S. Keith, & W. Marion (Eds.), *Assessment practices in undergraduate mathematics* (pp. 1–6). Washington, DC: Mathematical Association of America.

Suskie, L. (2000). Fair assessment practices: Giving students equitable opportunities to demonstrate learning. *AAHE Bulletin, 52*(9), 7–9. Retrieved June 2, 2003, from http://www.aahebulletin.com/public/archive/may2.asp

Suskie, L. (Ed.). (2001). *Assessment to promote deep learning: Insight from AAHE's 2000 and 1999 assessment conferences.* Washington, DC: American Association for Higher Education.

Upcraft, M. L., & Schuh, J. H. (1996). *Assessment in student affairs: A guide for practitioners.* San Francisco, CA: Jossey-Bass.

Walvoord, B. E., & Anderson, V. J. (1998). *Effective grading: A tool for learning and assessment.* San Francisco, CA: Jossey-Bass.

Wiggins, G. (1998). *Educative assessment: Designing assessments to inform and improve student performance*. San Francisco, CA: Jossey-Bass.

Other good general resources on assessment include:

- American Association for Higher Education (http://www.aahe.org)
- *Assessment Update*, a periodical published by Jossey-Bass (http://www.josseybass.com/wileyCDA/WileyTitle/productcd-AU.html)
- Association of American Colleges and Universities (http://www.aacu.org)
- *Internet Resources for Higher Education Outcomes Assessment* (http://www2.acs.ncsu.edu/UPA/assmt/resource.htm), a web site maintained by the Office of University Planning & Analysis at North Carolina State University
- ASSESS, a discussion list on assessment in higher education sponsored by the University of Kentucky (http://lsv.uky.edu/archives/assess.html)

Two organizations with a wealth of resources on assessing first-year experiences are the Policy Center on the First Year of College (http://www.brevard.edu/fyc) and the National Resource Center for the First-Year Experience and Students in Transition (http://www.sc.edu/fye).

Two organizations interested in assessment in student life programs are the American College Personnel Association (http://www.myacpa.org) and the National Association of Student Personnel Administrators (http://www.naspa.org/).

INDEX

academic freedom, 89–90

accountability, 13, 53

accreditation, 12

accreditation, disciplinary/specialized, *xi*, 13

accreditation, regional, *xi*, 12

action research, 8, 29, 36

active learning, 98

add-on assessments, 94, 103, 104

affective domain, assessment of, *See* attitudes and values

aligning goals, learning opportunities, and assessment, *See* matching goals, learning opportunities, and assessments

Allen, M. J., 318

alternative assessments, 102

alumni surveys, 97, 223

American Association for Higher Education, 31, 259, 315, 321

American College Personnel Association, 315, 321

American Educational Research Association, 259

analysis of assessment results, *See* results, analysis of assessment

analysis of thinking skills, 82, 83, 212, 216

Anderson, C., 260, 319

Anderson, J., 183

Anderson, J. A., 31

Anderson, L. W., 81, 91

Anderson, R. S., 318

Anderson, V. J., 7, 8, 16, 31, 127, 143, 150, 157, 160, 166, 182, 183, 321

Andrade, H. G., 150

Angelo, T. A., x, 4, 7, 16, 39, 46, 81, 87, 88, 91, 98, 119, 156, 166, 170, 183, 315, 318

application of thinking skills, 82, 212, 216

Aronson, J., 183

Aschbacher, P. R., 81, 92, 167

ASSESS discussion list, 321

assessment culture, *See* culture of assessment

assessment, definition, 3

assessment plans, *See* planning and implementing assessment programs

assessment principles of good practice, *See* principles of good practice, assessment

assessment results, *See* results, assessment

Assessment Update, 321

assignments (*See also* prompts), 152, 153, 154

Association of American Colleges and Universities, 8, 16, 32, 71, 92, 183, 315, 321

Astin, A. W., 119, 315, 318, 319

attitudes and values, assessment of, 86, 96, 169, 189

audiences for assessment, 53, 188, 281, 283, 294

Augustine, C., 319

authentic assessments, 102, 103

averages, 268

Ayala, F., Jr., 319

Badger, E., 31

Banning, J. H., 317

Banta, T. W., 16, 47, 48, 199, 260, 299, 318, 319, 320

Barr, R. B., 10, 16, 315

Barrera, F. D., 151

Bauer, K. W., 318

behavioral goals or behavioral objectives, 75